Shrī Bhagavad Gītā

Shrī Bhagavad Gītā

WINTHROP SARGEANT

State University of New York Press

Published by
State University of New York Press, Albany

Printed in the United States of America

For information, address
State University of New York Press,
State University Plaza, Albany, N.Y., 12246

Production by Cathleen Collins
Marketing by Dana Yanulavich

10 9 8 7 6 5 4 3 2

Gītā Dhyānam

Meditation on the Gita

1. Om pārthāya pratibodhitām bhagavatā
        nārāyaṇena svayaṁ
    vyāsena grathitām purāṇa muninā
        madhye mahābhāratam
    advaitāmṛtavarṣiṇīṁ bhagavatīm
        aṣṭādaśādhyāyinīm
    amba tvām anusandadhāmi bhagavad
        gīte bhavadveṣiṇīṁ

    Om. Bhagavad Gita, Divine Mother, with you Sri Krishna enlightened Arjuna. You were composed in eighteen chapters within the *Mahabharata* by Vyasa. You are the destroyer of rebirth, the source of the Advaita nectar. I meditate on you.

2. namo 'stu te vyāsa viśāla buddhe
        phullāravindāyata patra netra
    yena tvayā bhārata tailapūrṇaḥ
        prajvālito jñānamayaḥ pradīpaḥ

    Salutations, Vyasa, of high intellect with eyes like lotus petals. You have lighted the lamp of knowledge filled with the oil of the *Mahabharata*.

3. prapanna pārijātāya
        totravetraika pāṇaye
    jñāna mudrāya kṛṣṇāya
        gītāmṛta duhe namaḥ

Salutations to Sri Krishna, who satisfies all desires of those taking refuge in him, who holds the whip in one hand and the symbol of divine knowledge in the other. He is the milker of divine nectar from the *Bhagavad Gita.*

4. sarvopaniṣado gāvo
        dogdhā gopāla nandanaḥ
    pārtho vatsaḥ sudhir bhoktā
        dugdhaṁ gītāmṛtaṁ mahat

The Upanishads are the cows; the milker is Krshna; Arjuna, the cowherd, is the calf; men and women of purified intellect are the drinkers; the milk is the sublime nectar of the Gita.

5. vasudeva sutaṁ devaṁ
        kamsa cāṇūra mardanaṁ
    devakī paramānandaṁ
        kṛṣṇam vande jagad guruṁ

I am grateful to Sri Krishna, the universal Guru, the son of Vasudeva, the destroyer of Kamsa and Chanura, and the supreme bliss of Devaki.

6. bhiṣma droṇa taṭā jayadratha jalā
gāndhāra nīlotpalā
śalya grāhavatī kṛpeṇa vahanī
karṇena velākulā

aśvatthāma vikarṇa ghora makarā
duryodhanāvartinī
sottīrṇā khalu pāṇḍavai raṇa nadī
kaivartakaḥ keśavaḥ

With Krishna as the helmsman, the river of battle was crossed—the river whose banks were Bhishma and Drona, whose water was Jayadratha, whose blue lotus was the king of Gandhara, whose crocodile was Salya, whose current was Kripa, whose wave was Karna, whose awful alligators were Asvatthama and Vikarna, and whose whirlpool was Duryodhana.

7. pārāśarya vacaḥ sarojam amalaṁ
gītārtha gandhotkaṭaṁ
nānākhyānaka kesaraṁ hari kathā
saṁbodhanā bodhitaṁ

loke sajjana ṣaṭpadair aharahaḥ
pepīyamānaṁ mudā
bhūyād bhārata paṅkajaṁ kalimala
pradhvaṁsinaḥ śreyase

May the nectar from this lotus of the *Mahabharata,* drunk joyously by the bees, the good men and women of the world, nourish us everyday. This lotus was born in the lake of Vyasa's words, sweet with the fragrance of the meaning of the *Gita*, with many stories as its stamens, and fully opened by the discourses of Krishna, destroyer of impurities.

8. mūkaṁ karoti vācālaṁ
   paṅguṁ laṅghayate giriṁ
   yatkṛpā tam ahaṁ vande
   paramānanda mādhavaṁ

I offer gratitude to Krishna, the source of supreme bliss whose grace enables the dumb to be eloquent and crippled to climb mountains.

9. yaṁ brahmā varuṇendra rudra marutaḥ
   stunvanti divyaiḥ stavaiḥ
   vedaiḥ sāṅga pada kramopaniṣadair
   gāyanti yaṁ sāmagāḥ

   dhyānāvasthita tadgatena manasā
   paśyanti yaṁ yogino
   yasyāntam na viduḥ surāsuragaṇā
   devāya tasmai namaḥ

Salutations to that God who Brahma, Indra, Varuna, Rudra, and the Maruts praise with divine chants; who recitations of the Vedas and the Upanishads honor; who yogis see with their minds absorbed in meditation; and who the hosts of Devas and Asuras do not understand.

ONE

The Depression of Arjuna

atha prathamoddhyāyaḥ

1 धृतराष्ट्र उवाच । *dhṛtarāstra uvāca*

धर्मक्षेत्रे कुरुक्षेत्रे समवेता युयुत्सवः ।
मामकाः पाण्डवाश्चैव किम् अकुर्वत संजय ॥

dharmakṣetre kurukṣetre
samavetā yuyutsavaḥ
māmakāḥ pāṇḍavāś cāiva
kim akurvata samjayāca

Dhritarashtra spoke:

When they were in the field of virtue, in the field of the Kurus, assembled together, desiring to fight, what did my army and that of the sons of Pandu do, Sanjaya?

2 संजय उवाच । *sañjaya uvāca*

दृष्ट्वा तु पाण्डवानीकं व्यूढं दुर्योधनस् तदा ।
आचार्यमुपसंगम्य राजा वचनमब्रवीत् ॥

dṛṣṭvā tu pāṇḍavānīkaṁ
vyūḍhaṁ duryodhanas tadā
ācāryamupasaṁgamya
rājā vacanam abravīt

Sanjaya spoke:

Seeing indeed the army of the sons of Pandu arrayed, King Duryodhana, approaching his Master (Drona), spoke these words:

3 पश्यैतां पाण्डुपुत्राणाम् आचार्य महतीं चमूम् ।
व्यूढां द्रुपदपुत्रेण तव शिष्येण धीमता ।।
paśyāitāṁ pāṇḍuputrāṇām
ācārya mahatīṁ camūm
vyūḍhāṁ drupadaputreṇa
tava śiṣyeṇa dhīmatā

Behold O Master, this great army of the sons of Pandu arrayed by the son of Drupada, wise by your instruction.

4 अत्र शूरा महेष्वासा भीमार्जुनसमा युधि ।
युयुधानो विराटश्च द्रुपदश्च महारथः ।।
atra śūrā maheṣvāsā
bhīmārjunasamā yudhi
yuyudhāno virāṭaś ca
drupadaś ca mahārathaḥ

Here are heroes, mighty archers, equal in battle to Bhima and Arjuna, Yuyudhana and Virata, and Drupada, the great warrior;

5 धृष्टकेतुश्चेकितानः काशिराजश्च वीर्यवान् ।
पुरुजित् कुन्तिभोजश्च शैब्यश्च नरपुङ्गवः ।।
dhṛṣṭaketuś cekitānaḥ
kāśirājaś ca vīryavān
purujit kuntibhojaś ca
śāibyaś ca narapuṅgavaḥ

Dhrishtaketu, Chekitana, and the valorous King of Kashi, Purojit and Kuntibhoja and Shaibya, bull among men,

6 युधामन्युश्च विक्रान्त उत्तमौजश्च वीर्यवान् ।
सौभद्रो द्रौपदेयाश्च सर्व एव महारथाः ॥
yudhāmanyuś ca vikrānta
uttamāujaś ca vīryavān
sāubhadro drāupadesyāś ca
sarva eva mahārathāḥ

And mighty Yudhamanyu and valorous Uttamaujas; the son of Subhadra and the sons of Draupadi, all indeed great warriors.

7 अस्माकं तु विशिष्टा ये तान् निबोध द्विजोत्तम ।
नायका मम सैन्यस्य संज्ञार्थं तान् ब्रवीमि ते ॥
asmākaṁ tu viśiṣṭā ye
tān nibodha dvijottama
nāyakā mama sāinyasya
saṃjñārthaṁ tān bravīmi te

Those of ours who are indeed distinguished, know them! O Highest of the Twiceborn, the leaders of my army I name for you by proper names:

8 भवान् भीष्मश् च कर्णश् च कृपश्च समितिंजयः ।
अश्वत्थामा विकर्णश्च सौमदत्तिस्तथैव च ॥
bhavān bhīsmaś ca karṇaś ca
kṛpaś ca samitiṁjayaḥ
aśvatthāmā vikarṇaś ca
sāumadattis tathāiva ca

Your Lordship and Bhishma and Karna and Kripa, always victorious in battle, Ashvatthama and Vikarna and the son of Somadatta also;

9 अन्ये च बहव: शूरा मदर्थे त्यक्तजीविता:
नानाशस्त्रप्रहरणा सर्वे युद्धविशारदा: ।।
anye ca bahavaḥ śūrā
madarthe tyaktajīvitāḥ
nānāśastrapraharaṇāḥ
sarve yuddhaviśāradāḥ

And many other heroes whose lives are risked for my sake, attacking with various weapons, all skilled in battle.

10 अपर्याप्तं तद् अस्माकं बलं भीष्माभिरक्षितम् ।
पर्याप्तं त्विदम् एतेषां बलं भीमाभिरक्षितम् ।।
aparyāptam tad asmākaṁ
balaṁ bhīṣmābhirakṣitaṁ
paryāptaṁ tu idam eteṣām
balaṁ bhīmabhirakṣitam

Sufficient is that force of ours guarded by Bhishma; insufficient though is the force guarded by Bhima.

11 अयनेषु च सर्वेषु यथाभागम् अवस्थिता
भीष्मम् एवाभिरक्षन्तु भवन्त: सर्व एव हि ।।
ayaneṣu ca sarveṣu
yathābhāgam avasthitāḥ
bhīṣmam evābhirakṣantu
bhavantaḥ sarva eva hi

And in all movements, stationed each in his respective place, all of you, indeed, protect Bhishma!

12 तस्य संजनयन् हर्षं कुरुवृद्धः पितामहः ।
सिंहनादं विनद्योच्चैः शङ्खं दध्मौ प्रतापवान् ॥
tasya saṁjanayan harṣaṁ
kuruvṛddhaḥ pitāmahaḥ
siṁhanādaṁ vinadyoccāiḥ
śaṅkhaṁ dadhmāu pratāpavān

Making him (Duryodhana) happy, the aged Kuru, his grandsire, roaring like a lion, blew his conch horn powerfully.

13 ततः शङ्खाश्च भेर्यश्च पणवानकगोमुखाः ।
सहसैवाभ्यहन्यन्त स शब्दस् तुमुलो ऽभवत् ॥
tataḥ śaṅkhāś ca bheryaś ca
paṇavānakagomukhāḥ
sahasāivābhyahanyanta
sa śabdas tumulo 'bhavat

And thereupon the conch horns and the kettledrums, the cymbals, drums and trumpets all at once were sounded. The uproar was tremendous.

14 ततः श्वेतैर् हयैर् युक्ते महति स्यन्दने स्थितौ ।
माधवः पाण्डवश्चैव दिव्यौ शङ्खौ प्रदध्मतुः ॥
tataḥ śvetāir hayāir yukte
mahati syandane sthitāu
mādhavaḥ pāṇḍavaścāiva
divyāu śaṅkhāu pradadhmatuḥ

Then, standing in the great chariot yoked with white horses, Krishna and Arjuna sounded forth their divine conch horns.

15 पाञ्चजन्यं हृषीकेशो देवदत्तं धनंजयः ।
पौण्ड्रं दध्मौ महाशङ्खं भीमकर्मा वृकोदरः ॥
pāñcajanyaṁ hṛṣīkeśo
devadattaṁ dhanaṁjayaḥ
pāuṇḍraṁ dadhmāu mahāśaṅkhaṁ
bhīmakarmā vṛkodaraḥ

Krishna blew his Panchajanya; Arjuna blew Devadatta, while Bhima, terrible in action, blew the great conch horn Paundra.

16 अनन्तविजयं राजा कुन्तीपुत्रो युधिष्ठिरः ।
नकुलः सहदेवश्च सुघोषमणिपुष्पकौ ॥
anantavijayam rājā
kuntīputro yudhiṣṭhiraḥ
nakulaḥ sahadevaś cȧ
sughoṣamaṇipuṣpakāu

King Yudhishthira, son of Kunti, blew Anantavijaya; Nakula and Sahadeva blew Sughosa and Manipushpaka.

17 काश्यश्च परमेष्वासः शिखण्डी च महारथः ।
धृष्टद्युम्नो विराटश्च सात्यकिश्चापराजितः ॥
kāśyaś ca parameṣvāsaḥ
śikhaṇḍī ca mahārathaḥ
dhṛṣṭadyumno virāṭaś ca
sātyakiścāparājitaḥ

And the King of Kashi, supreme archer, and Shikhandi, that great warrior, Dhrishtadyumna and Virata and Satyaki, the invincible;

18 द्रुपदो द्रौपदेयाश्च सर्वशः पृथिवीपते ।
सौभद्रश्च महाबाहुः शङ्खान् दध्मुः पृथक् पृथक् ॥
drupado drāupadeyāś ca
sarvaśaḥ pṛthivīpate
sāubhadraś ca mahābāhuḥ
śaṅkhān dadhmuḥ pṛthak pṛthak

Drupada and the sons of Draupadi all together, O Lord of the Earth, and the strong armed son of Subhadra blew their conch horns, each his own.

19 स घोषो धार्तराष्ट्राणां हृदयानि व्यदारयत् ।
नभश्च पृथिवीं चैव तुमुलो व्यनुनादयन् ॥
sa ghoṣo dhārtarāṣṭrāṇāṁ
hṛdayāni vyadārayat
nabhaś ca pṛthivīṁ cāiva
tumulo vyanunādayan

The noise burst asunder the hearts of the sons of Dhritarashtra, and the tumult caused the sky and the earth to resound.

20 अथ व्यवस्थितान् दृष्ट्वा धार्तराष्ट्रान् कपिध्वजः ।
प्रवृत्ते शस्त्रसंपाते धनुर् उद्यम्य पाण्डवः ॥
atha vyavasthitān dṛṣṭvā
dhārtarāṣṭrān kapidhvajaḥ

pravṛtte śastrasaṁpāte
dhanur udyamya pāṇḍavaḥ

Then, Arjuna, having seen the sons of Dhritarashtra drawn up in battle array, raised his bow as the clash of weapons began.

21 हृषीकेशं तदा वाक्यम् इदम् आह महीपते ।
सेनयोर् उभयोर् मध्ये रथं स्थापय मे ऽच्युत ॥
hṛṣīkeśaṁ tadā vākyam
idam āha mahīpate
senayor ubhayor madhye
rathaṁ sthāpaya me 'cyuta

Arjuna then spoke these words to Krishna: O Lord of the earth, cause my chariot to stand in the middle between the two armies, imperishable one,

22 यावद् एतान् निरीक्षे ऽहं योद्धुकामान् अवस्थितान् ।
कैर् मया सह योद्धव्यम् अस्मिन् रणसमुद्यमे ॥
yāvad etān nirīkṣe 'haṁ
yoddhukāmān avasthitān
kāir mayā saha yoddhavyam
asmin raṇasamudyame

Until I behold these warriors, battle-hungry and arrayed. With whom must I fight in undertaking this battle?

23 योत्स्यमानान् अवेक्षे ऽहं य एते ऽत्र समागताः ।
धार्तराष्ट्रस्य दुर्बुद्धेर् युद्धे प्रियचिकीर्षवः ॥

yotsyamānān avekṣe 'haṁ
ya ete 'tra samāgatāḥ
dhārtarāṣṭrasya durbuddher
yuddhe priyacikīrṣavaḥ

I behold those who are about to give battle, having come together here, wishing to do service in warfare for the evil-minded son of Dhritarashtra (Duryodhana).

24 एवम् उक्तो हृषीकेशो गुडाकेशेन भारत।
सेनयोर् उभयोर् मध्ये स्थापयित्वा रथोत्तमम्॥
evam ukto hṛṣīkeśo
guḍākeśena bhārata
senayor ubhayor madhye
sthāpayitvā rathottamam

Thus Krishna was addressed by Arjuna, O Dhritarashtra, having caused the chief chariot to stand in the middle between the two armies.

25 भीष्मद्रोणप्रमुखत:सर्वेषां च महीक्षिताम्।
उवाच पार्थ पश्यैतान् समवेतान् कुरून् इति॥
bhīṣmadroṇapramukhataḥ
sarveṣāṁ ca mahīkṣitām
uvāca pārtha paśyāitān
samavetān kurūn iti

Before the eyes of Bhishma and Drona and all these rulers of the earth, Arjuna said: Behold these Kurus assembled.

26 तत्रापश्यत् स्थितान् पार्थः पितॄन् अथ पितामहान् ।
आचार्यान् मातुलान् भ्रातॄन् पुत्रान् पौत्रान् सखींस् तथा ॥

tatrāpaśyat sthitān pārthaḥ
pitṝn atha pitāmahān
ācāryān mātulān bhrātṝn
putrān pāutrān sakhīṅs tathā

Arjuna saw standing there fathers, then grandfathers, teachers, maternal uncles, brothers, sons, grandsons, friends as well;

27 श्वशुरान् सुहृदश्चैव सेनयोर् उभयोर् अपि ।
तान् समीक्ष्य स कौन्तेयः सर्वान् बन्धून् अवस्थितान् ॥

śvaśurān suhṛdaścāiva
senayor ubhayor api
tān samīkṣya sa kāunteyaḥ
sarvān bandhūn avasthitān

Arjuna saw fathers-in-law, companions, in the two armies, and contemplated all his kinsmen, arrayed.

28 कृपया परयाविष्टो विषीदन्न् इदम् अब्रवीत् ।
दृष्ट्वेमं स्वजनं कृष्ण युयुत्सुं समुपस्थितम् ॥

kṛpayā parayāviṣṭo
viṣīdann idam abravīt
dṛṣṭvemaṁ svajanaṁ kṛṣṇa
yuyutsuṁ samupasthitam

Filled with infinite pity, despondent, he said this: Having seen my own people, Krishna, desiring to fight, approaching,

29 सीदन्ति मम गात्राणि मुखं च परिशुष्यति।
वेपथुश्च शरीरे मे रोमहर्षश्च जायते ।।

sīdanti mama gātrāṇi
mukhaṁ ca pariśuṣyati
vepathuś ca śarīre me
romaharṣaś ca jāyate

My limbs sink down, my mouth dries up, my body trembles, and my hair stands on end;

30 गाण्डीवं स्रंसते हस्तात् त्वक् चैव परिदह्यते ।
न च शक्नोम्य् अवस्थातुं भ्रमतीव च मे मनः ।।

gāṇḍīvaṁ sraṁsate hastāt
tvak cāiva paridahyate
na ca śaknomy avasthātuṁ
bhramatīva ca me manaḥ

Gandiva (Arjuna's bow) falls from (my) hand, my skin burns, I am unable to remain as I am, and my mind seems to ramble.

31 निमित्तानि च पश्यामि विपरीतानि केशव ।
न च श्रेयो ऽनुपश्यामि हत्वा स्वजनम् आहवे ।।

nimittāni ca paśyāmi
viparītāni keśava
na ca śreyo 'nupaśyāmi
hatvā svajanam āhave

I perceive inauspicious omens,O Krishna, and I foresee misfortune in destroying my own people in battle.

32 न काङ्क्षे विजयं कृष्ण न च राज्यं सुखानि च।
किं नो राज्येन गोविन्द किं भोगैर् जीवितेन वा॥

na kāṅkṣe vijayam kṛṣṇa
na ca rājyaṁ sukhāni ca
kiṁ no rājyena govinda
kiṁ bhogāir jīvitena vā

I do not desire victory, Krishna, nor kingship nor pleasures. What is kingship to us, Krishna? What are enjoyments, even life?

33 येषाम् अर्थे काङ्क्षितं नो राज्यं भोगाः सुखानि च।
त इमे ऽवस्थिता युद्धे प्राणांस् त्यक्त्वा धनानि च॥

yeṣām arthe kāṅkṣitaṁ no
rājyaṁ bhogāḥ sukhāni ca
ta ime 'vasthitā yuddhe
prāṇāṅs tyaktvā dhanāni ca

Those for whose sake we desire kingship, enjoyments, and pleasures, they are arrayed here in battle, abandoning their lives and riches.

34 आचार्याः पितरः पुत्रास् तथैव च पितामहाः।
मातुलाः श्वशुराः पौत्राः श्यालाः संबन्धिनस् तथा॥

ācāryāḥ pitaraḥ putrās
tathāiva ca pitāmahāḥ
mātulāḥ śvaśurāḥ pāutrāḥ
śyālāḥ saṁbandhinas tathā

Teachers, fathers, sons, and also grandfathers, maternal uncles, fathers-in-law, grandsons, brothers-in-law, and other kinsmen.

35 एतान् न हन्तुम् इच्छामि घ्नतो ऽपि मधुसूदन ।
अपि त्रैलोक्यराज्यस्य हेतोः किं नु महीकृते ॥

etān na hantum icchāmi
ghnato 'pi madhusūdana
api trāilokyarājyasya
hetoḥ kiṁ nu mahīkṛte

I do not desire to kill them who are bent on killing, Krishna, even for the sovereignty of the three worlds. How much less then for the earth?

36 निहत्य धार्तराष्ट्रान् नः का प्रीतिः स्याज् जनार्दन ।
पापम् एवाश्रयेद् अस्मान् हत्वैतान् आततायिनः ॥

nihatya dhārtarāṣṭrān naḥ
kā prītiḥ syāj janārdana
pāpam evāśrayed asmān
hatvāitān ātatāyinaḥ

What joy would it be for us to strike down the sons of Dhritarashtra, O Krishna? Evil thus would cling to us, having killed these aggressors.

37 तस्मान् नार्हा वयं हन्तुं धार्तराष्ट्रान् स्वबान्धवान् ।
स्वजनं हि कथं हत्वा सुखिनः स्याम माधव ॥

tasmān nārhā vayaṁ hantuṁ
dhārtarāṣṭrān svabāndhavān

svajanam hi kathaṁ hatvā
sukhinaḥ syāma mādhava

Therefore we are not justified in killing the sons of Dhritarashtra, our own kinsmen. How, having killed our own people, could we be happy, Krishna?

38 यद्यप्येते न पश्यन्ति लोभोपहतचेतसः ।
कुलक्षयकृतं दोषं मित्रद्रोहे च पातकम् ।।

yadyapyete na paśyanti
lobhopahatacetasaḥ
kulakṣayakṛtaṁ doṣaṁ
mitradrohe ca pātakam

Even if those whose thoughts are overpowered by greed do not perceive the wrong caused by the destruction of the family, and the crime of treachery to friends,

39 कथं न ज्ञेयम् अस्माभिः पापाद् अस्मान् निवर्तितुम् ।
कुलक्षयकृतं दोषं प्रपश्यद्भिर् जनार्दन ।।

kathaṁ na jñeyam asmābhiḥ
pāpād asmān nivartitum
kulakṣayakṛtaṁ doṣaṁ
prapaśyadbhir janārdana

Why should we not know enough to turn back from this evil, through discernment of the wrong caused by the destruction of the family, O Krishna?

40 कुलक्षये प्रणश्यन्ति कुलधर्माः सनातनाः ।
धर्मे नष्टे कुलं कृत्स्नम् अधर्मो ऽभिभवत्युत ।।

kulakṣaye praṇaśyanti
kuladharmāḥ sanātanāḥ
dharme naṣṭe kulaṁ kṛtsnam
adharmo 'bhibhavatyuta

In the destruction of the family, the ancient family laws vanish; when the law has perished, lawlessness overpowers the entire family also.

41 अधर्माभिभवात् कृष्ण प्रदुष्यन्ति कुलस्त्रियः ।
स्त्रीषु दुष्टासु वार्ष्णेय जायते वर्णसंकरः ॥

adharmābhibhavāt kṛṣṇa
praduṣyanti kulastriyaḥ
strīṣu duṣṭāsu vārṣṇeya
jāyate varṇasaṁkaraḥ

Because of the ascendancy of lawlessness, Krishna, the family women are corrupted; when women are corrupted, O Krishna, the intermixture of caste is born.

42 संकरो नरकायैव कुलघ्नानां कुलस्य च ।
पतन्ति पितरो ह्येषां लुप्तपिण्डोदकक्रियाः ॥

saṁkaro narakāyāiva
kulaghnānāṁ kulasya ca
patanti pitaro hyeṣāṁ
luptapiṇḍodakakriyāḥ

Intermixture brings to hell the family destroyers and the family, too; the ancestors of these indeed fall, deprived of offerings of rice and water.

43 दोषैर् एतैः कुलघ्नानां वर्णसंकरकारकैः ।
उत्साद्यन्ते जातिधर्माः कुलधर्माश्च शाश्वताः ॥

doṣāir etāiḥ kulaghnānāṁ
varṇasaṁkarakārakāiḥ
utsādyante jātidharmāḥ
kuladharmāś ca śāśvatāḥ

By these wrongs of the family destroyers, producing intermixture of caste, caste duties are abolished, and eternal family laws also.

44 उत्सन्नकुलधर्माणां मनुष्याणां जनार्दन ।
नरके ऽनियतं वासो भवतीत्यनुशुश्रुम ॥

utsannakuladharmāṇāṁ
manuṣyāṇāṁ janārdana
narake 'niyataṁ vāso
bhavatītyanuśuśruma

Men whose family laws have been obliterated, O Krishna, dwell indefinitely in hell, thus we have heard repeatedly,

45 अहो बत महत् पापं कर्तुं व्यवसिता वयम् ।
यद् राज्यसुखलोभेन हन्तुं स्वजनम् उद्यताः ॥

aho bata mahat pāpaṁ
kartuṁ vyavasitā vayam
yad rājyasukhalobhena
hantuṁ svajanam udyatāḥ

Ah! Alas! We are resolved to do a great evil, which is to be intent on killing our own people, through greed for royal pleasures.

46 यदि माम् अप्रतीकारम् अशस्त्रं शस्त्रपाणयः ।
धार्तराष्ट्रा रणे हन्युस् तन् मे क्षेमतरं भवेत् ॥

yadi mām apratīkāram
aśastraṁ śastrapāṇayaḥ
dhārtarāṣṭrā raṇe hanyus
tan me kṣemataraṁ bhavet

If the armed sons of Dhritarashtra should kill me in battle while I was unresisting and unarmed, this would be a greater happiness for me.

47 एवम् उक्त्वा ऽर्जुन संख्ये रथोपस्थ उपाविशत् ।
विसृज्य सशरं चापं शोकसंविग्नमानसः ॥

evam uktvā 'rjuna saṁkhye
rathopastha upāviśat
visṛjya saśaraṁ cāpaṁ
śokasaṁvignamānasaḥ

Thus having spoken on the battlefield, Arjuna sat down upon the seat of the chariot, throwing down both arrow and bow, with a heart overcome by sorrow.

Hari Om Tat Sat
Iti Srimad Bhagavadgītāsūpaniṣatsu Brahmavidyāyām
Yogaśāstre Sri Kriṣnārjunasamvāde
Arjunaviṣādayogo Nāma Prathamoddhyāyaḥ.

Thus ends the first Chapter, entitled "The Depression of Arjuna," of the venerated Bhagavad Gita Upanishad, the Knowledge of the Absolute, the scripture of Yoga, the dialogue between Sri Krishna and Arjuna.

TWO

The Yoga of Knowledge

atha dvitiyoddhyāyaḥ

1 संजय उवाच । *sañjaya uvāca*

तं तथा कृपयाविष्टम् अश्रुपूर्णाकुलेक्षणम् ।
विषीदन्तम् इदं वाक्यम् उवाच मधुसूदनः ॥

taṁ tathā kṛpayāviṣṭam
aśrupūrṇākulekṣaṇam
viṣīdantam idaṁ vākyam
uvāca madhusūdanaḥ

Sanjaya spoke:
To him thus overcome by pity, despairing, whose eyes were filled with tears and downcast, Krishna spoke these words:

2 श्रीभगवान् उवाच । *śrībhagavān uvāca*

कुतस्त्वा कश्मलम् इदं विषमे समुपस्थितम् ।
अनार्यजुष्टम् अस्वर्ग्यम् अकीर्तिकरम् अर्जुन ॥

kutastvā kaśmalam idaṁ
viṣame samupasthitam
anāryajuṣṭam asvargyam
akīrtikaram arjuna

The Blessed Lord spoke:

Whence has this timidity of yours come to you in time of danger? It is not acceptable in you, does not lead to heaven, and causes disgrace, Arjuna.

3 क्लैब्यं मा स्म गमः पार्थ नैतत् त्वय्युपपद्यते ।
क्षुद्रं हृदयदौर्बल्यं त्यक्त्वोत्तिष्ठ परंतप ॥
klāibyaṁ mā sma gamaḥ pārtha
nāitat tvayyupapadyate
kṣudraṁ hṛdayadāurbalyaṁ
tyaktvottiṣṭha paraṁtapa

Do not become a coward, Arjuna. This is not suitable to you. Abandoning base faintheartedness, stand up, Arjuna!

4 अर्जुन उवाच *arjuna uvāca*
कथं भीष्मम् अहं संख्ये द्रोणं च मधुसूदन ।
इषुभिः प्रतियोत्स्यामि पूजार्हावरिसूदन ॥
kathaṁ bhīṣmam ahaṁ saṁkhye
droṇaṁ ca madhusūdana
iṣubhiḥ pratiyotsyāmi
pūjārhāvarisūdana

Arjuna spoke:

How can I kill in battle Bhishma and Drona, O Krishna? How can I fight with arrows against these two venerable men, O Krishna?

5 गुरून् अहत्वा हि महानुभावान् ।
श्रेयो भोक्तुं भैक्ष्यमपीह लोके

हत्वार्थकामांस् तु गुरूनिहैव
भुञ्जीय भोगान् रुधिरप्रदिग्धान् ।।

gurūn ahatvā hi mahānubhāvān
śreyo bhoktuṁ bhāikṣyamapīha loke
hatvārthakāmāṅs tu gurūn ihāiva
bhuñjīya bhogān rudhirapradigdhān

Indeed, instead of slaying these noble gurus it would be preferable to live on alms here on earth; having slain the gurus, with desire for worldly gain, I would enjoy here on earth delights smeared with blood.

6 न चैतद् विद्मः कतरन् नो गरीयो
यद् वा जयेम यदि वा नो जयेयुः ।
यान् एव हत्वा न जिजीविषामस्
ते ऽवस्थिताः प्रमुखे धार्तराष्ट्राः

na cāitad vidmaḥ kataran no garīyo
yad vā jayema yadi vā no jayeyuḥ
yān eva hatvā na jijīviṣāmas
te 'vasthitāḥ pramukhe dhārtarāṣṭrāḥ

And this we do not know: which for us is preferable, whether we should conquer them or they should conquer us. The sons of Dhritarashtra, having killed whom we would not wish to live, are standing before us.

7 कार्पण्यदोषोपहतस्वभावः
पृच्छामि त्वां धर्मसंमूढचेताः ।
यच्छ्रेयः स्यान् निश्चितं ब्रूहि तन् मे
शिष्यस् ते ऽहं शाधि मां त्वां प्रपन्नम् ।।

kārpaṇyadoṣopahataṣvabhāvaḥ
pṛcchāmi tvāṁ dharmasaṁmūḍhacetāḥ
yacchreyaḥ syān niścitaṁ brūhi tan me
śiṣyas te 'haṁ śādhi māṁ tvāṁ prapannam

My own being is overcome by pity and weakness. My mind is confused as to my duty. I ask you which is preferable, for certain? Tell that to me, your pupil. Correct me, I beg of you.

8 न हि प्रपश्यामि ममापनुद्याद्
यच्छोकम् उच्छोषणम् इन्द्रियाणाम् ।
अवाप्य भूमावसपत्नमृद्ध
राज्यं सुराणाम् अपि चाधिपत्यम् ॥

na hi prapaśyāmi mamāpanudyād
yacchokam ucchoṣaṇam indriyāṇām
avāpya bhūmāvasapatnaṁ ṛddhaṁ
rājyaṁ surāṇām api cādhipatyam

Indeed, I do not see what will dispel this sorrow of mine which dries up my senses, even if I should obtain on earth unrivaled and prosperous royal power, or even the sovereignty of the gods.

9 संजय उवाच । *sañjaya uvāca*

एवम् उक्त्वा हृषीकेशं गुडाकेशः परंतप ।
न योत्स्य इति गोविन्दम् उक्त्वा तूष्णीं बभूव ह ॥

evam uktvā hṛṣīkeśaṁ
guḍākeśaḥ paraṁtapa

na yotsya iti govindam
uktvā tūṣṇīṁ babhūva ha

Sanjaya spoke:
Thus having addressed Krishna, Arjuna said, "I shall not fight," and having spoken, he became silent.

10 तम् उवाच हृषीकेशः प्रहसन्न् इव भारत ।
सेनयोर् उभयोर् मध्ये विषीदन्तम् इदं वचः ॥
tam uvāca hṛṣīkeśaḥ
prahasann iva bhārata
senayor ubhayor madhye
viṣīdantam idaṁ vacaḥ

To him, the dejected Arjuna, Krishna, beginning to laugh, O Dhritarashtra, in the middle between the two armies, spoke these words:

11 श्रीभगवान् उवाच । *śrībhagavān uvāca*

अशोच्यान् अन्वशोचस् त्वं प्रज्ञावादांश्च भाषसे ।
गतासून् अगतासूंश्च नानुशोचन्ति पण्डिताः ॥
aśocyān anvaśocas tvaṁ
prajñāvādāṅś ca bhāṣase
gatāsūn agatāsūṅś ca
nānuśocanti paṇḍitāḥ

The Blessed Lord spoke:
You have mourned those that should not be mourned, and yet you speak words

as if with wisdom; the wise do not mourn for the dead or for the living.

12 न त्वेवाहं जातु नासं न त्वं नेमे जनाधिपाः ।
न चैव न भविष्यामः सर्वे वयम् अतः परम् ॥

na tvevāhaṁ jātu nāsaṁ
na tvaṁ neme janādhipāḥ
na cāiva na bhaviṣyāmaḥ
sarve vayam ataḥ param

Truly there was never a time when I was not, nor you, nor these lords of men; and neither will there be a time when we shall cease to be from this time onward.

13 देहिनो ऽस्मिन् यथा देहे कौमारं यौवनं जरा ।
तथा देहान्तरप्राप्तिर् धीरस् तत्र न मुह्यति ॥

dehino 'smin yathā dehe
kāumāraṁ yāuvanaṁ jarā
tathā dehāntaraprāptir
dhīras tatra na muhyati

Just as in the body childhood, adulthood, and old age happen to an embodied being, so also he (the embodied being) acquires another body. The wise one is not deluded about this.

14 मात्रास्पर्शास् तु कौन्तेय शीतोष्णसुखदुःखदाः ।
आगमापायिनो ऽनित्यास् तांस् तितिक्षस्व भारत ॥

mātrāsparśās tu kāunteya
śītoṣṇasukhaduḥkhadāḥ

āgamāpāyino 'nityās
tāṅs titikṣasva bhārata

Physical sensations, truly, Arjuna, causing cold, heat, pleasure, or pain, come and go and are impermanent. So manage to endure them, Arjuna.

15 यं हि न व्यथयन्त्येते पुरुषं पुरुषर्षभ ।
समदुःखसुखं धीरं सोऽमृतत्वाय कल्पते ॥
yaṁ hi na vyathayantyete
puruṣaṁ puruṣarṣabha
samaduḥkhasukhaṁ dhīraṁ
so 'mṛtatvāya kalpate

Indeed, the man whom these (i.e the sensations) do not afflict, O Arjuna, the wise one, to whom happiness and unhappiness are the same, is ready for immortality.

16 नासतो विद्यते भावो नाभावो विद्यते सतः ।
उभयोर् अपि दृष्टो ऽन्तस् त्वनयोस्तत्त्वदर्शिभिः ॥
nāsato vidyate bhāvo
nābhāvo vidyate sataḥ
ubhayor api dṛṣṭo 'ntas
tvanayor tattvadarśibhiḥ

It is found that the unreal has no being; it is found that there is no non-being of the real. The certainty of both these propositions is indeed surely seen by the perceivers of truth.

17 अविनाशि तु तद् विद्धि येन सर्वम् इदं ततम् ।
विनाशम् अव्ययस्यास्य न कश्चित् कर्तुम् अर्हति ।।

avināśi tu tad viddhi
yena sarvam idaṁ tatam
vināśam avyayasyāsya
na kaścit kartum arhati

Know that that by which all this universe is pervaded is indeed indestructible; no one is able to accomplish the destruction of the imperishable.

18 अन्तवन्त इमे देहा नित्यस्योक्ताः शरीरिणः ।
अनाशिनो ऽप्रमेयस्य तस्माद् युध्यस्व भारत ।।

antavanta ime dehā
nityasyoktāḥ śarīriṇaḥ
anāśino 'prameyasya
tasmād yudhyasva bhārata

These bodies inhabited by the eternal, the indestructible, the immeasurable embodied Self, are said to come to an end. Therefore fight, Arjuna!

19 य एनं वेत्ति हन्तारं यश्चैनं मन्यते हतम् ।
उभौ तौ न विजानीतो नायं हन्ति न हन्यते ।।

ya enaṁ vetti hantāraṁ
yaścāinaṁ manyate hatam
ubhāu tāu na vijānīto
nāyaṁ hanti na hanyate

He who imagines this (the embodied Self) the slayer and he who imagines this (the embodied Self) the slain, neither of them understands this (the embodied Self) does not slay, nor is it slain.

20 न जायते म्रियते वा कदाचिन्
नायं भूत्वा भविता वा न भूयः।
अजो नित्यः शाश्वतो ऽयं पुराणो
न हन्यते हन्यमाने शरीरे॥

na jāyate mriyate vā kadācin
nāyaṁ bhūtvā bhavitā vā na bhūyaḥ
ajo nityaḥ śāśvato 'yaṁ purāṇo
na hanyate hanyamāne śarīre

Neither is this (the embodied Self) born nor does it die at any time, nor, having been, will it again come not to be. Birthless, eternal, perpetual, primeval, it is not slain when the body is slain.

21 वेदाविनाशिनं नित्यं य एनम् अजम् अव्ययम्।
कथं स पुरुषः पार्थ कं घातयति हन्ति कम्॥

vedāvināśinaṁ nityaṁ
ya enam ajam avyayam
kathaṁ sa puruṣaḥ pārtha
kaṁ ghātayati hanti kam

He who knows this, the indestructible, the eternal, the birthless, the imperishable, in what way does this man cause to be slain, Arjuna? Whom does he slay?

22 वासांसि जीर्णानि यथा विहाय
नवानि गृह्णाति नरो ऽपराणि।

तथा शरीराणि विहाय जीर्णान्य्
अन्यानि संयाति नवानि देही ॥
vāsāṁsi jīrṇāni yathā vihāya
navāni gṛhṇāti naro 'parāṇi
tathā śarīrāṇi vihāya jīrṇāny
anyāni saṁyāti navāni dehī

As, after casting away worn out garments, a man later takes new ones, so, after casting away worn out bodies, the embodied Self encounters other, new ones.

23 नैनं छिन्दन्ति शस्त्राणि नैनं दहति पावकः ।
न चैनं क्लेदयन्त्यापो न शोषयति मारुतः ॥
nāinaṁ chindanti śastrāṇi
nāinaṁ dahati pāvakaḥ
na cāinaṁ kledayantyāpo
na śoṣayati mārutaḥ

Weapons do not pierce this (the embodied Self), fire does not burn this, water does not wet this, nor does the wind cause it to wither.

24 अच्छेद्यो ऽयम् अदाह्यो ऽयम् अक्लेद्यो ऽशोष्य एव च ।
नित्यः सर्वगतः स्थाणुर् अचलो ऽयं सनातनः ॥
acchedyo 'yam adāhyo 'yam
akledyo 'śoṣya eva ca
nityaḥ sarvagataḥ sthāṇur
acalo 'yaṁ sanātanaḥ

This cannot be pierced, burned, wetted or withered; this is eternal, all pervading, fixed; this is unmoving and primeval.

25 अव्यक्तो ऽयम् अचिन्त्यो ऽयम् अविकार्यो ऽयम् उच्यते ।
तस्माद् एवं विदित्वैनं नानुशोचितुम् अर्हसि ॥

avyakto 'yam acintyo 'yam
avikāryo 'yam ucyate
tasmād evaṁ viditvāinaṁ
nānuśocitum arhasi

It is said that this is unmanifest, unthinkable, and unchanging. Therefore, having understood in this way, you should not mourn.

26 अथ चैनं नित्यजातं नित्यं वा मन्यसे मृतम् ।
तथापि त्वं महाबाहो नैनं शोचितुमर्हसि ॥

atha cāinaṁ nityajātaṁ
nityaṁ vā manyase mṛtam
tathāpi tvaṁ mahābāho
nāinaṁ śocitumarhasi

And moreover even if you think this to be eternally born or eternally dead, even then you should not mourn for this, Arjuna.

27 जातस्य हि ध्रुवो मृत्युर् ध्रुवं जन्म मृतस्य च ।
तस्मादपरिहार्ये ऽर्थे न त्वं शोचितुमर्हसि ॥

jātasya hi dhruvo mṛtyur
dhruvaṁ janma mṛtasya ca
tasmādaparihārye 'rthe
na tvaṁ śocitumarhasi

For the born, death is certain; for the dead there is certainly birth. Therefore, for this, inevitable in consequence, you should not mourn.

28 अव्यक्तादीनि भूतानि व्यक्तमध्यानि भारत ।
अव्यक्तनिधानान्येव तत्र का परिदेवना ॥
avyaktādīni bhūtāni
vyaktamadhyāni bhārata
avyaktanidhānānyeva
tatra kā paridevanā

Beings are such that their beginnings are unmanifest, their middles are manifest, and their ends are unmanifest again. What complaint can there be over this?

29 आश्चर्यवत् पश्यति कश्चिदेनम्
आश्चर्यवद् वदति तथैव चान्यः ।
आश्चर्यवच्चैनम् अन्यः शृणोति
श्रुत्वाप्येनं वेद न चैव कश्चित् ॥
āścaryavat paśyati kaścidenam
āścaryavad vadati tathāiva cānyaḥ
āścaryavaccāinam anyaḥ śṛṇoti
śrutvāpyenaṁ veda na cāiva kaścit

Someone perceives this as a wonder, another declares this as a wonder, still another hears of this as a wonder; but even having heard of this, no one knows it.

30 देही नित्यं अवध्यो ऽयं देहे सर्वस्य भारत ।
तस्मात् सर्वाणि भूतानि न त्वं शोचितुमर्हसि ॥
dehī nityaṁ avadhyo 'yaṁ
dehe sarvasya bhārata
tasmāt sarvāṇi bhūtāni
na tvaṁ śocitumarhasi

This, the embodied Self, is eternally indestructible in the body of all, Arjuna. Therefore you should not mourn for any being.

31 स्वधर्मम् अपि चावेक्ष्य न विकम्पितुम् अर्हसि ।
धर्म्याद् धि युद्धाच्छ्रेयो ऽन्यत् क्षत्रियस्य न विद्यते ।।

svadharmam api cāvekṣya
na vikampitum arhasi
dharmyād dhi yuddhācchreyo 'nyat
ksatriyasya na vidyate

And, perceiving your own caste duty, you should not tremble. Indeed, anything superior to righteous battle does not exist for the kshatriya (man of warrior caste).

32 यदृच्छया चोपपन्नं स्वर्गद्वारम् अपावृतम् ।
सुखिनः क्षत्रियाः पार्थ लभन्ते युद्धम् ईदृशम् ।।

yadṛcchayā copapannaṁ
svargadvāram apāvṛtam
sukhinaḥ kṣatriyāḥ pārtha
labhante yuddham īdṛśam

And if by good fortune they gain the open gate of heaven, happy are the kshatriyas, Arjuna, when they encounter such a fight.

33 अथ चेत् त्वम् इमं धर्म्यं संग्रामं न करिष्यसि ।
ततः स्वधर्मं कीर्तिं च हित्वा पापम् अवाप्स्यसि ।।

atha cet tvam imaṁ dharmyaṁ
saṁgrāmaṁ na kariṣyasi
tataḥ svadharmaṁ kīrtiṁca
hitvā pāpam avāpsyasi

Now, if you will not undertake this righteous war, thereupon, having avoided your own duty and glory, you shall incur evil.

34 अकीर्तिं चापि भूतानि कथयिष्यन्ति ते ऽव्ययाम् ।
संभावितस्य चाकीर्तिर् मरणाद् अतिरिच्यते ॥
akīrtiṁ cāpi bhūtāni
kathayiṣyanti te 'vyayām
saṁbhāvitasya cākīrtir
maraṇād atiricyate

And also people will relate your undying infamy; and, for one who has been honored, disgrace is worse than dying.

35 भयाद् रणाद् उपरतं मंस्यन्ते त्वां महारथाः
येषां च त्वं वहुमतो भूत्वा यास्यसि लाघवम् ॥
bhayād raṇād uparataṁ
maṅsyante tvāṁ mahārathāḥ
yeṣāṁ ca tvaṁ bahumato
bhūtvā yāsyasi lāghavam

The great warriors will think that you have abstained from the battle through fear, and among those by whom you have been held in high esteem you shall come to be held lightly.

36 अवाच्यवादांश्च बहून् वदिष्यन्ति तवाहिताः ।
निन्दन्तस् तव सामर्थ्यं ततो दुःखतरं तु किम् ।।
avācyavādāṅśca bahūn
vadiṣyanti tavāhitāḥ
nindantas tava sāmarthyaṁ
tato duḥkhataraṁ tu kim

And your enemies will speak many words of you that should not be spoken, deriding your capacity. What greater hardship is there than that?

37 हतो वा प्राप्स्यसि स्वर्गं जित्वा वा भोक्ष्यसे महीम् ।
तस्माद् उत्तिष्ठ कौन्तेय युद्धाय कृतनिश्चयः ।।
hato vā prāpsyasi svargaṁ
jitvā vā bhokṣyase mahīm
tasmād uttiṣṭha kāunteya
yuddhāya kṛtaniścayaḥ

Either, having been slain, you shall attain heaven, or, having conquered, you shall enjoy the earth. Therefore stand up, Arjuna, resolved to fight.

38 सुखदुःखे समे कृत्वा लाभालाभौ जयाजयौ ।
ततो युद्धाय युज्यस्व नैवं पापम् अवाप्स्यसि ।।
sukhaduḥkhe same kṛtvā
lābhālābhāu jayājayāu
tato yuddhāya yujyasva
nāivaṁ pāpam avāpsyasi

Holding pleasure and pain to be alike, likewise gain and loss, victory and defeat, then engage in battle! Thus you shall not incur evil.

39 एषा ते ऽभिहिता सांख्ये बुद्धिर् योगे त्विमां शृणु ।
बुद्ध्या युक्तो यया पार्थ कर्मबन्धं प्रहास्यसि ॥
eṣā te 'bhihitā sāṁkhye
buddhir yoge tvimāṁ śṛṇu
buddhyā yukto yayā pārtha
karmabandhaṁ prahāsyasi

This (insight) is wisdom, as declared in the theory of Sankhya; now hear it as applied in arduous practice; yoked with this determination, Arjuna, you shall rid yourself of the bondage of karma.

40 नेहाभिक्रमनाशो ऽस्ति प्रत्यवायो न विद्यते ।
स्वल्पम् अप्य् अस्य धर्मस्य त्रायते महतो भयात् ॥
nehābhikramanāśo 'sti
pratyavāyo na vidyate
svalpam apy asya dharmasya
trāyate mahato bhayāt

Here (in the yoga doctrine of practice) no effort is lost, nor is any loss of progress found. Even a little of this discipline protects one from great danger.

41 व्यवसायात्मिका बुद्धिर् एकेह कुरुनन्दन ।
बहुशाखा ह्यनन्ताश्च बुद्धयो ऽव्यवसायिनाम् ॥
vyavasāyātmikā buddhir
ekeha kurunandana

bahuśākhā hyanantāś ca
buddhayo 'vyavasāyinām

Here there is a single resolute understanding, Arjuna. The thoughts of the irresolute have many branches and are, indeed, endless.

42 याम् इमां पुष्पितां वाचं प्रवदन्त्यविपश्चितः ।
वेदवादरताः पार्थ नान्यद् अस्तीति वादिनः ॥
yām imāṁ puṣpitāṁ vācaṁ
pravadantyavipaścitaḥ
vedavādaratāḥ pārtha
nānyad astīti vādinaḥ

The ignorant ones proclaim this flowery discourse, Arjuna, delighting in the letter of the Veda and saying, "There is nothing else."

43 कामात्मानः स्वर्गपरा जन्मकर्मफलप्रदाम् ।
क्रियाविशेषबहुलां भोगैश्वर्यगतिं प्रति ॥
kāmātmānaḥ svargaparā
janmakarmaphalapradām
kriyāviśeṣabahulāṁ
bhogāiśvaryagatiṁ prati

Full of desires, intent on heaven, they offer rebirth as the fruit of action, and are addicted to many specific rites aimed at the goal of enjoyment and power.

44 भोगैश्वर्यप्रसक्तानां तयापहृतचेतसाम् ।
व्यवसायात्मिका बुद्धिः समाधौ न विधीयते ॥

bhogāiśvaryaprasaktānāṁ
tayāpahṛtacetasām
vyavasāyātmikā buddhiḥ
samādhāu na vidhīyate

To those (the ignorant ones) attached to enjoyment and power, whose thought is stolen away by this kind of talk, resolute insight in meditation is not granted.

45 त्रैगुण्यविषया वेदा निस्त्रैगुण्यो भवार्जुन ।
निर्द्वन्द्वो नित्यसत्त्वस्थो निर्योगक्षेम आत्मवान् ॥
trāiguṇyaviṣayā vedā
nistrāiguṇyo bhavārjuna
nirdvandvo nityasattvastho
niryogakṣema ātmavān

The Vedas are such that their scope is confined to the three qualities; be free from those three qualities, Arjuna, indifferent toward the pairs of opposites, eternally fixed in truth, free from thoughts of acquisition and comfort, and possessed of the Self.

46 यावानर्थ उदपाने सर्वतः संप्लुतोदके ।
तावान्सर्वेषु वेदेषु ब्राह्मणस्य विजानतः ॥
yāvān artha udapāne
sarvataḥ saṁplutodake
tāvān sarveṣu vedeṣu
brāhmaṇasya vijānataḥ

As much value as there is in a well when water is flooding on every side, so much is the value in all the Vedas for a brahman who knows.

47 कर्मण्येवाधिकारस्ते मा फलेषु कदाचन ।
मा कर्मफलहेतुर् भूर् मा ते सङ्गो ऽस्त्व् अकर्मणि ॥
karmaṇyevādhikāraste
mā phaleṣu kadācana
mā karmaphalahetur bhūr
mā te sañgo 'stv akarmani

Your right is to action alone; never to its fruits at any time. Never should the fruits of action be your motive; never let there be attachment to inaction in you.

48 योगस्थः कुरु कर्माणि सङ्गं त्यक्त्वा धनंजय ।
सिद्ध्यसिद्ध्योः समो भूत्वा समत्वं योग उच्यते ॥
yogasthaḥ kuru karmāṇi
sañgaṁ tyaktvā dhanaṁjaya
siddhyasiddhyoḥ samo bhūtvā
samatvaṁ yoga ucyate

Fixed in yoga, perform actions, having abandoned attachment, Arjuna, and having become indifferent to success or failure. It is said that evenness of mind is yoga.

49 दूरेण ह्यवरं कर्म बुद्धियोगाद् धनंजय ।
बुद्धौ शरणम् अन्विच्छ कृपणाः फलहेतवः ॥
dūreṇa hyavaraṁ karma
buddhiyogād dhanaṁjaya
buddhāu śaraṇam anviccha
kṛpaṇāḥ phalahetavaḥ

Action is inferior by far to the yoga of wisdom, Arjuna. Seek refuge in wisdom! Despicable are those whose motives are based on the fruit of action.

50 बुद्धियुक्तो जहातीह उभे सुकृतदुष्कृते ।
तस्माद् योगाय युज्यस्व योगः कर्मसु कौशलम् ॥
buddhiyukto jahātīha
ubhe sukṛtaduṣkṛte
tasmād yogāya yujyasva
yogaḥ karmasu kāuśalam

He whose wisdom is established casts off, here in the world, both good and evil actions; therefore devote yourself to yoga! Yoga is skill in action.

51 कर्मजं बुद्धियुक्ता हि फलं त्यक्त्वा मनीषिणः ।
जन्मबन्धविनिर्मुक्ताः पदं गच्छन्त्य् अनामयम् ॥
karmajaṁ buddhiyuktā hi
phalaṁ tyaktvā manīṣiṇaḥ
janmabandhavinirmuktāḥ
padam gacchanty anāmayam

Those who are established in wisdom, the wise ones, who have abandoned the fruit born of action, and are freed from the bondage of rebirth, go to the place that is free from pain.

52 यदा ते मोहकलिलं बुद्धिर् व्यतितरिष्यति ।
तदा गन्तासि निर्वेदं श्रोतव्यस्य श्रुतस्य च ॥
yadā te mohakalilaṁ
buddhir vyatitariṣyati

tadā gantāsi nirvedaṁ
śrotavyasya śrutasya ca

When your intellect crosses beyond the thicket of delusion, then you shall become disgusted with that which is yet to be heard and with that which has been heard (in the Veda).

53 श्रुतिविप्रतिपन्ना ते यदा स्थास्यति निश्चला ।
समाधावचलाबुद्धिस् तदा योगम् अवाप्स्यसि ।।
śrutivipratipannā te
yadā sthāsyati niścalā
samādhāvacalābuddhis
tadā yogam avāpsyasi

When your intellect stands fixed in deep meditation, unmoving, disregarding Vedic doctrine, then you shall attain Self-realization.

54 अर्जुन उवाच । *arjuna uvāca*

स्थितप्रज्ञस्य का भाषा समाधिस्थस्य केशव ।
स्थितधीः किं प्रभाषेत किम् आसीत व्रजेत किम् ।।
sthitaprajñasya kā bhāṣā
samādhisthasya keśava
sthitadhīḥ kiṁ prabhāṣeta
kim āsīta vrajeta kim

Arjuna spoke:

How does one describe him who is of steady wisdom, who is steadfast in deep meditation, Krishna? How does he who is steady in wisdom speak? How does he sit? How does he move?

55 श्रीभगवान् उवाच। *śrībhagavān uvāca*

प्रजहाति यदा कामान् सर्वान् पार्थ मनोगतान्।
आत्मन्येवात्मना तुष्टः स्थितप्रज्ञस्तदोच्यते॥

prajahāti yadā kāmān
sarvān pārtha manogatān
ātmanyevātmanā tuṣṭaḥ
sthitaprajñastadocyate

The Blessed Lord spoke:

When he leaves behind all desires emerging from the mind, Arjuna, and is contented in the Self by the Self, then he is said to be one whose wisdom is steady.

56 दुःखेष्वनुद्विग्नमनाः सुखेषु विगतस्पृहः।
वीतरागभयक्रोधः स्थितधीर् मुनिर् उच्यते॥

duḥkheṣvanudvignamanāḥ
sukheṣu vigataspṛhaḥ
vītarāgabhayakrodhaḥ
sthitadhīr munir ucyate

He whose mind is not agitated in misfortune, whose desire for pleasures has disappeared, whose passion, fear, and anger have departed, and whose meditation is steady, is said to be a sage.

57 यः सर्वत्रानभिस्नेहस् तत्तत् प्राप्य शुभाशुभम्।
नाभिनन्दति न द्वेष्टि तस्य प्रज्ञा प्रतिष्ठिता॥

yaḥ sarvatrānabhisnehas
tattat prāpya śubhāśubham
nābhinandati na dveṣṭi
tasya prajñā pratiṣṭhitā

He who is without attachment on all sides, encountering this or that, pleasant or unpleasant, neither rejoicing nor disliking; his wisdom stands firm.

58 यदा संहरते चायं कूर्मो ऽङ्गानीव सर्वशः ।
इन्द्रियाणीन्द्रियार्थेभ्यस् तस्य प्रज्ञा प्रतिष्ठिता ॥
yadā saṁharate cāyaṁ
kūrmo 'ṅgānīva sarvaśaḥ
indriyāṇīndriyārthebhyas
tasya prajñā pratiṣṭhitā

And when he withdraws completely the senses from the objects of the senses, as a tortoise withdraws its limbs into its shell, his wisdom stands firm.

59 विषया विनिवर्तन्ते निराहारस्य देहिनः ।
रसवर्जं रसो ऽप्यस्य परं दृष्ट्वा निवर्तते ॥
viṣayā vinivartante
nirāhārasya dehinaḥ
rasavarjaṁ raso 'pyasya
paraṁ dṛṣṭvā nivartate

Sense objects turn away from the abstinent man, but the taste for them remains; but the taste also turns away from him who has seen the Supreme.

60 यततो ह्यपि कौन्तेय पुरुषस्य विपश्चितः ।
इन्द्रियाणि प्रमाथीनि हरन्ति प्रसभं मनः ॥
yatato hyapi kāunteya
puruṣasya vipaścitaḥ
indriyāṇi pramāthīni
haranti prasabhaṁ manaḥ

The turbulent senses carry away forcibly the mind, Arjuna, even of the striving man of wisdom.

61 तानि सर्वाणि संयम्य युक्त आसीत मत्परः ।
वशे हि यस्येन्द्रियाणि तस्य प्रज्ञा प्रतिष्ठिता ॥
tāni sarvāṇi saṁyamya
yukta āsīta matparaḥ
vaśe hi yasyendriyāṇi
tasya prajñā pratiṣṭhitā

Restraining all these senses, disciplined, he should sit, intent on Me; he whose senses are controlled, his wisdom stands firm.

62 ध्यायतो विषयान् पुंसः सङ्गस् तेषूपजायते ।
सङ्गात् संजायते कामः कामात् क्रोधो ऽभिजायते ॥
dhyāyato viṣayān puṁsaḥ
saṅgas teṣūpajāyate
saṅgāt saṁjāyate kāmaḥ
kāmāt krodho 'bhijāyate

For a man dwelling on the objects of the senses, an attachment to them is born; from attachment, desire is born; from desire, anger is born;

63 क्रोधाद् भवति संमोहः संमोहात् स्मृतिविभ्रमः।
स्मृतिभ्रंशाद् बुद्धिनाशो बुद्धिनाशात् प्रणश्यति ॥

krodhād bhavati saṁmohaḥ
saṁmohāt smṛtivibhramaḥ
smṛtibhraṁśād buddhināśo
buddhināśāt praṇaśyati

From anger arises delusion; from delusion, loss of the memory; from loss of the memory, destruction of discrimination; from destruction of discrimination one is lost.

64 रागद्वेषवियुक्तस्तु विषयान् इन्द्रियैश्चरन्।
आत्मवश्यैर् विधेयात्मा प्रसादम् अधिगच्छति ॥

rāgadveṣaviyuktas tu
viṣayān indriyāiścaran
ātmavaśyāir vidheyātmā
prasādam adhigacchati

With the elimination of desire and hatred, even though moving among the objects of the senses, he who is controlled by the Self, by self-restraint, attains tranquility.

65 प्रसादे सर्वदुःखानां हानिर् अस्योपजायते।
प्रसन्नचेतसो ह्याशु बुद्धिः पर्यवतिष्ठते ॥

prasāde sarvaduḥkhānāṁ
hānir asyopajāyate
prasannacetaso hyāśu
buddhiḥ paryavatiṣṭhate

In tranquility the cessation of all sorrows is born for him. Indeed, for the tranquil-minded the intellect at once becomes steady.

66 नास्ति बुद्धिर् अयुक्तस्य न चायुक्तस्य भावना ।
न चाभावयतः शान्तिर् अशान्तस्य कुतः सुखम् ॥
nāsti buddhir ayuktasya
na cāyuktasya bhāvanā
na cābhāvayataḥ śāntir
aśāntasya kutaḥ sukham

There is no wisdom in him who is uncontrolled, and there is likewise no concentration in him who is uncontrolled, and in him who does not concentrate, there is no peace. How can there be happiness for him who is not peaceful?

67 इन्द्रियाणां हि चरतां यन् मनो ऽनुविधीयते ।
तदस्य हरति प्रज्ञां वायुर् नावम् इवाम्भसि ॥
indriyāṇāṁ hi caratāṁ
yan mano 'nuvidhīyate
tadasya harati prajñāṁ
vāyur nāvam ivāmbhasi

When the mind runs after the wandering senses, then it carries away one's understanding, as the wind carries away a ship on the waters.

68 तस्माद् यस्य महाबाहो निगृहीतानि सर्वशः ।
इन्द्रियाणीन्द्रियार्थेभ्यस् तस्य प्रज्ञा प्रतिष्ठिता ॥

tasmād yasya mahābāho
nigṛhītāni sarvaśaḥ
indriyāṇīndriyārthebhyas
tasya prajñā pratiṣṭhitā

Therefore, O Arjuna, the wisdom of him whose senses are withdrawn from the objects of the senses; that wisdom stands firm.

69 या निशा सर्वभूतानां तस्यां जागर्ति संयमी ।
यस्यां जाग्रति भूतानि सा निशा पश्यतो मुनेः ॥
yā niśā sarvabhūtānāṁ
tasyāṁ jāgarti saṁyamī
yasyāṁ jāgrati bhūtāni
sā niśā paśyato muneḥ

The man of restraint is awake in that which is night for all beings; the time in which all beings are awake is night for the sage who sees.

70 आपूर्यमाणम् अचलप्रतिष्ठं
समुद्रम् आपः प्रविशन्ति यद्वत् ।
तद्वत् कामा यं प्रविशन्ति सर्वे
स शान्तिम् आप्नोति न कामकामी ॥
āpūryamaṇam acalapratiṣṭhaṁ
samudram āpaḥ praviśanti yadvat
tadvat kāmā yaṁ praviśanti sarve
sa śāntim āpnoti na kāmakāmī

Like the ocean, which becomes filled yet remains unmoved and stands still as the waters enter it, he whom all desires enter and who remains unmoved attains peace; not so the man who is full of desire.

71 विहाय कामान् यः सर्वान् पुमांश्चरति निःस्पृहः ।
निर्ममो निरहंकारः स शान्तिम् अधिगच्छति ॥
vihāya kāmān yaḥ sarvān
pumāṅścarati niḥspṛhaḥ
nirmamo nirahaṁkāraḥ
sa śāntim adhigacchati

The man who abandons all desires acts free from longing. Indifferent to possessions, free from egotism, he attains peace.

72 एषा ब्राह्मी स्थितिः पार्थ नैनां प्राप्य विमुह्यति ।
स्थित्वा ऽस्याम् अन्तकाले ऽपि ब्रह्मनिर्वाणम् ऋच्छति ॥
eṣā brāhmī sthitiḥ pārtha
nāināṁ prāpya vimuhyati
sthivā 'syām antakāle 'pi
brahmanirvāṇam ṛcchati

This is the divine state, Arjuna. Having attained this, he is not deluded; fixed in it, even at the hour of death, he reaches the bliss of God.

Hari Om Tat Sat
Iti Srimad Bhagavadgītāsūpaniṣatsu Brahmavidyāyām
Yogaśāstre Sri Kriṣnārjunasamvāde
Sānkhyayogo Nāma Dvitiyoddhyāyaḥ.

Thus ends the second Chapter, entitled "The Yoga of Knowledge," of the venerated Bhagavad Gita Upanishad, the Knowledge of the Absolute, the scripture of Yoga, the dialogue between Sri Krishna and Arjuna.

THREE

The Yoga of Action

atha tritiyoddhyāyaḥ

1 अर्जुन उवाच। *arjuna uvāca*

ज्यायसी चेत् कर्मणस् ते मता बुद्धिर्जनार्दन।
तत्किं कर्मणि घोरे मां नियोजयसि केशव॥

jyāyasī cet karmaṇas te
matā buddhirjanārdana
tatkiṁ karmaṇi ghore māṁ
niyojayasi keśava

Arjuna spoke:
If it is Your conviction that knowledge is better than action, O Krishna, then why do You urge me to engage in this terrible action?

2 व्यामिश्रेणेव वाक्येन बुद्धिं मोहयसीव मे।
तद् एकं वद निश्चित्य येन श्रेयो ऽहम् आप्नुयाम्॥

vyāmiśreṇeva vākyena
buddhiṁ mohayasīva me
tad ekaṁ vada niścitya
yena śreyo 'ham āpnuyām

With speech that seems equivocal, You confuse my intelligence. Tell me surely this one thing: how should I attain the highest good?

3 श्रीभगवान् उवाच । *śrībhagavān uvāca*

लोके ऽस्मिन् द्विविधा निष्ठा पुरा प्रोक्ता मया ऽनघ ।
ज्ञानयोगेन सांख्यानां कर्मयोगेन योगिनाम् ॥

loke 'smin dvividhā niṣṭhā
purā proktā mayā 'nagha
jñānayogena sāṁkhyānāṁ
karmayogena yoginām

The Blessed Lord spoke:

In this world there is a two-fold basis (of devotion) taught since ancient times by Me, O Arjuna: that of knowledge—the yoga of the followers of Samkhya and that of action—the yoga of the yogins.

4 न कर्मणाम् अनारम्भान् नैष्कर्म्यं पुरुषो ऽश्नुते ।
न च संन्यसनादेव सिद्धिं समधिगच्छति ॥

na karmaṇām anārambhān
nāiṣkarmyaṁ puruṣo 'śnute
na ca saṁnyasanādeva
siddhiṁ samadhigacchati

Not by abstention from actions does a man attain the state beyond karma, and not by renunciation alone does he approach perfection.

5 न हि कश्चित् क्षणमपि जातु तिष्ठत्यकर्मकृत् ।
कार्यते ह्यवशः कर्म सर्वः प्रकृतिजैर् गुणैः ॥

na hi kaścit kṣaṇamapi
jātu tiṣṭhatyakarmakṛt
kāryate hyavaśaḥ karma
sarvaḥ prakṛtijāir guṇāiḥ

Indeed, no one, even in the twinkling of an eye, ever exists without performing action; everyone is forced to perform action, even action which is against his will, by the qualities which originate in material nature.

6 कर्मेन्द्रियाणि संयम्य य आस्ते मनसा स्मरन् ।
इन्द्रियार्थान् विमूढात्मा मिथ्याचारः स उच्यते ।।
karmendriyāṇi saṁyaṁya
ya āste manasā smaran
indriyārthān vimūḍhātmā
mithyācāraḥ sa ucyate

He who sits, restraining his organs of action, while in his mind brooding over the objects of the senses, with a deluded mind, is said to be a hypocrite.

7 यस् त्विन्द्रियाणि मनसा नियम्यारभते ऽर्जुन ।
कर्मेन्द्रियैः कर्मयोगम् असक्तः स विशिष्यते ।।
yas tvindriyāṇi manasā
niyamyārabhate 'rjuna
karmendriyāiḥ karmayogam
asaktaḥ sa viśiṣyate

But he who undertakes the control of the senses by the mind, Arjuna, and, without attachment, engages the organs of action in the yoga of action, is superior.

8 नियतं कुरु कर्म त्वं कर्म ज्यायो ह्यकर्मणः ।
शरीरयात्रापि च ते तैर् दत्तान् अप्रदायैभ्यो
niyataṁ kuru karma tvaṁ
karma jyāyo hyakarmaṇaḥ
śarīrayātrāpi ca te
na prasiddhyed akarmaṇaḥ

Perform your duty, for action is indeed better than non-action, and even the mere maintenance of your body could not be accomplished without action.

9 यज्ञार्थात् कर्मणो ऽन्यत्र लोको ऽयं कर्मबन्धनः ।
तदर्थं कर्म कौन्तेय मुक्तसङ्गः समाचर ॥
yajñārthāt karmaṇo 'nyatra
loko 'yaṁ karmabandhanaḥ
tadarthaṁ karma kāunteya
muktasaṅgaḥ samācara

Aside from action for the purpose of sacrifice, this world is bound by action. Perform action for the purpose of sacrifice, Arjuna, free from attachment.

10 सहयज्ञाः प्रजाः सृष्ट्वा पुरोवाच प्रजापतिः ।
अनेन प्रसविष्यध्वम् एष वो ऽस्त्विष्टकामधुक्
sahayajñāḥ prajāḥ sṛṣṭvā
purovāca prajāpatiḥ
anena prasaviṣyadhvam
eṣa vo 'stviṣṭakāmadhuk

Having created mankind along with sacrifice, Prajapati, (the Lord of Creatures) anciently said, "By this (i.e. sacrifice), may you bring forth; may this be your wish-fulfilling cow."

11 देवान् भावयतानेन ते देवा भावयन्तु वः।
परस्परं भावयन्तः श्रेयः परम् अवाप्स्यथ ॥

devān bhāvayatānena
te devā bhāvayantu vaḥ
parasparaṁ bhāvayantaḥ
śreyaḥ param avāpsyatha

"By this (i.e. sacrifice) may you nourish the gods and may the gods nourish you; by nourishing each other, you shall attain the "highest welfare."

12 इष्टान् भोगान् हि वो देवा दास्यन्ते यज्ञभाविता:।
यो भुङ्क्ते स्तेन एव सः॥ न प्रसिद्ध्येद् अकर्मणः॥

iṣṭān bhogān hi vo devā
dāsyante yajñabhāvitāḥ
tāir dattān apradāyāibhyo
yo bhuṅkte stena eva saḥ

"The gods, nourished by the sacrifice, will indeed give you desired enjoyments; he who enjoys these gifts while not offering to them in return, is a thief."

13 यज्ञशिष्टाशिनः सन्तो मुच्यन्ते सर्वकिल्बिषैः।
भुञ्जते ते त्वघं पापा ये पचन्त्यात्मकारणात् ॥

yajñaśiṣṭāśinaḥ santo
mucyante sarvakilbiṣāiḥ
bhuñjate te tvaghaṁ pāpā
ye pacantyātmakāraṇāt

The good, who eat the remainder of the sacrifice, are released from all evils; but the wicked, who cook only for their own sake, eat their own impurity.

14 अन्नाद् भवन्ति भूतानि पर्जन्याद् अन्नसंभवः ।
यज्ञाद् भवति पर्जन्यो यज्ञः कर्मसमुद्भवः ॥
annād bhavanti bhūtāni
parjanyād annasaṁbhavaḥ
yajñād bhavati parjanyo
yajñaḥ karmasamudbhavaḥ

Beings exist from food, food is brought into being by rain, rain from sacrifice, and sacrifice is brought into being by action.

15 कर्म ब्रह्मोद्भवं विद्धि ब्रह्माक्षरसमुद्भवम् ।
तस्मात् सर्वगतं ब्रह्म नित्यं यज्ञे प्रतिष्ठितम् ॥
karma brahmodbhavaṁ viddhi
brahmākṣarasamudbhavam
tasmāt sarvagataṁ brahma
nityaṁ yajñe pratiṣṭhitam

Know that ritual action originates in Brahman (the Vedas) and Brahman arises from the Imperishable; therefore the all-pervading Brahman is eternally established in sacrifice.

16 एवं प्रवर्तितं चक्रं नानुवर्तयतीह यः ।
अघायुरिन्द्रियारामो मोघं पार्थ स जीवति ॥

evaṁ pravartitaṁ cakraṁ
nānuvartayatīha yaḥ
aghāyurindriyārāmo
moghaṁ pārtha sa jīvati

He who does, here on earth, turn the wheel thus set in motion, lives, Arjuna, maliciously, full of sense delights, and in vain.

17 यस्त्वात्मरतिरेव स्याद् आत्मतृप्तश्च मानवः ।
आत्मन्येव च संतुष्टस् तस्य कार्यं न विद्यते ॥

yastvātmaratireva syād
ātmatṛptaśca mānavaḥ
ātmanyeva ca saṁtuṣṭas
tasya kāryaṁ na vidyate

He whose delight is only in the Self, whose satisfaction is in the Self, and who is content only in the Self; for him the need to act does not exist.

18 नैव तस्य कृतेनार्थो नाकृतेनेह कश्चन ।
न चास्य सर्वभूतेषु कश्चिद् अर्थव्यपाश्रयः ॥

nāiva tasya kṛtenārtho
nākṛteneha kaścana
na cāsya sarvabhūteṣu
kaścid arthavyapāśrayaḥ

He has no purpose at all in action, or in non-action, and he has no need of any being for any purpose whatsoever.

19 तस्माद् असक्तः सततं कार्यं कर्म समाचर।
असक्तो ह्याचरन्कर्म परम् आप्नोति पूरुषः॥

tasmād asaktaḥ satataṁ
kāryaṁ karma samācara
asakto hyācarankarma
param āpnoti pūruṣaḥ

Therefore, constantly unattached, perform that action which is your duty. Indeed, by performing action while unattached, man attains the Supreme.

20 कर्मणैव हि संसिद्धिम् आस्थिता जनकादयः।
लोकसंग्रहमेवापि संपश्यन् कर्तुमर्हसि॥

karmaṇāiva hi saṁsiddhim
āsthitā janakādayaḥ
lokasaṁgrahamevāpi
saṁpaśyan kartum arhasi

Perfection was attained by kings like Janaka with action alone. For the mere maintenance of the world, you should act.

21 यद्यद् आचरति श्रेष्ठस् तत्तद् एवेतरो जनः।
स यत् प्रमाणं कुरुते लोकस्तदनुवर्तते॥

yadyad ācarati śreṣṭhas
tattad evetaro janaḥ
sa yat pramāṇaṁ kurute
lokastadanuvartate

Whatever the greatest man does, thus do the rest; whatever standard he sets, the world follows that.

22 न मे पार्थास्ति कर्तव्यं त्रिषु लोकेषु किंचन।
नानवाप्तमवाप्तव्यं वर्त एव च कर्मणि ॥

na me pārthāsti kartavyaṁ
trisu lokeṣu kiṁcana
nānavāptamavāptavyaṁ
varta eva ca karmaṇi

For Me, O Arjuna, there is nothing whatever to be done in the three worlds, nor is there anything not attained to be attained. Nevertheless I engage in action.

23 यदि ह्यहं न वर्तेयं जातु कर्मण्यतन्द्रितः।
मम वर्त्मानुवर्तन्ते मनुष्याः पार्थ सर्वशः ॥

yadi hyahaṁ na varteyaṁ
jātu karmaṇyatandritaḥ
mama vartmānuvartante
manuṣyāḥ pārtha sarvaśaḥ

Indeed, if I, unwearied, should not engage in action at all, mankind would follow My path everywhere, O Arjuna.

24 उत्सीदेयुर् इमे लोका न कुर्यां कर्म चेदहम्।
संकरस्य च कर्ता स्याम् उपहन्याम् इमाः प्रजाः ॥

utsīdeyur ime lokā
na kuryāṁ karma cedaham
saṁkarasya ca kartā syām
upahanyām imāḥ prajāḥ

If I did not perform action, these worlds would perish and I would be the cause of confusion; I would destroy these creatures.

25 सक्ताः कर्मण्यविद्वांसो यथा कुर्वन्ति भारत।
कुर्याद् विद्वांस् तथासक्तश् चिकीर्षुर् लोकसंग्रहम्॥

saktāḥ karmaṇyavidvāṁso
yathā kurvanti bhārata
kuryād vidvāṅs tathāsaktaś
cikīrṣur lokasaṁgraham

While those who are unwise act from attachment to action, O Arjuna, so the wise should act without attachment, intending to maintain the welfare of the world.

26 न बुद्धिभेदं जनयेद् अज्ञानां कर्मसङ्गिनां
जोषयेत् सर्वकर्माणि। विद्वान् युक्तः समाचरन्॥
na buddhibhedaṁ janayed
ajñānāṁ karmasaṅgināṁ
joṣayet sarvakarmāṇi
vidvān yuktaḥ samācaran

One should not unsettle the minds of the ignorant who are attached to action; the wise one should cause them to enjoy all actions, while himself performing actions in a disciplined manner.

27 प्रकृतेः क्रियमाणानि गुणैः कर्माणि सर्वशः।
अहंकारविमूढात्मा कर्ताहम् इति मन्यते॥
prakrteḥ kriyamāṇāni
guṇāiḥ karmāṇi sarvaśaḥ
ahaṁkāravimūḍhātmā
kartāham iti manyate

Actions in all cases are performed by the qualities of material nature; he whose mind is confused by egoism imagines, "I am the doer."

28 तत्त्ववित् तु महाबाहो गुणकर्मविभागयोः ।
गुणा गुणेषु वर्तन्त इति मत्वा न सज्जते ।।

tattvavit tu mahābāho
guṇakarmavibhāgayoḥ
guṇā guṇeṣu vartanta
iti matvā na sajjate

But he who knows the truth, O Arjuna, about the two roles of the qualities and action, thinking, "The qualities work among the qualities," is not attached.

29 प्रकृतेर् गुणसंमूढाः सज्जन्ते गुणकर्मसु ।
तान् अकृत्स्नविदो मन्दान् कृत्स्नविन् न विचालयेत् ।।

prakṛter guṇasaṁmūḍhāḥ
sajjante guṇakarmasu
tān akṛtsnavido mandān
kṛtsnavin na vicālayet

Those deluded by the qualities of material nature are attached to the actions of the qualities. The perfect knower should not disturb the foolish men of incomplete knowledge .

30 मयि सवाणि कर्माणि संन्यस्याध्यात्मचेतसा ।
निराशीर् निर्ममो भूत्वा युध्यस्व विगतज्वरः ।।

mayi sarvāṇi karmāṇi
saṁnyasyādhyātmacetasā
nirāśīr nirmamo bhūtvā
yudhyasva vigatajvaraḥ

Deferring all actions in Me, meditating on the supreme Spirit, having become free from desire and selfishness,with your fever departed, fight!

31 ये मे मतम् इदं नित्यम् अनुतिष्ठन्ति मानवाः ।
श्रद्धावन्तो ऽनसूयन्तो मुच्यन्ते ते ऽपि कर्मभिः ॥
ye me matam idaṁ nityam
anutiṣṭhanti mānavāḥ
śraddhāvanto 'nasūyanto
mucyante te 'pi karmabhiḥ

Men who constantly practice this teaching of Mine, believing, not sneering, are also released from the bondage of actions.

32 ये त्वेतद् अभ्यसूयन्तो नानुतिष्ठन्ति मे मतम् ।
सर्वज्ञानविमूढांस् तान् विद्धि नष्टान् अचेतसः ॥
ye tvetad abhyasūyanto
nānutiṣṭhanti me matam
sarvajñānavimūḍhāṅs tān
viddhi naṣṭān acetasaḥ

But those who, sneering at this, do not practice My teaching, confusing all wisdom, know them to be lost and mindless.

33 सदृशं चेष्टते स्वस्याः प्रकृतेर् ज्ञानवान् अपि ।
प्रकृतिं यान्ति भूतानि निग्रहः किं करिष्यति ॥

sadṛśam ceṣṭate svasyāḥ
prakṛter jñānavān api
prakṛtiṁ yānti bhūtāni
nigrahaḥ kim kariṣyati

One acts according to one's own material nature. Even the wise man does so. Beings follow their own material nature; what will restraint accomplish?

34 इन्द्रियस्येन्द्रियस्यार्थे रागद्वेषौ व्यवस्थितौ ।
तयोर् न वशम् आगच्छेत् तौ ह्यस्य परिपन्थिनौ ॥

indriyasyendriyasyārthe
rāgadveṣāu vyavasthitāu
tayor na vaśam āgacchet
tāu hyasya paripanthināu

Passion and hatred are seated in the senses in relation to their objects. One should not come under the power of these two; they are indeed one's enemies.

35 श्रेयान् स्वधर्मो विगुणः परधर्मात् स्वनुष्ठितात् ।
स्वधर्मे निधनं श्रेयः परधर्मो भयावहः ॥

śreyān svadharmo viguṇaḥ
paradharmāt svanuṣṭhitāt
svadharme nidhanam śreyaḥ
paradharmo bhayāvahaḥ

Better one's own duty though deficient than the duty of another well performed. Better is death in one's own duty; the duty of another invites danger.

36 अर्जुन उवाच। *arjuna uvāca*

अथ केन प्रयुक्तो ऽयं पापं चरति पूरुषः।
अनिच्छन्नपि वार्ष्णेय बलाद् इव नियोजितः॥

atha kena prayukto 'yaṁ
pāpaṁ carati pūruṣaḥ
anicchannapi vārṣṇeya
balād iva niyojitaḥ

Arjuna spoke:

Then impelled, by what does a man commit this evil, unwillingly even, O Krishna, as if urged by force?

37 श्रीभगवान् उवाच। *śrībhagavān uvāca*

काम एष क्रोध एष रजोगुणसमुद्भवः।
महाशनो महापाप्मा विद्ध्येनम् इह वैरिणम्॥

kāma eṣa krodha eṣa
rajoguṇasamudbhavaḥ
mahaśano mahāpāpmā
viddhyenam iha vāiriṇam

The Blessed Lord spoke:

This force is desire, this force is anger; its source is the rajas guna. Voracious and greatly injurious, know this to be the enemy.

38 धूमेनाव्रियते वह्निर् यथा ऽदर्शो मलेन च।
यथोल्बेनावृतो गर्भस् तथा तेनेदम् आवृतम्॥

dhūmenāvriyate vahnir
yathā 'darśo malena ca

yatholbenāvṛto garbhas
tathā tenedam āvṛtam

As fire is obscured by smoke, and a mirror by dust, as the embryo is enveloped by the membrane, so the intellect is obscured by passion.

39 आवृतं ज्ञानम् एतेन ज्ञानिनो नित्यवैरिणा ।
कामरूपेण कौन्तेय दुष्पूरेणानलेन च ॥
āvṛtaṁ jñānam etena
jñānino nityavāiriṇā
kāmarūpeṇa kāunteya
duṣpūreṇānalena ca

O Arjuna, the knowledge even of the wise ones is obscured by this eternal enemy, having the form of desire, which is as insatiable fire.

40 इन्द्रियाणि मनो बुद्धिर् अस्याधिष्ठानमुच्यते ।
एतैर् विमोहयत्येष ज्ञानम् आवृत्य देहिनम् ॥
indriyāṇi mano buddhir
asyādhiṣṭhānam ucyate
etāir vimohayatyeṣa
jñānam āvṛtya dehinam

The senses, the mind and the intellect are said to be its (i.e. the eternal enemy's) abode; with these, it confuses the embodied one, obscuring his knowledge.

41 तस्मात् त्वम् इन्द्रियाण्यादौ नियम्य भरतर्षभ ।
पाप्मानं प्रजहि ह्येनं ज्ञानविज्ञाननाशनम् ॥

tasmāt tvam indriyāṇyādāu
niyamya bharatarṣabha
pāpmānaṁ prajahi hyenaṁ
jñānavijñānanāśanam

Therefore, restraining the senses first, O Arjuna, kill this evil demon which destroys knowledge and discrimination.

42 इन्द्रियाणि पराण्याहुर् इन्द्रियेभ्यः परं मनः ।
मनसस् तु परा बुद्धिर् यो बुद्धेः परतस् तु सः ।।
indriyāṇi parāṇyāhur
indriyebhyaḥ paraṁ manaḥ
manasas tu parā buddhir
yo buddheḥ paratas tu saḥ

They say that the senses are superior. The mind is superior to the senses; moreover, the intellect is superior to the mind; that which is superior to the intellect is the Self.

43 एवं बुद्धेः परं बुद्ध्वा संस्तभ्यात्मानम् आत्मना ।
जहि शत्रु महाबाहो कामरूपं दुरासदम् ।।
evaṁ buddheḥ paraṁ buddhvā
saṁstabhyātmānam ātmanā
jahi śatruṁ mahābāho
kāmarūpaṁ durāsadam

Thus having known that which is higher than the intellect, sustaining the self by the Self, kill the enemy, O Arjuna, which has the form of desire and is difficult to conquer.

Hari Om Tat Sat
Iti Srimad Bhagavadgītāsūpaniṣatsu Brahmavidyāyām
Yogaśāstre Sri Kriṣnārjunasamvāde
Karmayogo Nāma Tritiyoddhyāyaḥ.

Thus ends the third Chapter, entitled "The Yoga of Action," of the venerated Bhagavad Gita Upanishad, the Knowledge of the Absolute, the scripture of Yoga, the dialogue between Sri Krishna and Arjuna.

FOUR

The Yoga of Wisdom

atha caturthoddhyāyaḥ

1 श्रीभगवान् उवाच । *śrībhagavān uvāca*

इमं विवस्वते योगं प्रोक्तवान् अहम् अव्ययम् ।
विवस्वान् मनवे प्राह मनुर् इक्ष्वाकवे ऽब्रवीत् ॥

imaṁ vivasvate yogaṁ
proktavān aham avyayam
vivasvān manave prāha
manur ikṣvākave 'bravīt

The Blessed Lord spoke:

I proclaimed this imperishable yoga to Vivasvat; Vivasvat communicated it to Manu, and Manu imparted it to Ikshvaku.

2 एवं परम्पराप्राप्तम् इमं राजर्षयो विदुः ।
स कालेनेह महता योगो नष्टः परंतप ॥

evaṁ paramparāprāptam
imaṁ rājarṣayo viduḥ
sa kāleneha mahatā
yogo naṣṭaḥ paraṁtapa

Thus received by succession, the royal seers knew this; after a long time here on earth, this yoga has been lost, Arjuna.

3 स एवायं मया ते ऽद्य योगः प्रोक्तः पुरातनः ।
भक्तो ऽसि मे सखा चेति रहस्यं ह्येतद् उत्तमम् ॥
sa evāyaṁ mayā te 'dya
yogaḥ proktaḥ purātanaḥ
bhakto 'si me sakhā ceti
rahasyaṁ hyetad uttamam

This ancient yoga is today declared by Me to you, since you are My devotee and friend. This secret is supreme indeed.

4 अर्जुन उवाच । *arjuna uvāca*

अपरं भवतो जन्म परं जन्म विवस्वतः ।
कथम् एतद् विजानीयां त्वम् आदौ प्रोक्तवान् इति ॥
aparaṁ bhavato janma
paraṁ janma vivasvataḥ
katham etad vijānīyāṁ
tvam ādāu proktavān iti

Arjuna spoke:
Your birth was later, the birth of Vivasvat earlier; how should I understand this, that You declared it in the beginning?

5 श्रीभगवान् उवाच । *śrībhagavān uvāca*

बहूनि मे व्यतीतानि जन्मानि तव चार्जुन ।
तान्यहं वेद सर्वाणि न त्वं वेत्थ परंतप ॥
bahūni me vyatītāni
janmāni tava cārjuna
tānyahaṁ veda sarvāṇi
na tvaṁ vettha paraṁtapa

Āratī Līјo

Refrain:
Āratī līјo aja avināśi
Pūraṇa nityānanda prakāśī
Pūraṇa muktānanda prakāśī (2x)
Āratī līјo

Nabha aura dharaṇī āratī thālā
Candra sūraja doū dīpa ujālā (2x)
Agara candana saba dhūpa birāje (2x)
Jhūlā merana cāvara tarana rāśī
(Refrain)

Phūla vanaspati haĩ ye sārī
Sātõ sāgara jala kī jhārī (2x)
Gagana anāhata bājẽ bāje (2x)
Gāje rāga ḍare yama pāśī
(Refrain)

Cāra prakāra ke anna gopālā
Soī tero bhoga rasālā (2x)
Loka caturdiśa mandira tero (2x)
Ghaṭa ghaṭa āsana svayaṁ vikāsī
(Refrain)

Mahāvākya vedon ke jo haĩ
So tero caraṇāmṛta so haĩ (2x)
Sadguru pujārī deo caraṇāmṛta (2x)
Pīyẽ narīnara bandha vināśī
(Refrain)

Śrī Guru Pādukā-Pañcakam

1. Om namo gurubhyo gurupādukābhyo
Namaḥ parebhyaḥ parapādukābhyaḥ,
Acārya-siddheśvara-pādukābhyo
Namo namaḥ śrīgurupādukābhyaḥ.

2. Aiṅkāra-hrīṅkāra-rahasya-yukta-
Śrīṅkāra-gūḍhārtha-mahāvibhūtyā,
Omkāra-marma-pratipādinībhyām
Namo namaḥ śrīgurupādukābhyām.

3. Hotrāgni-hautrāgni-haviṣya-hotṛ-
Homādi-sarvākṛti-bhāsamānam,
Yadbrahma tadbodha-vitāriṇībhyām
Namo namaḥ śrīgurupādukābhyām.

4. Kāmādi-sarpavraja-gāruḍābhyam
Viveka-vairāgya-nidhi-pradābhyām,
Bodhapradābhyām drutamokṣadābhyām
Namo namaḥ śrīgurupādukābhyām.

5. Ananta-samsāra-samudra-tāra-
Naukāyitābhyām sthirabhaktidābhyām,
Jāḍyābdhi-samśoṣaṇa-vāḍavābhyām
Namo namaḥ śrīgurupādukābhyām.

Om śāntiḥ śāntiḥ śāntiḥ

The Blessed Lord spoke:
Many of My births have passed away, and also yours, Arjuna. I know them all; you do not know them, Arjuna.

6 अजो ऽपि सन्न् अव्ययात्मा भूतानाम् ईश्वरो ऽपि सन् ।
प्रकृतिं स्वाम् अधिष्ठाय संभवाम्यात्ममायया ॥

ajo 'pi sann avyayātmā
bhūtānām īśvaro 'pi san
prakṛtiṁ svām adhiṣṭhāya
saṁbhavāmyātmamāyayā

Although I am birthless and My nature is imperishable, although I am the Lord of all beings, yet, by controlling My own material nature, I come into being by My own power.

7 यदा यदा हि धर्मस्य ग्लानिर् भवति भारत ।
अभ्युत्थानम् अधर्मस्य तदा ऽत्मानं सृजाम्यहम् ॥

yadā yadā hi dharmasya
glānir bhavati bhārata
abhyutthānam adharmasya
tadā 'tmānaṁ sṛjāmyaham

Whenever a decrease of righteousness exists, Arjuna, and there is a rising up of unrighteousness, then I manifest Myself.

8 परित्राणाय साधूनां विनाशाय च दुष्कृताम् ।
धर्मसंस्थापनार्थाय संभवामि युगे युगे ॥

paritrāṇāya sādhūnāṁ
vināśāya ca duṣkṛtām

dharmasaṁsthāpanārthāya
saṁbhavāmi yuge yuge

For the protection of the good and the destruction of evil doers, for the sake of establishing righteousness, I am born in every age.

9 जन्म कर्म च मे दिव्यम् एवं यो वेत्ति तत्त्वतः ।
त्यक्त्वा देहं पुनर्जन्म नैति माम् एति सोऽर्जुन ॥

janma karma ca me divyam
evaṁ yo vetti tattvataḥ
tyaktvā dehaṁ punarjanma
nāiti mām eti so 'rjuna

He who knows in truth My divine birth and action, having left his body, he is not reborn; he comes to Me, Arjuna.

10 वीतरागभयक्रोधा मन्मया माम् उपाश्रिताः ।
बहवो ज्ञानतपसा पूता मद्भावम् आगताः ॥

vītarāgabhayakrodhā
manmayā mām upāśritāḥ
bahavo jñānatapasā
pūtā madbhāvam āgatāḥ

Thinking solely of Me, resorting to Me, many whose greed, fear, and anger have departed, purified by the austerity of knowledge, have attained My state of being.

11 ये यथा मां प्रपद्यन्ते तांस् तथैव भजाम्यहम् ।
मम वर्त्मानुवर्तन्ते मनुष्याः पार्थ सर्वशः ॥

ye yathā māṁ prapadyante
tāṁs tathāiva bhajāmyaham
mama vartmānuvartante
manuṣyāḥ pārtha sarvaśaḥ

In whatever way, men take refuge in Me, I reward them. Men everywhere, Arjuna, follow My path.

12 काङ्क्षन्तः कर्मणां सिद्धिं यजन्त इह देवताः ।
क्षिप्रं हि मानुषे लोके सिद्धिर् भवति कर्मजा ।।
kāñksantaḥ karmaṇāṁ siddhiṁ
yajanta iha devatāh
kṣipraṁ hi mānuṣe loke
siddhir bhavati karmajā

Desiring the success of ritual acts, men sacrifice here on earth to the Vedic gods. Quickly indeed in the world of men ritual acts bring success.

13 चातुर्वर्ण्यं मया सृष्टं गुणकर्मविभागशः ।
तस्य कर्तारम् अपि मां विद्ध्यकर्तारम् अव्ययम् ।।
cāturvarṇyaṁ mayā sṛṣṭaṁ
guṇakarmavibhāgaśaḥ
tasya kartāram api māṁ
viddhyakartāram avyayam

The system of four castes was created by Me, according to the distribution of the qualities and their acts. Although I am the creator of this (the system), know Me to be the eternal non-doer.

14 न मां कर्माणि लिम्पन्ति न मे कर्मफले स्पृहा ।
इति मां यो ऽभिजानाति कर्मभिर न स बध्यते ॥

na māṁ karmāṇi limpanti
na me karmaphale spṛhā
iti māṁ yo 'bhijānāti
karmabhir na sa badhyate

Actions do not taint Me; I have no desire for the fruit of action; thus he who comprehends Me is not bound by actions.

15 एवं ज्ञात्वा कृतं कर्म पूर्वैर् अपि मुमुक्षुभिः ।
कुरु कर्मैव तस्मात् त्वं पूर्वैः पूर्वतरं कृतम् ॥

evaṁ jñātvā kṛtaṁ karma
pūrvāir api mumukṣubhiḥ
kuru karmāiva tasmāt tvaṁ
pūrvaiḥ pūrvataraṁ kṛtam

Having known this, the ancients, seeking release, also performed action. Therefore perform action as it was earlier performed by the ancients.

16 किं कर्म किम् अकर्मेति कवयो ऽप्य् अत्र मोहिताः ।
तत् ते कर्म प्रवक्ष्यामि यज् ज्ञात्वा मोक्ष्यसे ऽशुभात् ॥

kiṁ karma kim akarmeti
kavayo 'py atra mohitāḥ
tat te karma pravakṣyāmi
yaj jñātvā mokṣyase 'śubhāt

"What is action? What is inaction?" Thus, even the wise are confused in this matter. This action I shall explain to you, having

known which, you shall be released from evil.

17 कर्मणो ह्यपि बोद्धव्यं बोद्धव्यं च विकर्मणः ।
अकर्मणश्च बोद्धव्यं गहना कर्मणो गतिः ॥
karmaṇo hyapi boddhavyaṁ
boddhavyaṁ ca vikarmaṇaḥ
akarmaṇaśca boddhavyaṁ
gahanā karmaṇo gatiḥ

One must know the nature of action, the nature of wrong action, and also the nature of inaction. The way of action is profound.

18 कर्मण्यकर्म यः पश्येद् अकर्मणि च कर्म यः ।
स बुद्धिमान् मनुष्येषु स युक्तः कृत्स्नकर्मकृत् ॥
karmaṇyakarma yaḥ paśyed
akarmaṇi ca karma yaḥ
sa buddhimān manuṣyeṣu
sa yuktaḥ kṛtsnakarmakṛt

He who perceives inaction in action, and action in inaction, is wise among men; he is a yogi and performs all actions.

19 यस्य सर्वे समारम्भाः कामसंकल्पवर्जिताः ।
ज्ञानाग्निदग्धकर्माणं तम् आहुः पण्डितं बुधाः ॥

yasya sarve samārambhāḥ
kāmasaṁkalpavarjitāḥ
jñānāgnidagdhakarmāṇaṁ
tam āhuḥ paṇḍitaṁ budhāḥ

He who has excluded desire and motive from all his enterprises, and has consumed his karma in the fire of knowledge, him the wise men call a sage.

20 त्यक्त्वा कर्मफलासङ्गं नित्यतृप्तो निराश्रयः।
कर्मण्य् अभिप्रवृत्तो ऽपि नैव किंचित् करोति सः॥
tyaktvā karmaphalāsaṅgaṁ
nityatṛpto nirāśrayaḥ
karmaṇy abhipravṛtto 'pi
nāiva kiṁcit karoti saḥ

He who has abandoned all attachment to the fruits of action, always content, not dependent, even when performing action, does, in effect, nothing at all.

21 निराशीर् यतचित्तात्मा त्यक्तसर्वपरिग्रहः।
शारीरं केवलं कर्म कुर्वन् नाप्नोति किल्बिषम्॥
nirāśīr yatacittātmā
tyaktasarvaparigrahaḥ
śārīraṁ kevalaṁ karma
kurvan nāpnoti kilbiṣam

Performing action with the body alone, without wish, restrained in thought and self, with all motives of acquisition abandoned, he incurs no evil.

22 यदृच्छालाभसंतुष्टो द्वन्द्वातीतो विमत्सरः।
समः सिद्धाव् असिद्धौ च कृत्वा ऽपि न निबध्यते॥
yadṛcchālābhasaṁtuṣṭo
dvandvātīto vimatsaraḥ

samaḥ siddhāv asiddhāu ca
kṛtvā 'pi na nibadhyate

Content with whatever comes to him, transcending the dualities (i.e. pleasure, pain, etc.), free from envy, constant in mind whether in success or in failure, even though he acts, he is not bound.

23 गतसङ्गस्य मुक्तस्य ज्ञानावस्थितचेतसः ।
यज्ञायाचरतः कर्म समग्रं प्रविलीयते ॥
gatasaṅgasya muktasya
jñānāvasthitacetasaḥ
yajñāyācarataḥ karma
samagraṁ pravilīyate

The work of one who is free from attachment, who is liberated, whose thought is established in knowledge, who does work only as a sacrifice, is wholly dissolved.

24 ब्रह्मार्पणं ब्रह्म हविर् ब्रह्माग्नौ ब्रह्मणा हुतम् ।
ब्रह्मैव तेन गन्तव्यं ब्रह्मकर्मसमाधिना ॥
brahmārpaṇaṁ brahma havir
brahmāgnāu brahmaṇā hutam
brahmāiva tena gantavyaṁ
brahmakarmasamādhinā

Brahman is the offering, Brahman is the oblation poured out by Brahman into the fire of Brahman, Brahman is to be attained by him who always sees Brahman in action.

25 दैवम् एवापरे यज्ञं योगिनः पर्युपासते।
ब्रह्माग्नाव् अपरे यज्ञ यज्ञेनैवोपजुह्वति॥
dāivam evāpare yajñaṁ
yoginaḥ paryupāsate
brahmāgnāv apare yajnaṁ
yajñenāivopajuhvati

Some yogins perform sacrifice to the gods; others offer sacrifice, by sacrifice itself, in the fire of Brahman.

26 श्रोत्रादीनीन्द्रियाण्य् अन्ये संयमाग्निषु जुह्वति।
शब्दादीन् विषयान् अन्य इन्द्रियाग्निषु जुह्वति॥
śrotrādīnīndriyāṇy anye
saṁyamāgniṣu juhvati
śabdādīn viṣayān anya
indriyāgniṣu juhvati

Others offer senses like hearing in the fire of restraint; still others offer sound and other objects of the senses in the fire of the senses.

27 सर्वाणीन्द्रियकर्माणि प्राणकर्माणि चापरे।
आत्मसंयमयोगाग्नौ जुह्वति ज्ञानदीपिते॥
sarvāṇīṇdriyakarmāṇi
prāṇakarmāṇi cāpare
ātmasaṁyamayogāgnāu
juhvati jñānadīpite

Others offer all actions of the senses and actions of the vital breath in the fire of the yoga of self-restraint, which is kindled by knowledge.

28 द्रव्ययज्ञास् तपोयज्ञा योगयज्ञास् तथापरे ।
स्वाध्यायज्ञानयज्ञाश्च यतयः संशितव्रताः ।।
dravyayajñās tapoyajñā
yogayajñās tathāpare
svādhyāyajñānayajñāśca
yatayaḥ saṁśitavratāḥ

Some offer as sacrifice their material possessions or their austerities and practice of yoga, while ascetics of severe vows offer study of the scriptures and knowledge as sacrifice.

29 अपाने जुह्वति प्राणं प्राणे ऽपानं तथापरे ।
प्राणापानगती रुद्ध्वा प्राणायामपरायणाः ।।
apāne juhvati prāṇaṁ
prāṇe 'pānaṁ tathāpare
prāṇāpānagatī ruddhvā
prāṇāyāmaparāyaṇāḥ

Some offer inhalation into exhalation, and others exhalation into inhalation, restraining the path of inhalation and exhalation, intent on control of the vital breath.

30 अपरे नियताहाराः प्राणान् प्राणेषु जुह्वति ।
सर्वे ऽप्येते एते यज्ञविदो यज्ञक्षपितकल्मषाः ।।
apare niyatāhārāḥ
prāṇān prāṇeṣu juhvati

sarve 'pyete yajñavido
yajñakṣapitakalmaṣāḥ

Others who have restricted their foods offer the life breath into the life breath; all these are knowers of sacrifice, and their evils have been destroyed through sacrifice.

31 यज्ञशिष्टामृतभुजो यान्ति ब्रह्म सनातनम् ।
नायं लोको ऽस्त्य् अयज्ञस्य कुतो ऽन्यः कुरुसत्तम ।।
yajñaśiṣṭāmṛtabhujo
yānti brahma sanātanam
nāyaṁ loko 'sty ayajñasya
kuto 'nyaḥ kurusattama

The enjoyers of the nectar of the sacrificial remnants go to primeval Brahman. Not even this world is for the non-sacrificing; how then the other, Arjuna?

32 एवं बहुविधा यज्ञा वितता ब्रह्मणो मुखे ।
कर्मजान् विद्धि तान् सर्वान् एवं ज्ञात्वा विमोक्ष्यसे ।।
evaṁ bahuvidhā yajñā
vitatā brahmaṇo mukhe
karmajān viddhi tān sarvān
evaṁ jñātvā vimokṣyase

Thus sacrifices are of many kinds, spread out before Brahman. Know them all to be born of action. Thus knowing, you shall be released.

33 श्रेयान् द्रव्यमयाद् यज्ञाज् ज्ञानयज्ञः परंतप ।
सर्वं कर्माखिलं पार्थ ज्ञाने परिसमाप्यते ।।

śreyān dravyamayād yajñāj
jñānayajñaḥ paraṁtapa
sarvaṁ karmākhilaṁ pārtha
jñāne parisamāpyate

Better than the sacrifice of material possessions is the wisdom sacrifice, Arjuna; all action without exception, Arjuna, is fully comprehended in wisdom.

34 तद् विद्धि प्रणिपातेन परिप्रश्नेन सेवया ।
उपदेक्ष्यन्ति ते ज्ञानं ज्ञानिनस् तत्त्वदर्शिनः ॥
tad viddhi praṇipātena
paripraśnena sevayā
upadekṣyanti te jñānaṁ
jñāninas tattvadarśinaḥ

Know this! Through humble submission, through enquiry, through service (on your own part), the knowing ones, the perceivers of truth, will be led to teach you knowledge.

35 यज् ज्ञात्वा न पुनर् मोहम् एवं यास्यसि पाण्डव ।
येन भूतान्य् अशेषेण द्रक्ष्यस्य् आत्मन्य् अथो मयि ॥
yaj jñātvā na punar moham
evaṁ yāsyasi pāṇḍava
yena bhūtāny aśeṣeṇa
drakṣyasy ātmany atho mayi

Knowing that, you shall not again fall into delusion, Arjuna; and by that knowledge you shall see all beings in yourself, and also in Me.

36 अपि चेद् असि पापेभ्यः सर्वेभ्यः पापकृत्तमः ।
सर्वं ज्ञानप्लवेनैव वृजिनं संतरिष्यसि ॥
api ced asi pāpebhyaḥ
sarvebhyaḥ pāpakṛttamaḥ
sarvaṁ jñānaplavenāiva
vṛjinaṁ saṁtariṣyasi

Even if you were the most evil of all evildoers, you would cross over all wickedness by the boat of knowledge.

37 यथैधांसि समिद्धो ऽग्निर् भस्मसात्कुरुते ऽर्जुन ।
ज्ञानाग्निः सर्वकर्माणि भस्मसात् कुरुते तथा ॥
yathāidhāṁsi samiddho 'gnir
bhasmasāt kurute 'rjuna
jñānāgniḥ sarvakarmāṇi
bhasmasāt kurute tathā

As the kindled fire reduces firewood to ashes, Arjuna, so the fire of knowledge reduces all actions to ashes.

38 न हि ज्ञानेन सदृशं पवित्रम् इह विद्यते ।
तत् स्वयं योगसंसिद्धः कालेनात्मनि विन्दति ॥
na hi jñānena sadṛśaṁ
pavitram iha vidyate
tat svayaṁ yogasaṁsiddhaḥ
kālenātmani vindati

No purifier equal to knowledge is found here in the world; he who is himself perfected in yoga in time finds that knowledge in the Self.

39 श्रद्धावाँल् लभते ज्ञानं तत्परः संयतेन्द्रियः ।
ज्ञानं लब्ध्वा परां शान्तिम् अचिरेणाधिगच्छति ॥
śraddhāvāṁl labhate jñānaṁ
tatparaḥ saṁyatendriyaḥ
jñānaṁ labdhvā parāṁ śāntim
acireṇādhigacchati

He who possesses faith attains knowledge; devoted to that (knowledge), restraining his senses, having attained knowledge, he quickly attains supreme peace.

40 अज्ञश्चाश्रद्दधानश्च संशयात्मा विनश्यति ।
नायं लोको ऽस्ति न परो न सुखं संशयात्मनः ॥
ajñaścāśraddadhānaśca
saṁśayātmā vinaśyati
nāyaṁ loko 'sti na paro
na sukhaṁ saṁśayātmanaḥ

The man who is ignorant, and does not have faith, who is of a doubting nature, is destroyed. Neither this world nor that beyond, nor happiness, is for him who doubts.

41 योगसंन्यस्तकर्माणं ज्ञानसंछिन्नसंशयम् ।
आत्मवन्तं न कर्माणि निबध्नन्ति धनंजय ॥
yogasaṁnyastakarmāṇaṁ
jñānasaṁchinnasaṁśayam
ātmavantaṁ na karmāṇi
nibadhnanti dhanaṁjaya

Action does not bind him who has renounced action through yoga, whose doubt is cut away by knowledge, and who is possessed of the Self, Arjuna.

42 तस्माद् अज्ञानसंभूतं हृत्स्थं ज्ञानासिना ऽत्मनः ।
छित्त्वैनं संशयं योगम् आतिष्ठोत्तिष्ठ भारत ॥
tasmād ajñānasaṁbhūtaṁ
hṛtsthaṁ jñānāsinā 'tmanaḥ
chittvāinaṁ saṁśayaṁ yogam
ātiṣṭhottiṣṭha bhārata

Therefore, having cut away, with your own sword of knowledge, this doubt that proceeds from ignorance and abides in your heart, resort to yoga! Stand up, Arjuna.

Hari Om Tat Sat
Iti Srimad Bhagavadgītāsūpaniṣatsu Brahmavidyāyām
Yogaśāstre Sri Kriṣnārjunasamvāde
Jñānakarmasruyāsayogo Nāma Caturthoddhyāyaḥ.

Thus ends the fourth Chapter, entitled "The Yoga of Wisdom," of the venerated Bhagavad Gita Upanishad, the Knowledge of the Absolute, the scripture of Yoga, the dialogue between Sri Krishna and Arjuna.

FIVE

The Yoga of Renunciation of Action

atha pancamoddhyāyaḥ

1 अर्जुन उवाच । *arjuna uvāca*

संन्यासं कर्मणां कृष्ण पुनर् योगं च शंससि ।
यच्छ्रेय एतयोर् एकं तन् मे ब्रूहि सुनिश्चितम् ॥

saṁnyāsaṁ karmaṇāṁ kṛṣṇa
punar yogaṁ ca śaṁsasi
yacchreya etayor ekaṁ
tan me brūhi suniścitam

Arjuna spoke:
You praise renunciation of actions, and again You praise yoga, Krishna. Which one is the better of these two? Tell this to me definitely.

2 श्रीभगवान् उवाच । *śrībhagavān uvāca*

संन्यासः कर्मयोगश्च निःश्रेयसकराव् उभौ ।
तयोस् तु कर्मसंन्यासात् कर्मयोगो विशिष्यते ॥

saṁnyāsaḥ karmayogaśca
niḥśreyasakarāv ubhāu
tayos tu karmasaṁnyāsāt
karmayogo viśiṣyate

The Blessed Lord spoke:

Both renunciation and the yoga of action lead to incomparable bliss; of the two, however, the yoga of action is superior to the renunciation of action.

3 ज्ञेयः स नित्यसंन्यासी यो न द्वेष्टि न काङ्क्षति ।
निर्द्वन्द्वो हि महाबाहो सुखं बन्धात् प्रमुच्यते ॥

jñeyaḥ sa nityasaṁnyāsī
yo na dveṣṭi na kāṅkṣati
nirdvandvo hi mahābāho
sukhaṁ bandhāt pramucyate

He is to be known as the eternal sannyasi who neither hates nor desires, who is indifferent to the pairs of opposites, O Arjuna. He is easily liberated from bondage.

4 सांख्ययोगौ पृथग्बालाः प्रवदन्ति न पण्डिताः ।
एकम् अप्य् आस्थितः सम्यग् उभयोर् विन्दते फलम् ॥

sāṁkhyayogāu pṛthagbālāḥ
pravadanti na paṇḍitāḥ
ekam apy āsthitaḥ saṁyag
ubhayor vindate phalam

"Sankhya and yoga are different," the childish declare; not the wise. Even with one of them, practiced correctly, one finds the fruit of both.

5 यत् सांख्यैः प्राप्यते स्थानं तद् योगैर् अपि गम्यते ।
एकं सांख्यं च योगं च यः पश्यति स पश्यति ॥

yat sāṁkhyāiḥ prāpyate sthānaṁ
tad yogāir api gamyate
ekaṁ sāṁkhyaṁ ca yogaṁ ca
yaḥ paśyati sa paśyati

The place that is attained by the followers of Sankhya is also attained by the followers of yoga. Sankhya and yoga are one. He who perceives this, truly perceives.

6 संन्यासस् तु महाबाहो दुःखम् आप्तुम् अयोगतः ।
योगयुक्तो मुनिर् ब्रह्म नचिरेणाधिगच्छति ।।
samnyāsas tu mahābāho
duḥkham āptum ayogataḥ
yogayukto munir brahma
nacireṇādhigacchati

Renunciation indeed, O Arjuna, is difficult to attain without yoga; the sage who is disciplined in yoga quickly attains Brahman.

7 योगयुक्तो विशुद्धात्मा विजितात्मा जितेन्द्रियः ।
सर्वभूतात्मभूतात्मा कुर्वन्न् अपि न लिप्यते ।।
yogayukto viśuddhātmā
vijitātmā jitendriyaḥ
sarvabhūtātmabhūtātmā
kurvann api na lipyate

He who is devoted to yoga, whose self is purified, whose self is subdued, whose senses are conquered, whose self has become the self of all beings, is not tainted even when acting.

8 नैव किञ्चित् करोमीति युक्तो मन्यते तत्त्ववित्
पश्यञ्शृण्वन् स्पृशञ्जिघ्रन्न् अश्नन् गच्छन् स्वपञ्श्वसन्

nāiva kiñcit karomīti
yukto manyate tattvavit
paśyañśṛṇvan spṛśañjighrann
aśnan gacchan svapañśvasan

"I do not do anything," thus, steadfast in yoga, the knower of truth should think, whether seeing, hearing, touching, smelling, eating, walking, sleeping, breathing,

9 प्रलपन् विसृजन् गृह्णन्न् उन्मिषन् निमिषन्न् अपि ।
इन्द्रियाणीन्द्रियार्थेषु वर्तन्त इति धारयन् ॥

pralapan visṛjan gṛhṇann
unmiṣan nimiṣann api
indriyāṇīndriyārtheṣu
vartanta iti dhārayan

Talking, excreting, grasping, opening the eyes and shutting the eyes, believing "The senses abide in the objects of the senses."

10 ब्रह्मण्य् आधाय कर्माणि सङ्गं त्यक्त्वा करोति यः ।
लिप्यते न स पापेन पद्मपत्त्रम् इवाम्भसा ॥

brahmaṇy ādhāya karmāṇi
saṅgaṁ tyaktvā karoti yaḥ
lipyate na sa pāpena
padmapattram ivāmbhasā

Offering his actions to Brahman, having abandoned attachment, he who acts is not tainted by evil any more than a lotus leaf by water.

11 कायेन मनसा बुद्ध्या केवलैर् इन्द्रियैर् अपि ।
योगिनः कर्म कुर्वन्ति सङ्गं त्यक्त्वा ऽत्मशुद्धये ॥
kāyena manasā buddhyā
kevalāir indriyāir api
yoginaḥ karma kurvanti
saṅgaṁ tyaktvā 'tmaśuddhaye

With the body, with the mind, with the intellect, even merely with the senses, the yogins perform action toward self-purification, having abandoned attachment.

12 युक्तः कर्मफलं त्यक्त्वा शान्तिमाप्नोति नैष्ठिकीम् ।
अयुक्तः कामकारेण फले सक्तो निबध्यते ॥
yuktaḥ karmaphalaṁ tyaktvā
śāntimāpnoti nāiṣṭhikīm
ayuktaḥ kāmakāreṇa
phale sakto nibadhyate

He who is disciplined in yoga, having abandoned the fruit of action, attains steady peace; the undisciplined one, attached to fruit, is bound by actions prompted by desire.

13 सर्वकर्माणि मनसा संन्यस्यास्ते सुखं वशी ।
नवद्वारे पुरे देही नैव कुर्वन् न कारयन् ॥
sarvakarmāṇi manasā
saṁnyasyāste sukhaṁ vaśī

navadvāre pure dehī
nāiva kurvan na kārayan

Renouncing all actions with the mind, the embodied one sits happily, as the ruler within the city of nine gates, not acting at all, nor causing action.

14 न कर्तृत्वं न कर्माणि लोकस्य सृजति प्रभुः।
न कर्मफलसंयोगं स्वभावस् तु प्रवर्तते ॥
na kartṛtvaṁ na karmāṇi
lokasya sṛjati prabhuḥ
na karmaphalasaṁyogaṁ
svabhāvas tu pravartate

The Lord does not create either the agency (the means of action) or the actions of people, or the union of action with its fruit. Nature, on the other hand, proceeds (in all this).

15 नादत्ते कस्यचित् पापं न चैव सुकृतं विभुः।
अज्ञानेनावृतं ज्ञानं तेन मुह्यन्ति जन्तवः॥

nādatte kasyacit pāpaṁ
na cāiva sukrtaṁ vibhuḥ
ajñānenāvṛtaṁ jñānaṁ
tena muhyanti jantavaḥ

The Lord does not receive either the evil or the good deeds of anyone. Knowledge is enveloped by ignorance. By it (ignorance) people are deluded.

16 ज्ञानेन तु तद् अज्ञानं येषां नाशितम् आत्मनः ।
तेषाम् आदित्यवज् ज्ञानं प्रकाशयति तत् परम् ॥

jñānena tu tad ajñānaṁ
yeṣāṁ nāśitam ātmanaḥ
teṣām ādityavaj jñānaṁ
prakāśayati tat param

But for those in whom this ignorance of the Self is destroyed by knowledge, that knowledge of theirs causes the Supreme to shine like the sun.

17 तद्बुद्धयस् तदात्मानस् तन्निष्ठास् तत्परायणाः ।
गच्छन्त्यपुनरावृत्तिं ज्ञाननिर्धूतकल्मषाः ॥

tadbuddhayas tadātmānas
tanniṣṭhās tatparāyaṇāḥ
gacchantyapunarāvṛttim
jñānanirdhūtakalmaṣāḥ

They whose minds are absorbed in that (i.e. the Supreme), whose selves are fixed on that, whose basis is that, who hold that as the highest object, whose evils have been shaken off by knowledge, go to the end of rebirth.

18 विद्याविनयसंपन्ने ब्राह्मणे गवि हस्तिनि ।
शुनि चैव श्वपाके च पण्डिताः समदर्शिनः ॥

vidyāvinayasaṁpanne
brāhmaṇe gavi hastini
śuni cāiva śvapāke ca
paṇḍitāḥ samadarśinaḥ

The wise see the same (atman) in a brahman endowed with wisdom and cultivation, in a cow, in an elephant, and even in a dog or in an outcaste.

19 इहैव तैर् जितः सर्गो येषां साम्ये स्थितं मनः ।
निर्दोषं हि समं ब्रह्म तस्माद् ब्रह्मणि ते स्थिताः ॥

ihāiva tāir jitaḥ sargo
yeṣāṁ sāmye sthitaṁ manaḥ
nirdoṣaṁ hi samaṁ brahma
tasmād brahmaṇi te sthitāḥ

Even here on earth, rebirth is conquered by those whose mind is established in impartiality. Brahman is spotless and impartial; therefore they are established in Brahman.

20 न प्रहृष्येत् प्रियं प्राप्य नोद्विजेत् प्राप्य चाप्रियम् ।
स्थिरबुद्धिर् असंमूढो ब्रह्मविद् ब्रह्मणि स्थितः ॥

na prahṛṣyet priyaṁ prāpya
nodvijet prāpya cāpriyam
sthirabuddhir asammūḍho
brahmavid brahmaṇi sthitaḥ

One should not rejoice upon attaining what is pleasant, nor should one shudder upon encountering what is unpleasant; with firm intellect, undeluded, knowing Brahman, one is established in Brahman.

21 बाह्यस्पर्शेष्वसक्तात्मा विन्दत्यात्मनि यत् सुखम् ।
स ब्रह्मयोगयुक्तात्मा सुखम् अक्षयम् अश्नुते ॥

bāhyasparśeṣvasaktātmā
vindatyātmani yat sukham
sa brahmayogayuktātmā
sukham akṣayam aśnute

He whose self is unattached to external sensations, who finds happiness in the Self, whose Self is united with Brahman through yoga, reaches imperishable happiness.

22 ये हि संस्पर्शजा भोगा दुःखयोनय एव ते।
आद्यन्तवन्तः कौन्तेय न तेषु रमते बुधः॥
ye hi saṁsparśajā bhogā
duḥkhayonaya eva te
ādyantavantaḥ kāunteya
na teṣu ramate budhaḥ

Pleasures born of contact, indeed, are wombs (i.e. sources) of pain, since they have a beginning and an end (i.e. are not eternal), Arjuna. The wise man is not content with them.

23 शक्नोतीहैव यः सोढुं प्राक् शरीरविमोक्षणात्।
कामक्रोधोद्भवं वेगं स युक्तः स सुखी नरः॥
śaknotīhāiva yaḥ soḍhuṁ
prāk śarīravimokṣaṇāt
kāmakrodhodbhavaṁ vegaṁ
sa yuktaḥ sa sukhī naraḥ

He who is able to endure here on earth, before liberation from the body, the agitation that arises from desire and anger, is disciplined; he is a happy man.

24 यो ऽन्तःसुखो ऽन्तरारामस् तथान्तर्ज्योतिर् एव यः ।
स योगी ब्रह्मनिर्वाणं ब्रह्मभूतो ऽधिगच्छति ॥
yo 'ntaḥsukho 'ntārāramas
tathāntarjyotir eva yaḥ
sa yogī brahmanirvāṇam
brahmabhūto, 'dhigacchati

He who finds his happiness within, his delight within, and his light within, this yogin attains the bliss of Brahman, becoming Brahman.

25 लभन्ते ब्रह्मनिर्वाणम् ऋषयः क्षीणकल्मषाः ।
छिन्नद्वैधा यतात्मानः सर्वभूतहिते रताः ॥
labhante brahmanirvāṇam
ṛṣayaḥ kṣīṇakalmaṣāḥ
chinnadvāidhā yatātmānaḥ
sarvabhūtahite ratāḥ

The seers, whose evils have been destroyed, whose doubts have been cut away, whose selves are restrained, who delight in the welfare of all beings, attain the bliss of Brahman.

26 कामक्रोधवियुक्तानां यतीनां यतचेतसाम् ।
अभितो ब्रह्मनिर्वाणं वर्तते विदितात्मनाम् ॥
kāmakrodhaviyuktānāṁ
yatīnāṁ yatacetasām
abhito brahmanirvāṇaṁ
vartate viditātmanām

To those ascetics who have cast aside desire and anger, whose thought is controlled, who are knowers of the Self, the bliss of Brahman exists everywhere.

27 स्पर्शान् कृत्वा बहिर् बाह्यांश् चक्षुश्चैवान्तरे भ्रुवोः ।
प्राणापानौ समौ कृत्वा नासाभ्यन्तरचारिणौ ॥

sparśan kṛtvā bahir bāhyāṁś
cakṣuścāivāntare bhruvoḥ
prāṇāpānāu samāu kṛtvā
nāsābhyantaracāriṇāu

Expelling outside contacts and fixing the gaze between the two eyebrows, equalizing the inhalation and exhalation, moving within the nostrils,

28 यतेन्द्रियमनोबुद्धिर् मुनिर् मोक्षपरायणः ।
विगतेच्छाभयक्रोधो यः सदा मुक्त एव सः ॥

yatendriyamanobuddhir
munir mokṣaparāyaṇaḥ
vigatecchābhayakrodho
yah sadā mukta eva saḥ

The sage whose highest aim is release; whose senses, mind and intellect are controlled; from whom desire, fear and anger have departed, is forever liberated.

29 भोक्तारं यज्ञतपसां सर्वलोकमहेश्वरम् ।
सुहृदं सर्वभूतानां ज्ञात्वा मां शान्तिमृच्छति ॥

bhoktāraṁ yajñatapasāṁ
sarvalokamaheśvaram
suhṛdaṁ sarvabhūtānāṁ
jñātvā māṁ śāntimṛcchati

Having known Me, the enjoyer of sacrifices and austerities, the mighty Lord of all the world, the friend of all creatures, he (the sage) attains peace.

Hari Om Tat Sat
Iti Srimad Bhagavadgītāsūpaniṣatsu Brahmavidyāyām
Yogaśāstre Sri Kriṣnārjunasamvāde
Karmasannyāsayogo Nāma Pancamoddhyāyaḥ.

Thus ends the fifth Chapter, entitled "The Yoga of Renunciation of Action," of the venerated Bhagavad Gita Upanishad, the Knowledge of the Absolute, the scripture of Yoga, the dialogue between Sri Krishna and Arjuna.

SIX

The Yoga of Meditation

atha ṣaśtoddhyāyaḥ

1 श्रीभगवान् उवाच। *śrībhagavān uvāca*

अनाश्रितः कर्मफलं कार्यं कर्म करोति यः।
स संन्यासी च योगी च न निरग्निर् न चाक्रियः॥

anāśritaḥ karmaphalaṁ
kāryaṁ karma karoti yaḥ
sa saṁnyāsī ca yogī ca
na niragnir na cākriyaḥ

The Blessed Lord spoke:

He who performs that action which is his duty, while renouncing the fruit of action, is a renunciant and a yogin; not he who is without a consecrated fire, and who fails to perform sacred rites.

2 यं संन्यासम् इति प्राहुर् योगं तं विद्धि पाण्डव।
न ह्य् असंन्यस्तसंकल्पो योगी भवति कश्चन॥

yaṁ saṁnyāsam iti prāhur
yogaṁ taṁ viddhi pāṇḍava
na hy asaṁnyastasaṁkalpo
yogī bhavati kaścana

That which they call renunciation, know that to be yoga, Arjuna. Without renouncing selfish purpose, no one becomes a yogin.

3 आरुरुक्षोर् मुनेर् योगं कर्म कारणम् उच्यते ।
योगारूढस्य तस्यैव शमः कारणम् उच्यते ॥
ārurukṣor muner yogaṁ
karma kāraṇam ucyate
yogārūḍhasya tasyāiva
śamaḥ kāraṇam ucyate

For the sage desirous of attaining yoga, action is said to be the means; for him who has already attained yoga, tranquility is said to be the means.

4 यदा हि नेन्द्रियार्थेषु न कर्मस्व् अनुसज्जते ।
सर्वसंकल्पसंन्यासी योगारूढस् तदोच्यते ॥
yadā hi nendriyārtheṣu
na karmasv anusajjate
sarvasaṁkalpasaṁnyāsī
yogārūḍhas tadocyate

When he is attached neither to the objects of the senses nor to actions, and has renounced all purpose, he is then said to have attained yoga.

5 उद्धरेद् आत्मनाऽत्मानं नात्मानम् अवसादयेत् ।
आत्मैव ह्यात्मनो बन्धुर् आत्मैव रिपुर् आत्मनः ॥
uddhared ātmanā 'tmānaṁ
nātmānam avasādayet
ātmāiva hyātmano bandhur
ātmāiva ripur ātmanaḥ

One should uplift oneself by the Self; one should not degrade oneself; for the Self alone can be a friend to oneself, and the Self alone can be an enemy of oneself.

6 बन्धुर् आत्मा ऽत्मनस् तस्य येनात्मैवात्मना जितः ।
अनात्मनस् तु शत्रुत्वे वर्तेतात्मैव शत्रुवत् ॥

bandhur ātmā 'tmanas tasya
yenātmāivātmanā jitaḥ
anātmanas tu śatrutve
vartetātmāiva śatruvat

For him who has conquered himself by the Self, the Self is a friend; but for him who has not conquered himself, the Self remains hostile, like an enemy.

7 जितात्मनः प्रशान्तस्य परमात्मा समाहितः ।
शीतोष्णसुखदुःखेषु तथा मानापमानयोः ॥

jītātmanaḥ praśāntasya
paramātmā samāhitaḥ
śītoṣṇasukhaduḥkheṣu
tathā mānāpamānayoḥ

The highest Self of him who has conquered himself and is peaceful, is steadfast in cold, heat, pleasure, and pain; thus also in honor and dishonor.

8 ज्ञानविज्ञानतृप्तात्मा कूटस्थो विजितेन्द्रियः ।
युक्त इत्युच्यते योगी समलोष्टाश्मकाञ्चनः ॥

jñānavijñānatṛptātmā
kūṭastho vijitendriyaḥ
yukta ityucyate yogī
samaloṣṭāśmakāñcanaḥ

The yogin who is satisfied with knowledge and discrimination, who is unchanging, with conquered senses, to whom a clod, a stone, and gold are the same, is said to have attained samadhi.

9 सुहृन्मित्रार्युदासीन मध्यस्थद्वेष्यबन्धुषु ।
साधुष्व् अपि च पापेषु समबुद्धिर् विशिष्यते ।।
suhṛnmitrāryudāsīna-
madhyasthadveṣyabāndhuṣu
sādhuṣv api ca pāpeṣu
samabuddhir viśiṣyate

He who is equal-minded toward friend, companion, and enemy, who is neutral among enemies and kinsmen, and who is impartial among the righteous and also among the evil, is to be distinguished among men.

10 योगी युञ्जीत सततम् आत्मानं रहसि स्थितः ।
एकाकी यतचित्तात्मा निराशीर् अपरिग्रहः ।।
yogī yuñjīta satatam
ātmānaṁ rahasi sthitaḥ
ekākī yatacittātmā
nirāśīr aparigrahaḥ

The yogin should concentrate constantly on the Self, remaining in solitude, alone, with controlled mind and body, having no desires and destitute of possessions.

11 शुचौ देशे प्रतिष्ठाप्य स्थिरम् आसनम् आत्मनः ।
नात्युच्छ्रितं नातिनीचं चैलाजिनकुशोत्तरम् ॥

śucāu deśe pratiṣṭhāpya
sthiram āsanam ātmanaḥ
nātyucchritaṁ nātinīcaṁ
cāilājinakuśottaram

Establishing a firm seat for himself in a clean place, not too high, not too low, covered with a cloth, an antelope skin, and kusha grass,

12 तत्रैकाग्रं मनः कृत्वा यतचित्तेन्द्रियक्रियः ।
उपविश्यासने युञ्ज्याद् योगमात्मविशुद्धये ॥

tatrāikāgraṁ manaḥ kṛtvā
yatacittendriyakriyaḥ
upaviśyāsane yuñjād
yogamātmaviśuddhaye

There, having directed his mind to a single object, with his thought and the activity of the senses controlled, seating himself on the seat, he should practice yoga for the purpose of self-purification.

13 समं कायशिरोग्रीवं धारयन्न् अचलं स्थिरः ।
संप्रेक्ष्य नासिकाग्रं स्वं दिशश्चानवलोकयन् ॥

samaṁ kāyaśirogrīvaṁ
dhārayann acalaṁ sthiraḥ
saṁprekṣya nāsikāgraṁ svaṁ
diśaścānavalokayan

Holding the body, head and neck erect, motionless and steady, gazing at the tip of his own nose and not looking in any direction,

14 प्रशान्तात्मा विगतभीर् ब्रह्मचारिव्रते स्थितः ।
मनः संयम्य मच्चित्तो युक्त आसीत मत्परः ॥
praśāntātmā vigatabhīr
brahmacārivrate sthitaḥ
manaḥ saṁyamya maccitto
yukta āsīta matparaḥ

With quieted mind, banishing fear, established in the brahmacharin vow of celibacy, controlling the mind, with thoughts fixed on Me, he should sit, concentrated, devoted to Me.

15 युञ्जन्न् एवं सदा ऽत्मानं योगी नियतमानसः ।
शान्तिं निर्वाणपरमां मत्संस्थाम् अधिगच्छति ॥
yuñjann evaṁ sadā 'tmānaṁ
yogī niyatamānasaḥ
śāntiṁ nirvāṇaparamāṁ
matsaṁsthām adhigacchati

Thus, continually disciplining himself, the yogin whose mind is subdued goes to nirvana, to supreme peace, to union with Me.

16 नात्यश्नतस् तु योगो ऽस्ति न चैकान्तम् अनश्नतः ।
न चातिस्वप्नशीलस्य जाग्रतो नैव चार्जुन ॥

nātyaśnatas tu yogo 'sti
na cāikāntam anaśnataḥ
na cātisvapnaśīlasya
jāgrato nāiva cārjuna

Yoga is not eating too much, nor is it not eating at all, and not the habit of sleeping too much, and not keeping awake either, Arjuna.

17 युक्ताहारविहारस्य युक्तचेष्टस्य कर्मसु ।
युक्तस्वप्नावबोधस्य योगो भवति दुःखहा ॥
yuktāhāravihārasya
yuktaceṣṭasya karmasu
yuktasvapnāvabodhasya
yogo bhavati duḥkhahā

For him who is moderate in food and diversion, whose actions are disciplined, who is moderate in sleep and waking, yoga destroys all sorrow.

18 यदा विनियतं चित्तम् आत्मन्य् एवावतिष्ठते ।
निःस्पृहः सर्वकामेभ्यो युक्त इत्य् उच्यते तदा ॥
yadā viniyataṁ cittam
ātmany evāvatiṣṭhate
niḥspṛhaḥ sarvakāmebbyo
yukta ity ucyate tadā

When he is absorbed in the Self alone, with controlled mind, free from longing, from all desires, then he is said to be a saint.

19 यथा दीपो निवातस्थो नेङ्गते सोपमा स्मृता ।
योगिनो यतचित्तस्य युञ्जतो योगम् आत्मनः ॥

yathā dīpo nivātastho
neṅgate sopamā smṛtā
yogino yatacittasya
yuñjato yogam ātmanaḥ

As a lamp in a windless place does not flicker, to such is compared the yogin of controlled mind, performing the yoga of the Self.

20 यत्रोपरमते चित्तं निरुद्धं योगसेवया ।
यत्र चैवात्मना ऽत्मानं पश्यन्न् आत्मनि तुष्यति ॥

yatroparamate cittaṁ
niruddhaṁ yogasevayā
yatra cāivātmanā 'tmānaṁ
paśyann ātmani tuṣyati

When the mind comes to rest, restrained by the practice of yoga, and when beholding the Self, by the self, he is content in the Self,

21 सुखम् आत्यन्तिकं यत् तद् बुद्धिग्राह्यम् अतीन्द्रियम् ।
वेत्ति यत्र न चैवायं स्थितश्चलति तत्त्वतः ॥

sukham ātyantikaṁ yat tad
buddhigrāhyam atīndriyam
vetti yatra na cāivāyaṁ
sthitaścalati tattvataḥ

He knows that infinite happiness which is grasped by the intellect and transcends the senses, and, established there, does not deviate from the truth.

22 यं लब्ध्वा चापरं लाभं मन्यते नाधिकं ततः।
यस्मिन् स्थितो न दुःखेन गुरुणापि विचाल्यते ॥
yaṁ labdhvā cāparaṁ lābhaṁ
manyate nādhikaṁ tataḥ
yasmin sthito na duḥkhena
guruṇāpi vicālyate

Having attained this, no greater gain can he imagine; established in this, he is not moved even by profound sorrow.

23 तं विद्याद् दुःखसंयोग वियोगं योगसंज्ञितम्।
स निश्चयेन योक्तव्यो योगो ऽनिर्विण्णचेतसा ॥
taṁ vidyād duḥkhasaṁyoga
viyogaṁ yogasaṁjñitam
sa niścayena yoktavyo
yogo 'nirviṇṇacetasā

Let this, the dissolution of union with pain, be known as yoga; this yoga is to be practiced with determination and with an undismayed mind.

24 संकल्पप्रभवान् कामांस् त्यक्त्वा सर्वान् अशेषतः।
मनसैवेन्द्रियग्रामं विनियम्य समन्ततः ॥
saṁkalpaprabhavān kāmāṅs
tyaktvā sarvān aśeṣataḥ
manasāivendriyagrāmam
viniyamya samantatah

Abandoning those desires whose origins lie in one's intention, all of them, without exception, and completely restraining the multitude of senses with the mind,

25 शनैः शनैर् उपरमेद् बुद्ध्या धृतिगृहीतया ।
आत्मसंस्थं मनः कृत्वा न किंचिद् अपि चिन्तयेत् ॥
śanāiḥ śanāir uparamed
buddhyā dhṛtigṛhītayā
ātmasaṁsthaṁ manaḥ kṛtvā
na kiṁcid api cintayet

Little by little, he should come to rest, with the intellect firmly held. His mind having been established in the Self, he should not think of anything.

26 यतो यतो निश्चरति मनश्चञ्चलम् अस्थिरम् ।
ततस्ततो नियम्यैतद् आत्मन्य् एव वशं नयेत् ॥
yato yato niścarati
manaścañcalam asthiram
tatastato niyamyāitad
ātmany eva vaśaṁ nayet

Whenever the unsteady mind, moving to and fro, wanders away, he should restrain it and control it in the Self.

27 प्रशान्तमनसं ह्येनं योगिनं सुखम् उत्तमम् ।
उपैति शान्तरजसं ब्रह्मभूतम् अकल्मषम् ॥

praśantamanasaṁ hyenaṁ
yoginaṁ sukham uttamam

upāiti śantarajasaṁ
brahmabhūtam akalmaṣam

The yogin whose mind is peaceful, whose passions are calmed, who is free of evil and has become one with Brahman, attains the highest bliss.

28 युञ्जन्न् एवं सदा ऽत्मानं योगी विगतकल्मषः ।
सुखेन ब्रह्मसंस्पर्शम् अत्यन्त सुखम् अश्नुते ॥
yuñjann evaṁ sadā 'tmānaṁ
yogī vigatakalmaṣaḥ
sukhena brahmasaṁsparśam
atyantaṁ sukham aśnute

Thus constantly disciplining himself, the yogin, freed from evil, easily encountering Brahman, attains happiness beyond end.

29 सर्वभूतस्थम् आत्मानं सर्वभूतानि चात्मनि ।
ईक्षते योगयुक्तात्मा सर्वत्र समदर्शनः ॥
sarvabhūtastham ātmānaṁ
sarvabhūtāni cātmani
īkṣate yogayuktātmā
sarvatra samadarśanaḥ

He who is disciplined by yoga sees the Self present in all beings, and all beings present in the Self. He sees the same (Self) at all times.

30 यो मां पश्यति सर्वत्र सर्वं च मयि पश्यति
तस्याहं न प्रणश्यामि स च मे न प्रणश्यति ॥

yo māṁ paśyati sarvatra
sarvaṁ ca mayi paśyati
tasyāhaṁ na praṇaśyāmi
sa ca me na praṇaśyati

He who sees Me everywhere, and sees all things in Me; I am not lost to him, and he is not lost to Me.

31 सर्वभूतस्थितं यो मां भजत्य् एकत्वम् आस्थितः ।
सर्वथा वर्तमानो ऽपि स योगी मयि वर्तते ।।
sarvabhūtasthaṁ yo māṁ
bhajaty ekatvam āsthitaḥ
sarvathā vartamāno 'pi
sa yogī mayi vartate

The yogin who, established in oneness, honors Me as abiding in all beings, in whatever way he otherwise acts, dwells in Me.

32 आत्मौपम्येन सर्वत्र समं पश्यति यो ऽर्जुन ।
सुखं वा यदि वा दुःखं स योगी परमो मतः ।।
ātmāupamyena sarvatra
samaṁ paśyati yo 'rjuna
sukhaṁ vā yadi vā duḥkhaṁ
sa yogī paramo mataḥ

He who sees equality in everything in the image of his own Self, Arjuna, whether in pleasure or in pain, is thought to be a supreme yogin.

33 अर्जुन उवाच । *arjuna uvāca*

योऽयं योगस् त्वया प्रोक्तः साम्येन मधुसूदन ।
एतस्याहं न पश्यामि चञ्चलत्वात् स्थितिं स्थिराम् ॥

yo 'yaṁ yogas tvayā proktaḥ
sāmyena madhusūdana
etasyāhaṁ na paśyāmi
cañcalatvāt sthitiṁ sthirām

Arjuna spoke:

This yoga which is declared by You as evenness of mind, Krishna, I do not perceive the steady continuance of this because of (the mind's) instability.

34 चञ्चलं हि मनः कृष्ण प्रमाथि बलवद् दृढम् ।
तस्याहं निग्रहं मन्ये वायोर् इव सुदुष्करम् ॥

cañcalaṁ hi manaḥ kṛṣṇa
pramāthi balavad dṛḍham
tasyāhaṁ nigrahaṁ manye
vāyor iva suduṣkaram

The mind, indeed, is unstable, Krishna, turbulent, powerful and obstinate; I think it is as difficult to control as the wind.

35 श्रीभगवान् उवाच । *śrībhagavān uvāca*

असंशयं महाबाहो मनो दुर्निग्रहं चलम् ।
अभ्यासेन तु कौन्तेय वैराग्येण च गृह्यते ॥

asaṁśayaṁ mahābāho
mano durnigrahaṁ calam

abhyāsena tu kāunteya
vāirāgyeṇa ca gṛhyate

The Blessed Lord spoke:

Without doubt, O Arjuna, the mind is unsteady and difficult to restrain; but by practice, Arjuna, and by indifference to worldly objects, it is restrained.

36 असंयतात्मना योगो दुष्प्राप इति मे मतिः ।
वश्यात्मना तु यतता शक्योऽवाप्तुम् उपायतः ॥

asaṁyatātmanā yogo
duṣprāpa iti me matiḥ
vaśyātmanā tu yatatā
śakyo 'vāptum upāyataḥ

I agree that yoga is difficult to attain by him whose self is uncontrolled; but by him whose self is controlled, by striving, it is possible to attain through proper means.

37 अर्जुन उवाच । *arjuna uvāca*

अयतिः श्रद्धयोपेतो योगाच्चलितमानसः ।
अप्राप्य योगसंसिद्धिं कां गतिं कृष्ण गच्छति ॥

ayatiḥ śraddhayopeto
yogāccalitamānasaḥ
aprāpya yogasaṁsiddhiṁ
kāṁ gatiṁ kṛṣṇa gacchati

Arjuna spoke:

One who is uncontrolled though he has faith, whose mind has fallen away from yoga, who does not attain perfection in yoga, which way, Krishna, does he go?

38 कच्चिन् नोभयविभ्राष्टश् छिन्नाभ्रम् इव नश्यति ।
अप्रतिष्ठो महाबाहो विमूढो ब्रह्मणः पथि ॥
kaccin nobhayavibhraṣṭaś
chinnābhram iva naśyati
apratiṣṭho mahābāho
vimūḍho brahmaṇaḥ pathi

Is he not lost like a disappearing cloud, having fallen from both worlds, having no solid ground, O Krishna, confused on the path of Brahman?

39 एतन् मे संशयं कृष्ण छेत्तुम् अर्हस्य् अशेषतः ।
त्वदन्यः संशयस्यास्य छेत्ता न ह्य् उपपद्यते ॥
etan me saṁśayaṁ kṛṣṇa
chettum arhasy aśeṣataḥ
tvadanyaḥ saṁśayasyāsya
chettā na hy upapadyate

You are able, Krishna, to dispel the totality of this doubt of mine; other than You, no one comes forth to help me erase this doubt.

40 श्रीभगवान् उवाच *śrībhagavān uvāca*

पार्थ नैवेह नामुत्र विनाशस् तस्य विद्यते ।
न हि कल्याणकृत् कश्चिद् दुर्गतिं तात गच्छति ॥

pārtha nāiveha nāmutra
vinaśas tasya vidyate
na hi kalyāṇakṛt kaścid
durgatiṁ tāta gacchati

The Blessed Lord spoke:

Arjuna, neither here on earth nor in heaven above is there found to be destruction of him; no one who does good goes to misfortune, My Son.

41 प्राप्य पुण्यकृतां लोकान् उषित्वा शाश्वतीः समाः ।
शुचीनां श्रीमतां गेहे योगभ्रष्टोऽभिजायते ॥
prāpya puṇyakṛtāṁ lokān
uṣitvā śāśvatīḥ samāḥ
śucīnāṁ śrīmatāṁ gehe
yogabhraṣṭo 'bhijāyate

Attaining the worlds of the meritorious, having dwelt there for endless years, he who has fallen from yoga is born again in the dwelling of the radiant and the illustrious.

42 अथवा योगिनाम् एव कुले भवति धीमताम् ।
एतद् धि दुर्लभतरं लोके जन्म यद् ईदृशम् ॥
athavā yogināṁ eva
kule bhavati dhīmatām
etad dhi durlabhataram
loke janma yad īdṛśam

Or he may be born in the family of wise yogins; such a birth as this is very difficult to attain in the world.

43 तत्र तं बुद्धिसंयोगं लभते पौर्वदेहिकम् ।
यतते च ततो भूयः संसिद्धौ कुरुनन्दन ।।

tatra taṁ buddhisaṁyogaṁ
labhate pāurvadehikam
yatate ca tato bhūyaḥ
saṁsiddhāu kurunandana

There he regains the knowledge derived from a former body, and he strives onward once more toward perfection, Arjuna.

44 पूर्वाभ्यासेन तेनैव ह्रियते ह्य् अवशो ऽपि सः ।
जिज्ञासुर् अपि योगस्य शब्दब्रह्मातिवर्तते ।।

pūrvābhyāsena tenāiva
hriyate hy avaśo 'pi saḥ
jijñāsur api yogasya
śabdabrahmātivartate

He is carried on, even against his will, by prior practice; he who even wishes to know of yoga transcends Brahman in the form of sound (i.e. Vedic recitation).

45 प्रयत्नाद् यतमानस् तु योगी संशुद्धकिल्बिषः ।
अनेकजन्मसंसिद्धस् ततो याति परां गतिं ।।

prayatnād yatamānas tu
yogī saṁśuddhakilbiṣaḥ
anekajanmasaṁsiddhas
tato yāti parām gatiṁ

Through persevering effort and controlled mind, the yogin, completely cleansed of evil, and perfected through many births, then goes to the supreme goal.

46 तपस्विभ्यो ऽधिको योगी ज्ञानिभ्यो ऽपि मतो ऽधिकः ।
कर्मिभ्यश् चाधिको योगी तस्माद् योगी भवार्जुन ।।

tapasvibhyo 'dhiko yogī
jñānibhyo 'pi mato 'dhikaḥ
karmibhyaś cādhiko yogī
tasmād yogī bhavārjuna

The yogin is superior to the ascetics, he is also thought to be superior to the learned, and the yogin is superior to those who perform ritual works. Therefore, be a yogin, Arjuna.

47 योगिनाम् अपि सर्वेषां मद्गतेनान्तरात्मना ।
श्रद्धावान् भजते यो मां स मे युक्ततमो मतः ।।

yoginām api sarveṣāṁ
madgatenāntarātmanā
śraddhāvān bhajate yo māṁ
sa me yuktatamo mataḥ

Of all these yogins, he who has merged his inner Self in Me, honors Me, full of faith, is thought to be the most devoted to Me.

Hari Om Tat Sat
Iti Srimad Bhagavadgītāsūpaniṣatsu Brahmavidyāyām
Yogaśāstre Sri Kriṣnārjunasamvāde
Ātmasamyamayogo Nāma Ṣaśtoddhyāyaḥ.

Thus ends the sixth Chapter, entitled "The Yoga of Meditation," of the venerated Bhagavad Gita Upanishad, the Knowledge of the Absolute, the scripture of Yoga, the dialogue between Sri Krishna and Arjuna.

SEVEN

The Yoga of Wisdom and Realization

atha saptamoddhyāyaḥ

1 श्रीभगवान् उवाच । *śrībhagavān uvāca*

मय्य् आसक्तमनाः पार्थ योगं युञ्जन् मदाश्रयः ।
असंशयं समग्रं मां यथा ज्ञास्यसि तच्छृणु ॥

mayy āsaktamanāḥ pārtha
yogaṁ yuñjan madāśrayaḥ
asaṁśayaṁ samagraṁ māṁ
yathā jñāsyasi tac chṛṇui

The Blessed Lord spoke:

With mind absorbed in Me, Arjuna, practicing yoga, dependent on Me, you shall know Me completely, without doubt; hear that!

2 ज्ञानं ते ऽहं सविज्ञानम् इदं वक्ष्याम्य् अशेषतः ।
यज् ज्ञात्वा नेह भूयो ऽन्यज् ज्ञातव्यम् अवशिष्यते ॥

jñānaṁ te 'haṁ savijñānam
idaṁ vakṣyāmy aśeṣataḥ
yaj jñātvā neha bhūyo 'nyaj
jñātavyam avaśiṣyate

To you I shall explain in full this knowledge, along with realization, which, having been understood, nothing further remains to be known here in the world.

3 मनुष्याणां सहस्रेषु कश्चिद् यतति सिद्धये।
यतताम् अपि सिद्धानां कश्चिन् मां वेत्ति तत्त्वतः॥

manuṣyāṇāṁ sahasreṣu
kaścid yatati siddhaye
yatatām api siddhānāṁ
kaścin māṁ vetti tattvataḥ

Of thousands of men, scarcely anyone strives for perfection; even of the striving and the perfected, scarcely anyone knows Me in truth.

4 भूमिर् आपो ऽनलो वायुः खं मनो बुद्धिर् एव च।
अहंकार इतीयं मे भिन्ना प्रकृतिर् अष्टधा॥

bhūmir āpo 'nalo vāyuḥ
khaṁ mano buddhir eva ca
ahaṁkāra itīyaṁ me
bhinnā prakṛtir aṣṭadhā

Earth, water, fire, air, ether, mind, intellect—and egoism—this, My material nature, is divided into eight parts.

5 अपरेयम् इतस् त्व् अन्यां प्रकृतिं विद्धि मे पराम्।
जीवभूतां महाबाहो ययेदं धार्यते जगत्॥

apareyam itas tv anyāṁ
prakṛtiṁ viddhi me parām
jīvabhūtāṁ mahābāho
yayedaṁ dhāryate jagat

Such is My inferior nature, but know it as different from My highest nature, the

Self, O Arjuna, by which this universe is sustained.

6 एतद्योनीनि भूतानि सर्वाणीत्य् उपधारय।
अहं कृत्स्नस्य जगतः प्रभवः प्रलयस् तथा॥
etadyonīni bhūtāni
sarvāṇīty upadhāraya
ahaṁ kṛtsnasya jagataḥ
prabhavaḥ pralayas tathā

All creatures have their birth in this, My highest nature. Understand this! I am the origin and also the dissolution of the entire universe.

7 मत्तः परतरं नान्यत् किंचिद् अस्ति धनंजय।
मयि सर्वम् इदं प्रोतं सूत्रे मणिगणा इव॥
mattaḥ parataraṁ nānyat
kiṁcid asti dhanaṁjaya
mayi sarvam idaṁ protaṁ
sūtre maṇigaṇā iva

Nothing higher than Me exists, O Arjuna. On Me all this universe is strung like pearls on a thread.

8 रसो ऽहम् अप्सु कौन्तेय प्रभास्मि शशिसूर्ययोः।
प्रणवः सर्ववेदेषु शब्दः खे पौरुषं नृषु॥
raso 'ham apsu kāunteya,
prabhāsmi śaśisūryayoḥ
praṇavaḥ sarvavedeṣu
śabdaḥ khe pāuruṣaṁ nṛṣu

I am the liquidity in the waters, Arjuna, I am the radiance in the moon and sun, the sacred syllable (Om) in all the Vedas, the sound in the air, and the manhood in men.

9 पुण्यो गन्धः पृथिव्यां च तेजश्चास्मि विभावसौ ।
जीवनं सर्वभूतेषु तपश्चास्मि तपस्विषु ॥
puṇyo gandhaḥ pṛthivyāṁ ca
tejaścāsmi vibhāvasāu
jīvanaṁ sarvabhūteṣu
tapaścāsmi tapasviṣu

I am the pure fragrance in the earth, and the brilliance in the fire, the life in all beings, and the austerity in ascetics.

10 बीजं मां सर्वभूतानां विद्धि पार्थ सनातनम्
बुद्धिर् बुद्धिमताम् अस्मि तेजस् तेजस्विनाम् अहम् ॥
bījaṁ māṁ sarvabhūtānāṁ
viddhi pārtha sanātanam
buddhir buddhimatām asmi
tejas tejasvinām aham

Know Me to be the primeval seed of all creatures, Arjuna; I am the intelligence of the intelligent; the splendor of the splendid, am I.

11 बलं बलवतां चाहं कामरागविवर्जितम् ।
धर्माविरुद्धो भूतेषु कामो ऽस्मि भरतर्षभ ॥
balaṁ balavatāṁ cāham
kāmarāgavivarjitam

dharmāviruddho bhūtesu
kāmo 'sṃi bharatarṣabha

And the might of the mighty I am, which is freed from lust and passion, and I am that desire in beings which is according to law, Arjuna.

12 ये चैव सात्त्विका भावा राजसास् तामसाश्च ये ।
मत्त एवेति तान् विद्धि न त्व् अहं तेषु ते मयि ॥
ye cāiva sāttvikā bhāvā
rājasās tāmasāśca ye
matta eveti tān viddhi
na tv ahaṁ teṣu te mayi

And those states of being which are sattvic, and those which are rajasic and tamasic, know that they proceed from Me. But I am not in them; they are in Me.

13 त्रिभिर् गुणमयैर् भावैर् एभिः सर्वम् इदं जगत् ।
मोहितं नाभिजानाति माम् एभ्यः परम् अव्ययम् ॥
tribhir guṇamayāir bhāvāir
ebhiḥ sarvam idaṁ jagat
mohitaṁ nābhijānāti
mām ebhyaḥ param avyayam

All this universe is deluded by these three states of being, composed of the qualities. It does not recognize Me, who am higher than these, and eternal.

14 दैवी ह्य् एषा गुणमयी मम माया दुरत्यया ।
माम् एव ये प्रपद्यन्ते मायाम् एतां तरन्ति ते ॥

dāivī hy eṣā guṇamayī
mama māyā duratyayā
mām eva ye prapadyante
māyām etāṁ taranti te

Divine indeed is this illusion of Mine made up of the three qualities, and difficult to penetrate; only those who resort to Me transcend this illusion.

15 न मां दुष्कृतिनो मूढाः प्रपद्यन्ते नराधमाः ।
माययापहृतज्ञाना आसुरं भावम् आश्रिताः ॥

na māṁ duṣkṛtino mūḍhāḥ
prapadyante narādhamāḥ
māyayāpahṛtajñānā
āsuraṁ bhāvam āśritāḥ

Evil doers, lowest of men, deprived of knowledge by illusion, do not seek Me, attached as they are to a demoniacal existence.

16 चतुर्विधा भजन्ते मां जनाः सुकृतिनो ऽर्जुन ।
आर्तो जिज्ञासुर् अर्थार्थी ज्ञानी च भरतर्षभ ॥

caturvidhā bhajante māṁ
janāḥ sukṛtino 'rjuna
ārto, jijñāsur arthārthī
jñānī ca bharatarṣabha

Among benevolent men, four kinds worship Me, Arjuna: the distressed, those who desire wealth, those who desire knowledge, and the man of wisdom, Arjuna.

17 तेषां ज्ञानी नित्ययुक्त एकभक्तिर् विशिष्यते ।
प्रियो हि ज्ञानिनो ऽत्यर्थम् अहं स च मम प्रियः ॥

teṣām jñānī nityayukta
ekabhaktir viśiṣyate
priyo hi jñānino 'tyartham
ahaṁ sa ca mama priyaḥ

Of them the man of wisdom, eternally steadfast, devoted to the One alone, is preeminent. I am indeed exceedingly fond of the man of wisdom, and he is fond of Me.

18 उदाराः सर्व एवैते ज्ञानी त्व् आत्मैव मे मतम् ।
आस्थितः स हि युक्तात्मा माम् एवानुत्तमां गतिम् ॥

udārāḥ sarva evāite
jñānī tv ātmāiva me matam
āsthitaḥ sa hi yuktātmā
mām evānuttamāṁ gatim

All these are indeed noble, but the man of wisdom is thought to be My very Self. He, indeed, whose mind is steadfast, abides in Me, the supreme goal.

19 बहूनां जन्मनाम् अन्ते ज्ञानवान् मां प्रपद्यते ।
वासुदेवः सर्वम् इति स महात्मा सुदुर्लभः ॥

bahūnāṁ janmanām ante
jñānavān māṁ prapadyate

vāsudevaḥ sarvam iti
sa mahātmā sudurlabhaḥ

At the end of many births, the man of wisdom resorts to Me, thinking "Vasudeva (Krishna) is all." Such a great soul is hard to find.

20 कामैस् तैस्तैर् हृतज्ञानाः प्रपद्यन्ते ऽन्यदेवताः ।
तंतं नियमम् आस्थाय प्रकृत्या नियताः स्वया ॥
kāmāis tāistāir hṛtajñānāḥ
prapadyante 'nyadevatāḥ
taṁtaṁ niyamam āsthāya
prakṛtyā niyayāḥ svayā

Men whose knowledge has been carried away by these and those desires, resort to other gods, having recourse to this and that religious rite, constrained by their own material natures.

21 यो यो यां यां तनुं भक्तः श्रद्धयार्चितुम् इच्छति ।
तस्य तस्याचलां श्रद्धां ताम् एव विदधाम्य् अहम् ॥
yo yo yāṁ yāṁ tanuṁ bhaktaḥ
śraddhayārcitum icchati
tasya tasyācalāṁ śraddhāṁ
tām eva vidadhāmy aham

Whoever desires to honor with belief whatever worshiped form, on him I bestow immovable faith.

22 स तया श्रद्धया युक्तस् तस्याराधनम् ईहते ।
लभते च ततः कामान् मयैव विहितान् हि तान् ॥
sa tayā śraddhayā yuktas
tasyārādhanam īhate
labhate ca tataḥ kāmān
mayāiva vihitān hi tān

He, who, endowed with this faith, desires to propitiate that form, receives from it his desires because those desires are decreed by Me.

23 अन्तवत् तु फलं तेषां तद् भवत्य् अल्पमेधसाम् ।
देवान् देवयजो यान्ति मद्भक्ता यान्ति माम् अपि ॥
antavat tu phalaṁ teṣāṁ
tad bhavaty alpamedhasām
devān devayajo yānti
madbhaktā yānti mām api

But temporary is the fruit for those of small understanding. To the gods the god-worshipers go; My worshipers come surely to Me.

24 अव्यक्तं व्यक्तिम् आपन्नं मन्यन्ते माम अबुद्धयः ।
परं भावम् अजानन्तो ममाव्ययम् अनुत्तमम् ॥
avyaktaṁ vyaktim āpannaṁ
manyante mām abuddhayaḥ
paraṁ bhāvam ajānanto
mamāvyayam anuttamam

Though I am unmanifest, the unintelligent think of Me as having manifestation, not knowing My higher being which is imperishable and unsurpassed.

25 नाहं प्रकाशः सर्वस्य योगमायासमावृतः ।
मूढो ऽयं नाभिजानाति लोको माम् अजम् अव्ययम् ॥
nāhaṁ prakāśaḥ sarvasya
yogamāyāsamāvṛtaḥ
mūḍho 'yaṁ nābhijānāti
loko mām ajam avyayam

I am not manifest to all, being enveloped in yoga maya; this deluded world does not recognize Me, the birthless and imperishable.

26 वेदाहं समतीतानि वर्तमानानि चार्जुन ।
भविष्याणि च भूतानि मां तु वेद न कश्चन ॥
vedāhaṁ samatītāni
vartamānāni cārjuna
bhaviṣyāṇi ca bhūtāni
māṁ tu veda na kaścana

I know the departed beings and the living, Arjuna, and those who are yet to be; but no one knows Me.

27 इच्छाद्वेषसमुत्थेन द्वन्द्वमोहेन भारत ।
सर्वभूतानि संमोहं सर्गे यान्ति परंतप ॥
icchādveṣasamutthena
dvandvamohena bhārata
sarvabhūtāni saṁmohaṁ
sarge yānti paraṁtapa

Because of the arising of desire and hatred, because of the deluding (power) of the opposites, Arjuna, all beings fall into delusion at birth.

28 येषां त्व् अन्तगतं पापं जनानां पुण्यकर्मणाम् ।
ते द्वन्द्वमोहनिर्मुक्ता भजन्ते मां दृढव्रताः ॥

yeṣāṁ tv antagataṁ pāpaṁ
janānāṁ puṇyakarmaṇām
te dvandvamohanirmuktā
bhajante mām dṛḍhavratāḥ

But those in whom evil has come to an end, those men whose actions are pure; they, liberated from the deluding power of the opposites, worship Me with firm vows.

29 जरामरणमोक्षाय माम् आश्रित्य यतन्ति ये ।
ते ब्रह्म तद् विदुः कृत्स्नम् अध्यात्मं कर्म चाखिलम् ॥

jarāmaraṇamokṣāya
mām āśritya yatanti ye
te brahma tad viduḥ kṛtsnam
adhyātmaṁ karma cākhilam

Those who strive toward release from old age and death, depending on Me, know Brahman thoroughly, as well as the Self and all action.

30 साधिभूताधिदैवं मां साधियज्ञं च ये विदुः ।
प्रयाणकाले ऽपि च मां ते विदुर् युक्तचेतसः ॥

sādhibhūtādhidāivaṁ māṁ
sādhiyajñaṁ ca ye viduḥ
prayāṇakāle 'pi ca māṁ
te vidur yuktacetasaḥ

They who know Me as the Adhibhuta and the Adhidaiva, as well as the chief of sacrifice, they truly know Me with steadfast thought even at the hour of death.

Hari Om Tat Sat
Iti Srimad Bhagavadgītāsūpaniṣatsu Brahmavidyāyām
Yogaśāstre Sri Kriṣnārjunasamvāde
Jnānavijñānayogo Nāma Saptamoddhyāyaḥ.

Thus ends the seventh Chapter, entitled "The Yoga of Wisdom and Realization," of the venerated Bhagavad Gita Upanishad, the Knowledge of the Absolute, the scripture of Yoga, the dialogue between Sri Krishna and Arjuna.

EIGHT

The Yoga of the Imperishable Absolute

atha aṣṭamoddhyāyaḥ

1 अर्जुन उवाच । *arjuna uvāca*

किं तद् ब्रह्म किम् अध्यात्मं किं कर्म पुरुषोत्तम ।
अधिभूतं च किं प्रोक्तम् अधिदैवं किम् उच्यते ॥

kim tad brahma kim adhyātmam
kim karma purusottama
adhibhūtam ca kim proktam
adhidāivam kim ucyate

Arjuna spoke:

What is this Brahman? What is the Adhyatma? What is action, O highest among Spirits? And the Adhibhuta, what is it declared to be? And the Adhidaiva, what is it said to be?

2 अधियज्ञः कथं को ऽत्र देहे ऽस्मिन् मधुसूदन ।
प्रयाणकाले च कथं ज्ञेयो ऽसि नियतात्मभिः ॥

adhiyajñaḥ kathaṁ ko 'tra
dehe 'smin madhusūdana
prayāṇakāle ca kathaṁ
jñeyo 'si niyatātmabhiḥ

In what manner, and what, is the Adhiyajna here in this body, O Krishna?

And how at the hour of death are You to be known by those who are self-controlled?

3 श्रीभगवान् उवाच । *śrībhagavān uvāca*

अक्षरं ब्रह्म परमं स्वभावो ऽध्यात्मम् उच्यते ।
भूतभावोद्भवकरो विसर्गः कर्मसंज्ञितः ॥
akṣaraṁ brahma paramaṁ
svabhāvo 'dhyātmam ucyate
bhūtabhāvodbhavakaro
visargaḥ karmasaṁjñitaḥ

The Blessed Lord spoke:

Brahman is the supreme imperishable; the Adhyatma is said to be the inherent nature of the individual, which originates the being of creatures; action is known as the creative power (of the individual, which causes him to be reborn in this or that condition of being).

4 अधिभूतं क्षरो भावः पुरुषश्चाधिदैवतम् ।
अधियज्ञो ऽहम् एवात्र देहे देहभृतां वर ॥
adhibhūtaṁ kṣaro bhāvaḥ
puruṣaścādhidāivatam
adhiyajño 'ham evātra
dehe dehabhṛtāṁ vara

The Adhibhuta is the perishable nature of being (or the sphere of the supreme Spirit in acting on the individual, i.e. nature). The Adhidaivata is the supreme divine Agent itself (the purusha). The Adhiyajna (Lord of

Sacrifice) is Myself, here in this body, O Arjuna.

5 अन्तकाले च माम् एव स्मरन् मुक्त्वा कलेवरम् ।
यः प्रयाति स मद्भावं याति नास्त्य् अत्र संशयः ॥
antakāle ca mām eva
smaran muktvā kalevaram
yaḥ prayāti sa madbhāvaṁ
yāti nāsty atra saṁśayaḥ

And at the hour of death, he who dies remembering Me, having relinquished the body, goes to My state of being. In this matter there is no doubt.

6 यं यं वापि स्मरन् भावं त्यजत्य् अन्ते कलेवरम् ।
तं तं एवैति कौन्तेय सदा तद्भावभावितः ॥
yaṁ yaṁ vāpi smaran bhāvaṁ
tyajaty ante kalevaram
taṁ ṭaṁ evāiti kāunteya
sadā tadbhāvabhāvitaḥ

Moreover, whatever state of being he remembers when he gives up the body at the end, he goes respectively to that state of being, Arjuna, transformed into that state of being.

7 तस्मात् सर्वेषु कालेषु माम् अनुस्मर युद्य च ।
मय्य् अर्पितमनोबुद्धिर् माम् एवैष्यस्य् असंशयम् ॥
tasmāt sarveṣu kāleṣu
mām anusmara yudhya ca

mayy arpitamanobuddhir
mām evāiṣyasy asaṁśayam

Therefore, at all times meditate on Me, with your mind and intellect fixed on Me. In this way, you shall surely come to Me.

8 अभ्यासयोगयुक्तेन चेतसा नान्यगामिना ।
परमं पुरुषं दिव्यं याति पार्थानुचिन्तयन् ॥

abhyāsayogayuktena
cetasā nānyagāminā
paramaṁ puruṣaṁ divyaṁ
yāti pārthānucintayan

With a mind disciplined by the practice of yoga, which does not turn to anything else, to the divine supreme Spirit he goes, Arjuna, meditating on Him.

9 कविं पुराणम् अनुशासितारम्
अणोर् अणीयांसम् अनुस्मरेद् यः ।
सर्वस्य धातारम् अचिन्त्यरूपम्
आदित्यवर्णं तमसः परस्तात् ॥

kaviṁ purāṇam anuśāsitāram
aṇor aṇīyāṁsam anusmared yaḥ
sarvasya dhātāram acintyarūpam
ādityavarṇaṁ tamasaḥ parastāt

He who meditates on the ancient seer, the ruler, smaller than the atom, who is the supporter of all, whose form is unthinkable, and who is effulgent like the sun, beyond darkness;

10 प्रयाणकाले मनसाचलेन
भक्त्या युक्तो योगबलेन चैव ।
भ्रुवोर् मध्ये प्राणम् आवेश्य सम्यक्
स तं परं पुरुषम् उपैति दिव्यम् ।।

prayāṇakāle manasācalena
bhaktyā yukto yogabalena cāiva
bhruvor madhye prāṇam āveśya samyak
sa taṁ paraṁ purusam upāiti divyam

At the hour of death, with unmoving mind, endowed with devotion and with the power of yoga, having made the vital breath enter between the two eyebrows, he reaches this divine supreme Spirit.

11 यद् अक्षरं वेदविदो वदन्ति
विशन्ति यद् यतयो वीतरागाः ।
यद् इच्छन्तो ब्रह्मचर्यं चरन्ति
तत् ते पदं संग्रहेण प्रवक्ष्ये ।।

yad akṣaraṁ vedavido vadanti
viśanti yad yatayo vītarāgāḥ
yad icchanto brahmacaryaṁ caranti
tat te padaṁ saṁgraheṇa pravakṣye

That which those who know the Vedas call the imperishable, which the ascetics, free from passion, enter, desiring which they follow a life of chastity, that path I shall explain to you briefly.

12 सर्वद्वाराणि संयम्य मनो हृदि निरुध्य च।
मूर्ध्न्य् आधायात्मनः प्राणम् आस्थितो योगधारणाम्॥

sarvadvārāṇi saṁyamya
mano hṛdi nirudhya ca
mūrdhny ādhāyātmanaḥ prāṇam
āsthito yogadhāraṇām

Closing all the gates of the body, and confining the mind in the heart, having placed the vital breath in the head, established in yoga concentration,

13 ओम् इत्य् एकाक्षरं ब्रह्म व्याहरन् माम् अनुस्मरन्।
यः प्रयाति त्यजन् देहं स याति परमां गतिम्॥

om ity ekākṣaraṁ brahma
vyāharan mām anusmaran
yaḥ prayāti tyajan dehaṁ
sa yāti paramāṁ gatim

Uttering the single-syllable "Om"—Brahman—meditating on Me, he who goes forth, renouncing the body, goes to the supreme goal.

14 अनन्यचेताः सततं यो मां स्मरति नित्यशः।
तस्याहं सुलभः पार्थ नित्ययुक्तस्य योगिनः॥

ananyacetāḥ satataṁ
yo māṁ smarati nityaśaḥ
tasyāhaṁ sulabhaḥ pārtha
nityayuktasya yoginaḥ

He who thinks of Me constantly, whose mind does not ever go elsewhere, for him, the yogin who is constantly devoted, I am easy to reach, Arjuna.

15 माम् उपेत्य पुनर्जन्म दुःखालयम् अशाश्वतम् ।
नाप्नुवन्ति महात्मानः संसिद्धिं परमां गताः ॥

mām upetya punarjanma
duḥkhālayam aśāśvatam
nāpnuvanti mahātmānaḥ
saṁsiddhiṁ paramāṁ gatāḥ

Approaching Me, those whose souls are great, who have gone to supreme perfection, do not incur rebirth, that impermanent home of misfortune.

16 आ ब्रह्मभुवनाल् लोकाः पुनरावर्तिनो ऽर्जुन ।
माम् उपेत्य तु कौन्तेय पुनर्जन्म न विद्यते ॥

ā brahmabhuvanāl lokāḥ
punarāvartino 'rjuna
mām upetya tu kāunteya
punarjanma na vidyate

Up to Brahma's realm of being, the worlds are subject to successive rebirths, Arjuna; but he who reaches Me is not reborn.

17 सहस्रयुगपर्यन्तम् अहर् यद् ब्रह्मणो विदुः ।
रात्रिं युगसहस्रान्तां ते ऽहोरात्रविदो जनाः ॥

sahasrayugaparyantam
ahar yad brahmano viduḥ

rātriṁ yugasahasrāntāṁ
te 'horātravido janāḥ

They who know that the day of Brahma extends as far as a thousand yugas, and that the night of Brahma ends only in a thousand yugas; they are men who know day and night.

18 अव्यक्ताद् व्यक्तयः सर्वाः प्रभवन्त्य् अहरागमे ।
रात्र्यागमे प्रलीयन्ते तत्रैवाव्यक्तसंज्ञके ॥

avyaktād vyaktayaḥ sarvāḥ
prabhavanty ahārāgame
rātryāgame pralīyante
tatrāivāvyaktasaṁjñake

From the unmanifest, all manifestations come forth at the arrival of (Brahma's) day; at the arrival of (Brahma's) night, they are dissolved, at that point to be known as the unmanifest again.

19 भूतग्रामः स एवायं भूत्वा भूत्वा प्रलीयते ।
रात्र्यागमे ऽवशः पार्थ प्रभवत्य् अहरागमे ॥

bhūtagrāmaḥ sa evāyaṁ
bhūtvā bhūtvā pralīyate
rātryāgame 'vaśaḥ pārtha
prabhavaty ahārāgame

This multitude of beings, having come to be again and again, is dissolved helplessly at the arrival of night, Arjuna, and it comes into existence again at the arrival of day.

20 परस् तस्मात् तु भावो ऽन्यो ऽव्यक्तो ऽव्यक्तात् सनातनः ।
यः स सर्वेषु भूतेषु नश्यत्सु न विनश्यति ।।

paras tasmāt tu bhāvo 'nyo
'vyakto 'vyaktāt sanātanaḥ
yaḥ sa sarveṣu bhūteṣu
naśyatsu na vinaśyati

But higher than this state of being is another unmanifest state of being higher than the primeval unmanifest, which, when all beings perish, does not perish.

21 अव्यक्तो ऽक्षर इत्य् उक्तस् तम् आहुः परमां गतिम् ।
यं प्राप्य न निवर्तन्ते तद् धाम परमं मम ।।

avyakto 'kṣara ity uktas
tam āhuḥ paramāṁ gatim
yaṁ prāpya na nivartante
tad dhāma paramaṁ mama

This unmanifest is the imperishable, thus it is said. They call it the supreme goal, attaining which, they do not return. This is My supreme dwelling place.

22 पुरुषः स परः पार्थ भक्त्या लभ्यस् त्व् अनन्यया ।
यस्यान्तःस्थानि भूतानि येन सर्वम् इदं ततम् ।।

puruṣaḥ sa paraḥ pārtha
bhaktyā labhyas tv ananyayā

yasyāntaḥsthāni bhūtāni
yena sarvam idaṁ tatam

This is the supreme Spirit, Arjuna, attainable by one-pointed devotion, within which all beings stand, and by which all this universe is pervaded.

23 यत्र काले त्व् अनावृत्तिम् आवृत्तिं चैव योगिनः ।
प्रयाता यान्ति तं कालं वक्ष्यामि भरतर्षभ ॥
yatra kāle tv anāvṛttim
āvṛttiṁ cāiva yoginaḥ
prayātā yānti taṁ kālaṁ
vaksyāmi bharatarṣabha

But at which times the yogins return or do not return, as they depart at death, of these times I shall speak, Arjuna.

24 अग्निर् ज्योतिर् अहः शुक्लः षण्मासा उत्तरायणम् ।
तत्र प्रयाता गच्छन्ति ब्रह्म ब्रह्मविदो जनाः ॥
agnir jyotir ahaḥ śuklaḥ
ṣaṇmāsā uttarāyaṇam
tatra prayātā gacchanti
brahma brahmavido janāḥ

Fire, brightness, day, the bright lunar fortnight, the six months of the northern course of the sun: departing then, the men who know Brahman go forth to Brahman.

25 धूमो रात्रिस् तथा कृष्णः षण्मासा दक्षिणायनम् ।
तत्र चान्द्रमसं ज्योतिर् योगी प्राप्य निवर्तते ॥

dhūmo rātris tathā kṛṣṇaḥ
ṣaṇmāsā dakṣiṇāyanam
tatra cāndramasaṁ jyotir
yogī prāpya nivartate

Smoke, night, the dark lunar fortnight, the six months of the southern course of the sun; attaining by these the lunar light, the yogin is born again.

26 शुक्लकृष्णे गती ह्येते जगतः शाश्वते मते
एकया यात्य् अनावृत्तिम् अन्ययावर्तते पुनः ॥
śuklakṛṣṇe gatī hyete
jagataḥ śāśvate mate
ekayā yāty anāvṛttim
anyayāvartate punaḥ

These are the two paths, light and dark, thought to be eternal for the universe. By one he does not return; by the other he returns again.

27 नैते सृती पार्थ जानन् योगी मुह्यति कश्चन ।
तस्मात् सर्वेषु कालेषु योगयुक्तो भवार्जुन ॥
nāite sṛtī pārtha jānan
yogī muhyati kaścana
tasmāt sarveṣu kāleṣu
yogayukto bhavārjuna

Knowing these two paths the yogin is not confused at all. Therefore, at all times, be steadfast in yoga, Arjuna.

28 वेदेषु यज्ञेषु तपःसु चैव
दानेषु यत् पुण्यफलं प्रदिष्टम् ।
अत्येति तत् सर्वम् इदं विदित्वा
योगी परं स्थानम् उपैति चाद्यम् ।।
vedeṣu yajñeṣu tapaḥsu cāiva
dāneṣu yat puṇyaphalaṁ pradiṣṭam
atyeti tat sarvam idaṁ viditvā
yogī paraṁ sthānam upāiti cādyam

The yogin, having known all this, goes beyond the pure fruit of action which comes from study of the Vedas, sacrifices, austerities, and gifts, and goes to the supreme primal state.

Hari Om Tat Sat
Iti Srimad Bhagavadgītāsūpaniṣatsu Brahmavidyāyām
Yogaśāstre Sri Kriṣnārjunasamvāde
Akṣarabrahmayogo Nāma Aṣtamoddhyāyaḥ.

Thus ends the eighth Chapter, entitled "The Yoga of the Imperishable Absolute," of the venerated Bhagavad Gita Upanishad, the Knowledge of the Absolute, the scripture of Yoga, the dialogue between Sri Krishna and Arjuna.

NINE

The Yoga of Sovereign Knowledge

atha navamoddhyāyaḥ

1 श्रीभगवान् उवाच । *śrībhagavān uvāca*

इदं तु ते गुह्यतमं प्रवक्ष्याम्य् अनसूयवे ।
ज्ञानं विज्ञानसहितं यज् ज्ञात्वा मोक्ष्यसे ऽशुभात् ॥

idaṁ tu te guhyatamaṁ
pravakṣyāmy anasūyave
jñānaṁ vijñānasahitaṁ
yaj jñātvā mokṣyase 'śubhāt

The Blessed Lord spoke:

But this most secret thing I shall declare to you, who do not disbelieve: knowledge and realization combined, having learned which you shall be released from evil.

2 राजविद्या राजगुह्यं पवित्रम् इदम् उत्तमम् ।
प्रत्यक्षावगमं धर्म्यं सुसुखं कर्तुम् अव्ययम् ॥

rājavidyā rājaguhyaṁ
pavitram idam uttamam
pratyakṣāvagamaṁ dharmyaṁ
susukhaṁ kartum avyayam

This is royal knowledge, a royal secret, a supreme purifier, plainly intelligible, righteous, easy to practice, imperishable.

3 अश्रद्दधानाः पुरुषा धर्मस्यास्य परंतप।
अप्राप्य मां निवर्तन्ते मृत्युसंसारवर्त्मनि॥
aśraddadhānāḥ puruṣā
dharmasyāsya paraṁtapa
aprāpya māṁ nivartante
mṛtyusaṁsāravartmani

Men who have no faith in this knowledge, Arjuna, not attaining to Me, are born again in the path of death and transmigration.

4 मया ततम् इदं सर्वं जगद् अव्यक्तमूर्तिना।
मत्स्थानि सर्वभूतानि न चाहं तेष्व् अवस्थितः॥
mayā tatam idaṁ sarvaṁ
jagad avyaktamūrtinā
matsthāni sarvabhūtāni
na cāhaṁ teṣv avasthitaḥ

This whole universe is pervaded by Me in My unmanifest aspect. All beings abide in Me; I do not abide in them.

5 न च मत्स्थानि भूतानि पश्य मे योगम् ऐश्वरम्।
भूतभृन् न च भूतस्थो ममात्मा भूतभावनः॥
na ca matsthāni bhūtāni
paśya me yogam āiśvaram
bhūtabhṛn na ca bhūtastho
mamātmā bhūtabhāvanaḥ

And yet beings do not abide in Me. Behold my divine yoga! Sustaining beings and not dwelling in beings is my Self, causing beings to be.

6 यथाकाशस्थितो नित्यं वायुः सर्वत्रगो महान् ।
तथा सर्वाणि भूतानि मत्स्थानीत्य् उपधारय ॥

yathākāśasthito nityaṁ
vāyuḥ sarvatrago mahān
tathā sarvāṇi bhūtāni
matsthānīty upadhāraya

As the mighty wind, going everywhere, dwells eternally in space, so all beings dwell in Me. Consider this!

7 सर्वभूतानि कौन्तेय प्रकृतिं यान्ति मामिकाम् ।
कल्पक्षये पुनस् तानि कल्पादौ विसृजाम्य् अहम् ॥

sarvabhūtāni kāunteya
prakṛtiṁ yānti māmikām
kalpakṣaye punas tāni
kalpādāu visṛjāmy aham

All beings, Arjuna, go to My own material nature at the end of a kalpa; at the beginning of a kalpa, I send them forth.

8 प्रकृतिं स्वाम् अवष्टभ्य विसृजामि पुनः पुनः ।
भूतग्रामम् इमं कृत्स्नम् अवशं प्रकृतेर् वशात् ॥

prakṛtiṁ svām avaṣṭabhya
visṛjāmi punaḥ punaḥ
bhūtagrāmam imam kṛtsnam
avaśaṁ prakṛteṛ vaśāt

Resting on My own material nature, I send forth again and again this entire multi-

tude of beings, which is powerless, by the power of My material nature.

9 न च मां तानि कर्माणि निबध्नन्ति धनंजय ।
उदासीनवद् आसीनम् असक्तं तेषु कर्मसु ॥
na ca māṁ tāni karmāṇi
nibadhnanti dhanaṁjaya
udāsīnavad āsīnam
asaktaṁ teṣu karmasu

And these actions do not bind Me, Arjuna; I sit indifferently, unattached to these actions.

10 मयाध्यक्षेण प्रकृतिः सूयते सचराचरम् ।
हेतुनानेन कौन्तेय जगद् विपरिवर्तते ॥
mayādhyakṣeṇa prakṛtiḥ
sūyate sacarācaram
hetunānena kāunteya
jagad viparivartate

With Me as overseer, material nature produces all things animate and inanimate. From this cause, Arjuna, the universe revolves.

11 अवजानन्ति मां मूढा मानुषीं तनुम् आश्रितम् ।
परं भावम् अजानन्तो मम भूतमहेश्वरम् ॥
avajānanti māṁ mūḍhā
mānuṣīṁ tanum āśritam
paraṁ bhāvam ajānanto
mama bhūtamaheśvaram

The deluded despise Me, clad in human form, not knowing My higher being as the great Lord of beings.

12 मोघाशा मोघकर्माणो मोघज्ञाना विचेतसः ।
राक्षसीम् आसुरीं चैव प्रकृतिं मोहिनीं श्रिताः ॥

moghāśā moghakarmāṇo
moghajñānā vicetasaḥ
rākṣasīm āsurīṁ cāiva
prakṛtiṁ mohinīṁ śritāḥ

Those of vain hopes, vain actions, vain knowledge, devoid of discrimination, abide in a fiendish and demoniacal nature, which is deluding.

13 महात्मानस् तु मां पार्थ दैवीं प्रकृतिम् आश्रिताः ।
भजन्त्य् अनन्यमनसो ज्ञात्वा भूतादिम् अव्ययम् ॥

mahātmānas tu māṁ pārtha
dāivīṁ prakṛtim āśritāḥ
bhajanty ananyamanaso
jñātvā bhūtādim avyayam

But those whose souls are great, Arjuna, partaking of a celestial nature, worship Me single-mindedly, knowing Me as the origin of beings and as the imperishable.

14 सततं कीर्तयन्तो मां यतन्तश्च दृढव्रताः ।
नमस्यन्तश्च मां भक्त्या नित्ययुक्ता उपासते ॥

satataṁ kīrtayanto māṁ
yatantaśca dṛḍhavratāḥ

namasyantaśca māṁ bhaktyā
nityayuktā upāsate

Perpetually glorifying Me and striving with firm vows, and honoring Me with devotion, ever steadfast, they worship Me.

15 ज्ञानयज्ञेन चाप्य् अन्ये यजन्तो माम् उपासते ।
एकत्वेन पृथक्त्वेन बहुधा विश्वतोमुखम् ॥
jñānayajñena cāpy anye
yajanto mām upāsate
ekatvena pṛthaktvena
bahudhā viśvatomukham

And by the wisdom sacrifice, others, sacrificing, worship Me as the one and as the manifold, variously manifested, facing in all directions (i.e. omniscient).

16 अहं क्रतुर् अहं यज्ञः स्वधाहम् अहम् औषधम् ।
मन्त्रो ऽहम् अहम् एवाज्यम् अहम् अग्निर् अहं हुतम् ॥
ahaṁ kratur ahaṁ yajñaḥ
svadhāham aham āusadham
mantro 'ham aham evājyam
aham agnir ahaṁ hutam

I am the ritual, I am the sacrifice, I am the offering, I am the medicinal herb, I am the sacred text, I am also the clarified butter, I am the fire, and I am the pouring out (of the oblation).

17 पिताहम् अस्य जगतो माता धाता पितामहः ।
वेद्यं पवित्रम् ओंकार ऋक् साम यजुर् एव च ॥
pitāham asya jagato
mātā dhātā pitāmahaḥ
vedyaṁ pavitram oṁkāra
ṛk sāma yajur eva ca

I am the father of the universe, the mother, the establisher, the grandfather, the object of knowledge, the purifier, the sacred syllable "Om," the Rig, Sama, and Yajur Vedas.

18 गतिर् भर्ता प्रभुः साक्षी निवासः शरणं सुहृत् ।
प्रभवः प्रलयः स्थानं निधानं बीजम् अव्ययम् ॥
gatir bhartā prabhuḥ sākṣī
nivāsaḥ śaraṇaṁ suhṛt
prabhavaḥ pralayaḥ sthānaṁ
nidhānaṁ bījam avyayam

I am the goal, the supporter, the great Lord, the witness, the abode, the refuge, the friend, the origin, the dissolution and the foundation, the treasure house and the imperishable seed.

19 तपाम्य् अहम् अहं वर्षं निगृह्णाम्य् उत्सृजामि च ।
अमृतं चैव मृत्युश्च सद असच् चाहम् अर्जुन ॥
tapāmy aham ahaṁ varṣaṁ
nigṛhṇāmy utsṛjāmi ca
amṛtaṁ cāiva mṛtyuśca
sad asac cāham arjuna

I radiate heat, I withhold and send forth the rain; and I am both immortality and death, being and non-being, Arjuna.

20 त्रैविद्या मां सोमपाः पूतपापा
यज्ञैर् इष्ट्वा स्वर्गतिं प्रार्थयन्ते ।
ते पुण्यम् आसाद्य सुरेन्द्रलोकम्
अश्नन्ति दिव्यान् दिवि देवभोगान् ॥
trāividyā māṁ somapāḥ pūtapāpā
yajñāir iṣṭvā svargatiṁ prārthayante
te puṇyam āsādya surendralokam
aśnanti divyān divi devabhogān

Those who know the three Vedas, the soma drinkers, those whose evils are cleansed, worship Me with sacrifices and seek to go to heaven. They, attaining the pure world of the Lord of the gods, enjoy in heaven the gods' celestial pleasures.

21 ते तं भुक्त्वा स्वर्गलोकं विशालं
क्षीणे पुण्ये मर्त्यलोकं विशन्ति ।
एवं त्रयीधर्मम् अनुप्रपन्ना
गतागतं कामकामा लभन्ते ॥
te taṁ bhuktvā svargalokaṁ viśālaṁ
kṣīṇe puṇye martyalokaṁ viśanti
evaṁ trayīdharmam anuprapannā
gatāgataṁ kāmakāmā labhante

Having enjoyed the vast world of heaven, they enter the world of mortals when their merit is exhausted. Thus conforming to the law of the three Vedas, desir-

ing enjoyments, they obtain the state of going and returning.

22 अनन्याश् चिन्तयन्तो मां ये जनाः पर्युपासते ।
तेषां नित्याभियुक्तानां योगक्षेमं वहाम्य् अहम् ॥
ananyāś cintayanto māṁ
ye janāḥ paryupāsate
teṣāṁ nityābhiyuktānāṁ
yogakṣemaṁ vahāmy aham

Those men who worship, directing their thoughts to Me, whose minds do not go elsewhere; for them, who are constantly steadfast, I secure what they lack and preserve what they already possess.

23 ये ऽप्य् अन्यदेवताभक्ता यजन्ते श्रद्धयान्विताः ।
ते ऽपि माम् एव कौन्तेय यजन्त्य् अविधिपूर्वकम् ॥
ye 'py anyadevatābhaktā
yajante śraddhayānvitāḥ
te 'pi mām eva kāunteya
yajanty avidhipūrvakam

Even those who worship other gods with faith, also worship Me, Arjuna, though they do so in ignorance.

24 अहं हि सर्वयज्ञानां भोक्ता च प्रभुर् एव च ।
न तु माम् अभिजानन्ति तत्त्वेनातश् च्यवन्ति ते ॥
ahaṁ hi sarvayajñānāṁ
bhoktā ca prabhur eva ca
na tu mām abhijānanti
tattvenātaś cyavanti te

For I am the enjoyer and the Lord of all sacrifices. But they do not recognize Me in truth; hence they fall.

25 यान्ति देवव्रता देवान् पितॄन् यान्ति पितृव्रताः ।
भूतानि यान्ति भूतेज्या यान्ति मद्याजिनोऽपि माम् ॥
yānti devavratā devān
pitṝn yānti pitṛvratāḥ
bhūtāni yānti bhūtejyā
yānti madyājino 'pi mām

Those who are devoted to the gods go to the gods; those who are devoted to the ancestors go to the ancestors; those who are devoted to the spirits go to the spirits; those who worship Me come surely to Me.

26 पत्त्रं पुष्पं फलं तोयं यो मे भक्त्या प्रयच्छति ।
तद् अहं भक्त्युपहृतम् अश्नामि प्रयतात्मनः ॥
pattraṁ puṣpaṁ phalaṁ toyaṁ
yo me bhaktyā prayacchati
tad ahaṁ bhaktyupahṛtam
aśnāmi prayatātmanaḥ

He who offers to Me with devotion and a pure heart a leaf, a flower, a fruit,or water, that offering of devotion I accept from him.

27 यत् करोषि यद् अश्नासि यज् जुहोषि ददासि यत् ।
यत् तपस्यसि कौन्तेय तत् कुरुष्व मदर्पणम् ॥
yat karoṣi yad aśnāsi
yaj juhoṣi dadāsi yat

yat tapasyasi kāunteya
tat kuruṣva madarpaṇam

Whatever you do, whatever you eat, whatever you offer, whatever you give, whatever austerities you perform, Arjuna, do that as an offering to Me.

28 शुभाशुभफलैर् एवं मोक्ष्यसे कर्मबन्धनैः ।
सन्यासयोगयुक्तात्मा विमुक्तो माम् उपैष्यते ॥

śubhāśubhaphalāir evaṁ
mokṣyase karmabandhanāiḥ
saṁnyāsayogayuktātmā
vimukto mām upāiṣyate

You shall certainly be liberated from the bonds of action which produce good and evil fruits; liberated, with your mind disciplined by the yoga of renunciation, you shall come to Me.

29 समो ऽहं सर्वभूतेषु न मे द्वेष्यो ऽस्ति न प्रियः ।
ये भजन्ति तु मां भक्त्या मयि ते तेषु चाप्य् अहम् ॥

samo 'haṁ sarvabhūteṣu
na me dveṣyo 'sti na priyaḥ
ye bhajanti tu māṁ bhaktyā
mayi te teṣu cāpy aham

I am the same (Self) in all beings; there is none disliked or dear to Me. But they who worship Me with devotion are in Me, and I am also in them.

30 अपि चेत् सुदुराचारो भजते माम् अनन्यभाक् ।
साधुर् एव स मन्तव्यः सम्यग् व्यवसितो हि सः ॥
api cet sudurācāro
bhajate mām ananyabhāk
sādhur eva sa mantavyaḥ
samyag vyavasito hi saḥ

If even the evil doer worships Me with undivided devotion, he is to be thought of as righteous, for he has indeed rightly resolved.

31 क्षिप्रं भवति धर्मात्मा शश्वच्छान्तिं निगच्छति ।
कौन्तेय प्रतिजानीहि न मे भक्तः प्रणश्यति ॥
kṣipraṁ bhavati dharmātmā
śaśvacchāntiṁ nigacchati
kāunteya pratijānīhi
na me bhaktaḥ praṇaśyati

Quickly he becomes virtuous and goes to everlasting peace. Arjuna, know for certain that no devotee of Mine is ever lost.

32 मां हि पार्थ व्यपाश्रित्य येऽपि स्युः पापयोनयः ।
स्त्रियो वैश्यास् तथा शूद्रास् तेऽपि यान्ति परां गतिम् ॥
māṁ hi pārtha vyapāśritya
ye 'pi syuḥ pāpayonayaḥ
striyo vāiśyās tathā śūdrās
te 'pi yānti parāṁ gatim

They who take refuge in Me, Arjuna, even if they are born of those whose wombs are evil (i.e. those of low origin), women,

Vaishyas, even Shudras, also go to the highest goal.

33 किं पुनर् ब्राह्मणाः पुण्या भक्ता राजर्षयस् तथा ।
अनित्यम् असुखं लोकम् इमं प्राप्य भजस्व माम् ॥
kiṁ punar brāhmaṇāḥ puṇyā
bhaktā rājarṣayas tathā
anityam asukhaṁ lokam
imaṁ prāpya bhajasva mām

How much more easily then, the pure Brahmins and the devoted royal seers! Having attained this impermanent and unhappy world, devote yourself to Me.

34 मन्मना भव मद्भक्तो मद्याजी मां नमस्कुरु ।
माम् एवैष्यसि युक्त्वैवम् आत्मानं मत्परायणः ॥
manmanā bhava madbhakto
madyājī māṁ namaskuru
mām evāiṣyasi yuktvāivam
ātmānaṁ matparāyaṇah

With mind fixed on Me, be devoted to Me; sacrificing to Me, make reverence to Me. Thus steadfast, with Me as your supreme aim, you yourself shall come to Me.

Hari Om Tat Sat
Iti Srimad Bhagavadgītāsūpaniṣatsu Brahmavidyāyām
Yogaśāstre Sri Krişnārjunasamvāde
Rājavidyā-rājaguhyayogo Nāma Navamoddhyāyaḥ.

Thus ends the ninth Chapter, entitled "The Yoga of Sovereign Knowledge," of the venerated Bhagavad Gita Upanishad, the Knowledge of the Absolute, the scripture of Yoga, the dialogue between Sri Krishna and Arjuna.

TEN

The Yoga of Manifestation

atha daṣamoddhyāyaḥ

1 श्रीभगवान् उवाच । *śrībhagavān uvāca*

भूय एव महाबाहो शृणु मे परमं वचः ।
यत् ते ऽहं प्रीयमाणाय वक्ष्यामि हितकाम्यया ॥
bhūya eva mahābāho
śṛṇu me paramaṁ vacaḥ
yat te 'haṁ prīyamāṇāya
vakṣyāmi hitakāmyayā

The Blessed Lord spoke:
Again, O Arjuna, hear My supreme word which I shall speak to you, who are beloved, with a desire for your welfare.

2 न मे विदुः सुरगणाः प्रभवं न महर्षयः ।
अहम् आदिर् हि देवानां महर्षीणां च सर्वशः ॥
na me viduḥ suragaṇāḥ
prabhavaṁ na maharṣayaḥ
aham ādir hi devānāṁ
maharṣīṇāṁ ca sarvaśaḥ

Neither the multitude of gods nor the great seers know My origin. In truth I am the source of the gods and the great seers.

3 यो माम् अजम् अनादिं च वेत्ति लोकमहेश्वरम् ।
असंमूढः स मर्त्येषु सर्वपापैः प्रमुच्यते ॥

yo mām ajam anādiṁ ca
vetti lokamaheśvaram
asaṁmūḍhaḥ sa martyeṣu
sarvapāpāiḥ pramucyate

He who knows Me, the birthless and the beginningless, the mighty Lord of the world, he among mortals is undeluded; he is released from all evils.

4 बुद्धिर् ज्ञानम् असंमोहः क्षमा सत्यं दमः शमः ।
सुखं दुःखं भवो ऽभवो भयं चाभयम् एव च ॥

buddhir jñānam asaṁmohaḥ
kṣamā satyaṁ damaḥ śamaḥ
sukhaṁ duḥkhaṁ bhavo 'bhavo
bhayaṁ cābhayam eva ca

Intellect, knowledge, freedom from delusion, patience, truth, self-restraint, tranquility, pleasure, pain, birth, death, and fear and fearlessness,

5 अहिंसा समता तुष्टिस् तपो दानं यशो ऽयशः ।
भवन्ति भावा भूतानां मत्त एव पृथग्विधाः ॥

ahiṁsā samatā tuṣṭis
tapo dānaṁ yaśo 'yaśaḥ
bhavanti bhāvā bhūtānāṁ
matta eva pṛthagvidhāḥ

Non-violence, impartiality, contentment, austerity, charity, fame, disrepute, the manifold conditions of beings, arise from Me alone.

6 महर्षयः सप्त पूर्वे चत्वारो मनवस् तथा
मद्भावा मानसा जाता येषां लोक इमाः प्रजाः ॥
maharṣayaḥ sapta pūrve
catvāro manavas tathā
madbhāvā mānasā jātā
yeṣāṁ loka imāḥ prajāḥ

The seven great seers of old, and also the four Manus, from whom have sprung these creatures of the world, originated from Me, born of My mind.

7 एतां विभूतिं योगं च मम यो वेत्ति तत्त्वतः ।
सो ऽविकम्पेन योगेन युज्यते नात्र संशयः ॥
etāṁ vibhūtiṁ yogaṁ ca
mama yo vetti tattvataḥ
so 'vikampena yogena
yujyate nātra saṁśayaḥ

He who knows in truth this, My manifested glory and power, is united with Me by unwavering yoga; of this there is no doubt.

8 अहं सर्वस्य प्रभवो मत्तः सर्वं प्रवर्तते ।
इति मत्वा भजन्ते मां बुधा भावसमन्विताः ॥
ahaṁ sarvasya prabhavo
mattaḥ sarvaṁ pravartate
iti matvā bhajante māṁ
budhā bhāvasamanvitāḥ

I am the origin of all; all proceeds from Me. Thinking thus, the intelligent ones,

9 मच्चित्ता मद्गतप्राणा बोधयन्तः परस्परम् ।
कथयन्तश्च मां नित्यं तुष्यन्ति च रमन्ति च ॥

maccittā madgataprāṇā
bodhayantaḥ parasparam
kathayantaśca māṁ nityaṁ
tuṣyanti ca ramanti ca

Those who think of Me, who absorb their lives in Me, enlightening each other, and speaking of Me constantly, they are content and rejoice.

10 तेषां सततयुक्तानां भजतां प्रीतिपूर्वकम् ।
ददामि बुद्धियोगं तं येन माम् उपयान्ति ते ॥

teṣāṁ satatayuktānāṁ
bhajatāṁ prītipūrvakam
dadāmi buddhiyogaṁ taṁ
yena mām upayānti te

To those who are constantly steadfast, those who worship Me with love, I give the yoga of discrimination by which they come to Me.

11 तेषाम् एवानुकम्पार्थम् अहम् अज्ञानजं तमः ।
नाशयाम्य् आत्मभावस्थो ज्ञानदीपेन भास्वता ॥

teṣām evānukampārtham
aham ajñānajaṁ tamaḥ
nāśayāmy ātmabhāvastho
jñānadīpena bhāsvatā

Out of compassion for them, I, who dwell within their own beings, destroy the darkness born of ignorance with the shining lamp of knowledge.

12 अर्जुन उवाच । *arjuna uvāca*

मरं ब्रह्मपरं धाम पवित्रं परमं भवान् ।
पुरुषं शाश्वतं दिव्यम् आदिदेवम् अजं विभुम् ।।

paraṁ brahma paraṁ dhāma
pavitraṁ paramaṁ bhavān
puruṣaṁ śāśvataṁ divyam
ādidevam ajaṁ vibhum

Arjuna spoke:

You are the supreme Brahman, the supreme abode, the supreme purifier, the eternal divine Spirit, the primal God, unborn and all-pervading.

13 आहुस् त्वाम् ऋषयः सर्वे देवर्षिर् नारदस् तथा ।
असितो देवलो व्यासः स्वयं चैव ब्रवीषि मे ।।

āhus tvām ṛṣayaḥ sarve
devarṣir nāradas tathā
asito devalo vyāsaḥ
svayaṁ cāiva bravīṣi me

Thus they call You, all the seers, the divine seer Narada, also Asita, Devala, and Vyasa, and You Yourself (now) tell me so.

14 सर्वम् एतद् ऋतं मन्ये यन् मां वदसि केशव ।
न हि ते भगवन् व्यक्तिं विदुर् देवा न दानवाः ।।

sarvam etad ṛtaṁ manye
yan māṁ vadasi keśava
na hi te bhagavan vyaktiṁ
vidur devā na dānavāḥ

All this which You speak to me, Krishna, I believe to be true; indeed, neither the gods nor the demons,O Blessed one, know Your manifestation.

15 स्वयम् एवात्मना ऽत्मानं वेत्थ त्वं पुरुषोत्तम ।
भूतभावन भूतेश देवदेव जगत्पते ।।
svayam evātmanā 'tmānaṁ
vettha tvaṁ puruṣottama
bhūtabhāvana bhūteśa
devadeva jagatpate

Supreme Being, O Lord of the universe,You know Yourself through Yourself alone, highest of spirits, source of welfare of beings, Lord of beings, God of gods, O Lord of the universe.

16 वक्तुम् अर्हस्य् अशेषेण दिव्या ह्य् आत्मविभूतयः ।
याभिर् विभूतिभिर् लोकान् इमांस् त्वं व्याप्य तिष्ठसि ।।
vaktum arhasy aśeṣeṇa
divyā hy ātmavibhūtayaḥ
yābhir vibhūtibhir lokān
imāṅs tvam vyāpya tiṣṭhasi

Please describe without reserve the divine self-manifestations by which You pervade these worlds, and abide in them.

17 कथं विद्याम् अहं योगिंस् त्वां सदा परिचिन्तयन् ।
केषुकेषु च भावेषु चिन्त्यो ऽसि भगवन् मया ॥

katharn vidyām aharn yogiṅs
tvārn sadā paricintayan
keṣukeṣu ca bhāveṣu
cintyo 'si bhagavan mayā

How may I know You, O Yogin, constantly meditating on You? And in what various aspects of being are You to be thought of by me, O Blessed One?

18 विस्तरेणात्मनो योगं विभूतिं च जनार्दन ।
भूयः कथय तृप्तिर् हि शृण्वतो नास्ति मे ऽमृतम् ॥

vistareṇātmano yogarn
vibhūtirn ca janārdana
bhūyaḥ kathaya tṛptir hi
śṛṇvato nāsti me 'mṛtam

Explain to me further in detail Your power and manifestation, O Krishna. I am never satiated with hearing Your nectar-like words.

19 श्रीभगवान् उवाच । *śrībhagavān uvāca*

हन्त ते कथयिष्यामि दिव्या ह्य् आत्मविभूतयः ।
प्राधान्यतः कुरुश्रेष्ठ नास्त्य् अन्तो विस्तरस्य मे ॥

hanta te kathayiṣyāmi
divyā hy ātmavibhūtayaḥ
prādhānyataḥ kuruśreṣṭha
nāsty anto vistarasya me

The Blessed Lord spoke:

Listen! I shall explain to you My divine self-manifestations; those only that are prominent, for there is no end to My extent.

20 अहम् आत्मा गुडाकेश सर्वभूताशयस्थितः ।
अहम् आदिश्च मध्यं च भूतानाम् अन्त एव च ॥
aham ātmā guḍākeśa
sarvabhūtāśayasthitaḥ
aham ādiśca madhyaṁ ca
bhūtānām anta eva ca

I am the Self, Arjuna, abiding in the heart of all beings; and I am the beginning and the middle of beings, and the end as well.

21 आदित्यानाम् अहं विष्णुर् ज्योतिषां रविर् अंशुमान् ।
मरीचिर् मरुताम् अस्मि नक्षत्राणाम् अहं शशी ॥
ādityānām ahaṁ viṣṇur
jyotiṣāṁ ravir aṁśuman
marīci marutām asmi
nakṣatrāṇām ahaṁ śaśī

Of the Adityas, I am Vishnu; of lights, the radiant sun; I am Marichi of the Maruts; among the heavenly bodies I am the moon.

22 वेदानां सामवेदो ऽस्मि देवानाम् अस्मि वासवः ।
इन्द्रियाणाम् मनश्चास्मि भूतानाम् अस्मि चेतना ॥
vedānāṁ sāmavedo 'smi
devānām asmi vāsavaḥ

indriyāṇām manaścāsmi
bhūtānām asmi cetanā

Of the Vedas, I am the Sama Veda; of the gods, I am Vasava; and of the senses, I am the mind, I am the consciousness of beings.

23 रुद्राणां शंकरश्चास्मि वित्तेशो यक्षरक्षसाम् ।
वसूनां पावकश्चास्मि मेरुः शिखरिणाम् अहम् ॥

rudrāṇām śaṁkaraścāsmi
vitteśo yakṣarakṣasām
vasūnāṁ pāvakaścāsmi
meruḥ śikhariṇām aham

And of the Rudras, I am Shankara; I am Kubera of the Yaksas and Rakshasas; I am fire of the Vasus and the Meru of mountains.

24 पुरोधसां च मुख्यं मां विद्धि पार्थ बृहस्पतिम् ।
सेनानीनाम् अहं स्कन्दः सरसाम् अस्मि सागरः ॥

purodhasāṁ ca mukhyaṁ māṁ
viddhi pārtha bṛhaspatim
senānīnām ahaṁ skandaḥ
sarasām asmi sāgaraḥ

Know that I am the chief of household priests, Brihaspati, Arjuna; of the commanders of armies, I am Skanda; of bodies of water, I am the ocean.

25 महर्षीणां भृगुर् अहं गिराम् अस्म्य् एकम् अक्षरम् ।
यज्ञानां जपयज्ञो ऽस्मि स्थावराणां हिमालयः ॥

maharṣīṇāṁ bhṛgur ahaṁ
girām asmy ekam akṣaram
yajñānāṁ japayajño 'smi
sthāvarāṇaṁ himālayaḥ

Of the great seers, I am Bhrigu; of words, I am the single syllable "Om;" of sacrifices, I am japa (silent repetition); of immovable things, the Himalayas.

26 अश्वत्थः सर्ववृक्षाणां देवर्षीणां च नारद ।
गन्धर्वाणां चित्ररथः सिद्धानां कपिलो मुनिः ॥
aśvatthaḥ sarvavṛkṣāṇāṁ
devarṣīṇāṁ ca nārada
gandharvāṇāṁ citrarathaḥ
siddhānāṁ kapilo muniḥ

Among all trees, I am the sacred fig tree; and of the divine seers, Narada; and of the Gandharvas, Chitraratha; and of the perfected, Kapila the sage.

27 उच्चैःश्रवसम् अश्वानां विद्ध माम् अमृतोद्भवम् ।
ऐरावतं गजेन्द्राणां नराणां च नराधिपम् ॥
uccāiḥśravasam aśvānāṁ
viddhi mām amṛtodbhavam
āirāvataṁ gajendrāṇāṁ
narāṇāṁ ca narādhipam

Know that I am Ucchaishravas of horses, born of nectar; Airavata of princely elephants; and of men, the king.

28 आयुधानाम् अहं वज्रं धेनूनाम् अस्मि कामधुक् ।
प्रजनश्चास्मि कन्दर्पः सर्पाणाम् अस्मि वासुकिः ॥

āyudhānām ahaṁ vajraṁ
dhenūnām asmi kāmadhuk
prajanaścāsmi kandarpaḥ
sarpāṇām asmi vāsukiḥ

Of weapons, I am the thunderbolt; of cows, I am the wish-fulfilling cow; I am the progenitor Kandarpa; and of serpents, I am Vasuki.

29 अनन्तश्चास्मि नागानां वरुणो यादसाम् अहम् ।
पितॄणाम् अर्यमा चास्मि यमः संयमताम् अहम् ॥

anantaścāsmi nāgānāṁ
varuṇo yādasām aham
pitṝṇām aryamā cāsmi
yamaḥ saṁyamatām aham

I am Ananta of the Nagas; Varuna of the water creatures; of the ancestors, I am Aryaman; and Yama of the controllers.

30 प्रह्लादश्चास्मि दैत्यानां कालः कलयताम् अहम् ।
मृगाणां च मृगेन्द्रो ऽहं वैनतेयश्च पक्षिणाम् ॥

prahlādaścāsmi dāityānāṁ
kālaḥ kalayatām aham
mṛgāṇāṁ ca mṛgendro 'haṁ
vāinateyaśca pakṣiṇām

I am Prahlada of the demons; time, of the calculators; of the beasts, I am the lion; and Garuda, of the bird's.

31 पवनः पवताम् अस्मि रामः शस्त्रभृताम् अहम् ।
झषानां मकरश्चास्मि स्रोतसाम् अस्मि जाह्नवी ।।

pavanaḥ pavatām asmi
rāmaḥ śastrabhṛtām aham
jhaṣānāṁ makaraścāsmi
srotasām asmi jāhnavś

Of purifiers, I am the wind; Rama of the warriors; of the sea monsters I am the alligators; and of rivers I am the Ganges.

32 सर्गाणाम् आदिर् अन्तश्च मध्यं चैवाहम् अर्जुन ।
अध्यात्मविद्या विद्यानां वादः प्रवदताम् अहम् ।।

sargāṇām ādir antaśca
madhyaṁ cāivāham arjuna
adhyātmavidyā vidyānāṁ
vādaḥ pravadatām aham

Of creations I am the beginning and the end, and also the middle, O Arjuna; of all knowledge, the knowledge of the supreme Self. I am the logic of those who debate.

33 अक्षराणाम् अकारो ऽस्मि द्वन्द्वः सामासिकस्य च ।
अहम् एवाक्षयः कालो धाताहं विश्वतोमुखः ।।

akṣarāṇām akāro 'smi
dvandvaḥ sāmāsikasya ca
aham evākṣayaḥ kālo
dhātāhaṁ viśvatomukhaḥ

Of letters I am the letter A, and the dual of compound words; I alone am infi-

nite time; I am the Establisher, facing in all directions (i.e. omniscient).

34 मृत्युः सर्वहरश्चाहम् उद्भवश्च भविष्यताम् ।
कीर्तिः श्रीर् वाक् च नारीणां स्मृतिर् मेधा धृतिः क्षमा ॥

mṛtyuḥ sarvaharaścaham
udbhavaśca bhaviṣyatām
kīrtiḥ śrīr vāk ca nārīṇām
smṛtir medhā dhṛtiḥ kṣamā

I am all-destroying death, and the origin of those things that are yet to be. Among the feminine qualities, I am fame, prosperity, speech, memory, wisdom, courage, and patience.

35 बृहत्साम तथा साम्नां गायत्री छन्दसाम् अहम् ।
मासानां मार्गशीर्षो ऽहम् ऋतूनां कुसुमाकरः ॥

bṛhatsāma tathā sāmnāṁ
gāyatrī chandasām aham
māsānāṁ mārgaśīrṣo 'ham
ṛtūnāṁ kusumākaraḥ

Of chants I am the Brihatsaman; of meters I am the Gayatri; of months, the Marga-shirsha; and of seasons, the spring, abounding with flowers.

36 द्यूतं छलयताम् अस्मि तेजस् तेजस्विनाम् अहम् ।
जयो ऽस्मि व्यवसायो ऽस्मि सत्त्वं सत्त्ववताम् अहम् ॥

dyūtaṁ chalayatām asmi
tejas tejasvinām aham

jayo 'smi vyavasāyo 'smi
sattvaṁ sattvavatām aham

I am the gambling of the dishonest, the splendor of the splendid; I am victory, I am effort, I am the goodness of the good.

37 वृष्णीनां वासुदेवो ऽस्मि पाण्डवानां धनंजयः ।
मुनीनाम् अप्य् अहं व्यासः कवीनाम् उशना कविः ॥
vṛṣṇīnām vāsudevo 'smi
pāṇḍavānāṁ dhanamjayaḥ
munīnām apy ahaṁ vyāsaḥ
kavīnām uśanā kaviḥ

Of the Vrishnis, I am Vasudeva; of the sons of Pandu, Arjuna; of the sages, moreover, I am Vyasa; of poets, the poet Ushana.

38 दण्डो दमयताम् अस्मि नीतिर् अस्मि जिगीषताम् ।
मौनं चैवास्मि गुह्यानां ज्ञानं ज्ञानवताम् अहम् ॥
daṇḍo damayatām asmi
nītir asmi jigīṣatām
māunaṁ cāivāsmi guhyānāṁ
jñānaṁ jñānavatām aham

Of punishers, I am the scepter, and I am the guidance of those desirous of victory; of secrets, I am silence and the knowledge of the wise.

39 यच् चापि सर्वभूतानां बीजं तद् अहम् अर्जुन ।
न तद् अस्ति विना यत् स्यान् मया भूतं चराचरम् ॥
yac cāpi sarvabhūtānāṁ
bījaṁ tad aham arjuna

na tad asti vinā yat syān
mayā bhūtaṁ carācaram

And also I am that which is the seed of all creatures, Arjuna; there is nothing that could exist without existing through Me, whether moving or not moving.

40 नान्तो ऽस्ति मम दिव्यानां विभूतीनां परंतप ।
एष तूद्देशतः प्रोक्तो विभूतेर् विस्तरो मया ॥
nānto 'sti mama divyānāṁ
vibhūtīnāṁ paraṁtapa
eṣa tūddeśataḥ prokto
vibhūter vistaro mayā

There is no end to My divine manifestations, Arjuna. This has been declared by Me as an example of the extent of My manifestations.

41 यद् यद् विभूतिमत् सत्त्वं श्रीमद् ऊर्जितम् एव वा ।
तत् तद् एवावगच्छ त्वं मम तेजों ऽशसंभवम् ॥
yad yad vibhūtimat sattvaṁ
śrīmad ūrjitam eva vā
tat tad evāvagaccha tvaṁ
mama tejo'ṁśasaṁbhavam

Whatever manifested being that is glorious and vigorous, indeed, understand that in every case he originates from a fraction of My splendor.

42 अथवा बहुनैतेन किं ज्ञातेन तवार्जुन ।
विष्टभ्याहम् इदं कृत्स्नम् एकांशेन स्थितो जगत् ॥

athavā bahunāitena
kiṁ jñātena tavārjuna
viṣṭabhyāham idaṁ kṛtsnam
ekāṁśena sthito jagat

But what is this extensive knowledge to you, Arjuna? I support this entire universe constantly with a single fraction of Myself.

Hari Om Tat Sat
Iti Srimad Bhagavadgītāsūpaniṣatsu Brahmavidyāyām
Yogaśāstre Sri Krişnārjunasamvāde
Vibhūtiyogo Nāma Daṣamoddhyāyaḥ.

Thus ends the tenth Chapter, entitled "The Yoga of Manifestation," of the venerated Bhagavad Gita Upanishad, the Knowledge of the Absolute, the scripture of Yoga, the dialogue between Sri Krishna and Arjuna.

ELEVEN

The Vision of the Cosmic Form

atha ekādaśoddhyāyaḥ

1 अर्जुन उवाच । *arjuna uvāca*

मदनुग्रहाय परमं गुह्यम् अध्यात्मसंज्ञितम् ।
यत् त्वयोक्तं वचस् तेन मोहो ऽयं विगतो मम ।।
madanugrahāya paramam
guhyam adhyātmasaṁjñitaṁ
yat tvayoktaṁ vacas tena
moho 'yam vigato mama

Arjuna spoke:

As a favor to me, You have spoken about the highest secret known as the supreme Self. With this my delusion is gone.

2 भवाप्ययौ हि भूतानां श्रुतौ विस्तरशो मया ।
त्वत्तः कमलपत्त्राक्ष माहात्म्यम् अपि चाव्ययम् ।।
bhavāpyayāu hi bhūtānāṁ
śrutāu vistaraśo mayā
tvattaḥ kamalapattrākṣa
māhātmyam api cāvyayam

The origin and the dissolution of beings have been heard in detail by me from You, O Krishna, and also Your imperishable majesty.

3 एवम् एतद् यथात्थ त्वम् आत्मानं परमेश्वर ।
द्रष्टुम् इच्छामि ते रूपम् ऐश्वरं पुरुषोत्तम ॥
evam etad yathāttha tvam
ātmānaṁ parameśvara
draṣṭum icchāmi te rūpam
āiśvaram puruṣottama

Thus, as You have described Yourself, O supreme Lord, I desire to see Your divine form, O Supreme Spirit.

4 मन्यसे यदि तच्छक्यं मया द्रष्टुम् इति प्रभो ।
योगेश्वर ततो मे त्वं दर्शयात्मानम् अव्ययम् ॥
manyase yadi tac chakyaṁ
mayā draṣṭum iti prabho
yogeśvara tato me tvaṁ
darśayātmānam avyayam

If You think it possible for me to see this, O Lord of Yogins, then show me Your imperishable Self.

5 श्रीभगवान् उवाच । *śrībhagavān uvāca*

पश्य मे पार्थ रूपाणि शतशो ऽथ सहस्रशः ।
नानाविधानि दिव्यानि नानावर्णाकृतीनि च ॥
paśya me pārtha rūpāṇi
śataśo 'tha sahasraśaḥ
nānāvidhāni divyāni
nānāvarṇākṛtīni ca

The Blessed Lord spoke:

Behold, Arjuna, My forms, a hundredfold, a thousandfold, various, divine, and of various colors and shapes.

6 पश्यादित्यान् वसून् रुद्रान् अश्विनौ मरुतस् तथा ।
बहून्य् अदृष्टपूर्वाणि पश्याश्चर्याणि भारत ॥
paśyādityān vasūn rudrān
aśvināu marutas tathā
bahūny adṛṣṭapūrvāṇi
paśyāścaryāṇi bhārata

Behold the Adityas, the Vasus, the Rudras, the two Asvins, the Maruts too; many wonders unseen before, behold, Arjuna!

7 इहैकस्थं जगत् कृत्स्नं पश्याद्य सचराचरम् ।
मम देहे गुडाकेश यच् चान्यद् द्रष्टुम् इच्छसि ॥
ihāikasthaṁ jagat kṛtsnaṁ
paśyādya sacarācaram
mama dehe guḍākeśa
yac cānyad draṣṭum icchasi

Behold now the entire universe, with everything moving and not moving, standing together here in My body, Arjuna, and whatever else you desire to see.

8 न तु माम् शक्यसे द्रष्टुम् अनेनैव स्वचक्षुषा ।
दिव्यं ददामि ते चक्षुः पश्य मे योगम् ऐश्वरम् ॥
na tu mām śakyase draṣṭum
anenāiva svacakṣuṣā
divyaṁ dadāmi te cakṣuḥ
pasya me yogam āiśvaram

But you are not able to see Me with your own eyes. I give to you a divine eye; behold My majestic power!

9 संजय उवाच । *sañjaya uvāca*

एवम् उक्त्वा ततो राजन् महायोगेश्वरो हरिः ।
दर्शयम् आस पार्थाय परमं रूपम् ऐश्वरम् ॥

evam uktvā tato rājan
mahāyogeśvaro hariḥ
darśayam āsa pārthāya
paramam rūpaṁ āiśvaram

Sanjaya spoke:

Having spoken thus, O King, the great Lord of yoga, Hari (Krishna), revealed to the Arjuna His majestic supreme form.

10 अनेकवक्त्रनयनम् अनेकाद्भुतदर्शनम् ।
अनेकदिव्याभरणं दिव्यानेकोद्यतायुधम् ॥

anekavaktranayanam
anekādbhutadarśanam
anekadivyābharaṇaṁ
divyānekodyatāyudham

Of many mouths and eyes, of many wondrous aspects, of many divine ornaments, of many uplifted divine weapons.

11 दिव्यमाल्याम्बरधरं दिव्यगन्धानुलेपनम् ।
सर्वाश्चर्यमयं देवम् अनन्तं विश्वतोमुखम् ॥

divyamālyāmbaradharaṁ
divyagandhānulepanam
sarvāścaryamayaṁ devam
anantaṁ visvatomukham

Wearing divine garlands and apparel, with divine perfumes and ointments, made up of all marvels, the resplendent Lord, endless, facing in all directions.

12 दिवि सूर्यसहस्रस्य भवेद् युगपद् उत्थिता ।
यदि भाः सदृशी सा स्याद् भासस् तस्य महात्मनः ॥
divi sūryasahasrasya
bhaved yugapad utthitā
yadi bhāḥ sadṛśī sā syād
bhāsas tasya mahātmanaḥ

If a thousand suns should rise all at once in the sky, such splendor would resemble the splendor of that great Being.

13 तत्रैकस्थं जगत् कृत्स्नं प्रविभक्तम् अनेकधा ।
अपश्यद् देवदेवस्य शरीरे पाण्डवस् तदा ॥
tatrāikasthaṁ jagat kṛtsnaṁ
pravibhaktam anekadhā
apaśyad devadevasya
śarīre pāṇḍavas tadā

There Arjuna then beheld the entire universe established in one, divided in many groups, in the body of the God of Gods.

14 ततः स विस्मयाविष्टो हृष्टरोमा धनंजयः ।
प्रणम्य शिरसा देवं कृताञ्जलिर् अभाषत ॥
tataḥ sa vismayāviṣṭo
hṛṣṭaromā dhanaṁjayaḥ
praṇamya śirasā devaṁ
kṛtāñjalir abhāṣata

Then Arjuna, who was filled with amazement, whose hair was standing on end, bowing his head to the Lord with joined palms, said:

15 अर्जुन उवाच । *arjuna uvāca*

पश्यामि देवांस् तव देव देहे
सर्वांस् तथा भूतविशेषसंघान् ।
ब्रह्माणम् ईशं कमलासनस्थम्
ऋषींश्च सर्वान् उरगांश्च दिव्यान् ॥

paśyāmi devāṅs tava deva dehe
sarvāṅs tathā bhūtaviśeṣasaṁghān
brahmāṇam īśaṁ kamalāsanastham
ṛṣīnśca sarvān uragāṅśca divyān

Arjuna spoke:

I see the gods, O God, in Your body, and all kinds of beings assembled; Lord Brahma on his lotus seat, and all the seers and divine serpents.

16 अनेकबाहूदरवक्त्रनेत्रं
पश्यामि त्वां सर्वतो ऽनन्तरूपम् ।
नान्तं न मध्यं न पुनस् तवादिं
पश्यामि विश्वेश्वर विश्वरूप ॥

anekabāhūdaravaktranetraṁ
paśyāmi tvāṁ sarvato 'nantarūpam
nāntaṁ na madhyaṁ na punas tavādiṁ
paśyāmi viśveśvara viśvarūpa

I see You everywhere, infinite in form, with many arms, bellies, faces, and eyes; not the end, nor the middle, nor yet the beginning of You do I see, O Lord of all, whose form is the universe.

17 किरीटिनं गदिनं चक्रिणं च
तेजोराशिं सर्वतो दीप्तिमन्तम् ।
पश्यामि त्वां दुर्निरीक्ष्यं समन्ताद्
दीप्तानलार्कद्युतिम् अप्रमेयम् ।।
kirīṭinaṁ gadinaṁ cakriṇaṁ ca
tejorāśiṁ sarvato dīptimantam
paśyāmi tvāṁ durnirīkṣyaṁ samantād
dīptānalārkadyutim aprameyam

Crowned, armed with a club and bearing a discus, a mass of splendor, shining on all sides, with the immeasurable radiance of the sun and blazing fire, I see You, who are difficult to behold.

18 त्वम् अक्षरं परमं वेदितव्यं
त्वम् अस्य विश्वस्य परं निधानम् ।
त्वमव्ययः शाश्वतधर्मगोप्ता
सनातनस् त्वं पुरुषो मतो मे ।।
tvam akṣaraṁ paramaṁ veditavyaṁ
tvam asya viśvasya paraṁ nidhānam
tvam avyayaḥ śāśvatadharmagoptā
sanātanas tvaṁ puruṣo mato me

You are the unchanging, the supreme object of knowledge; You are the ultimate resting place of all; You are the imperishable defender of the eternal law; You are the primeval Spirit, I believe.

19 अनादिमध्यान्तम् अनन्तवीर्यम्
अनन्तबाहुं शशिसूर्यनेत्रम् ।
पश्यामि त्वां दीप्तहुताशवक्त्रं
स्वतेजसा विश्वम् इदं तपन्तम् ।।
anādimadhyāntam anantavīryam
anantabāhuṁ śaśisūryanetram
paśyāmi tvāṁ dīptahutāśavaktraṁ
svatejasā viśvam idaṁ tapantam

With infinite power, without beginning, middle, or end, with innumerable arms, the moon and sun being Your eyes, I see You, the blazing fire Your mouth, burning all this universe with Your radiance.

20 द्यावापृथिव्योर् इदम् अन्तरं हि
व्याप्तं त्वयैकेन दिशश्च सर्वाः ।
दृष्ट्वाद्भुतं रूपम् उग्रं तवेदं
लोकत्रयं प्रव्यथितं महात्मन् ।।
dyāvāpṛthivyor idam antaraṁ hi
vyāptaṁ tvayāikena diśaśca sarvāḥ
dṛṣṭvādbhutaṁ rūpam ugraṁ tavedaṁ
lokatrayaṁ pravyathitaṁ mahātman

This space between heaven and earth, is pervaded by You alone in all directions. Seeing Your marvelous and terrible form, the three worlds tremble, O great Being.

21 अमी हि त्वां सुरसंघा विशन्ति
केचिद् भीताः प्राञ्जलयो गृणन्ति ।

स्वस्तीत्य् उक्त्वा महर्षिसिद्धसंघाः
स्तुवन्ति त्वां स्तुतिभिः पुष्कलाभिः ॥

amī hi tvāṁ surasaṁghā viśanti
kecid bhītāḥ prāñjalayo gṛṇanti
svastīty uktvā mahārṣisiddhasaṁghāḥ
stuvanti tvāṁ stutibhiḥ puṣkalābhiḥ

The throngs of gods enter into You, some, terrified, with reverent gestures praise You; saying "Hail," the throngs of great seers and perfected ones extol You with abundant praises.

22 रुद्रादित्या वसवो ये च साध्या
विश्वे ऽश्विनौ मरुतश्चोष्मपाश्च ।
गन्धर्वयक्षासुरसिद्धसंघा
वीक्षन्ते त्वां विस्मिताश्चैव सर्वे ॥

rudrādityā vasavo ye ca sādhyā
viśve 'śvināu marutaścoṣmapāś ca
gandharvayakṣāsurasiddhasaṁghā
vīkṣante tvāṁ vismitāścāiva sarve

The Rudras, Adityas, Vasus, the Sadhyas, the Vishve devas, the two Ashvins, the Maruts, and the Ushmapas, the throngs of Gandharvas, Yakshas, Asuras, and perfected ones, all behold You, amazed.

23 रूपं महत् ते बहुवक्त्रनेत्रं
महाबाहो बहुबाहूरुपादम् ।

बहूदरं बहुदंष्ट्राकरालं
दृष्ट्वा लोकाः प्रव्यथितास् तथा ऽहम् ॥
rūpaṁ mahat te bahuvaktranetram
mahābāho bahubāhūrupādam
bahūdaraṁ bahudaṁṣṭrākarālaṁ
dṛṣṭvā lokāḥ pravyathitās tathā 'ham

Having seen Your great form, which has many mouths and eyes, which has many arms, thighs, and feet, which has many bellies, and mouths gaping with many tusks, O Krishna, the worlds tremble, and so do I.

24 व्यात्ताननं दीप्तविशालनेत्रम् ।
नभःस्पृशं दीप्तम् अनेकवर्णं
दृष्ट्वा हि त्वां प्रव्यथितान्तरात्मा
धृतिं न विन्दामि शमं च विष्णो ॥
nabhaḥspṛśaṁ dīptam anekavarṇaṁ
vyāttānanam dīptaviśālanetram
dṛṣṭvā hi tvāṁ pravyathitāntarātmā
dhṛtiṁ na vindāmi śamaṁ ca viṣṇo

Having seen You touching the sky, blazing, many colored, gaping-mouthed, with enormous fiery eyes; I tremble indeed in my heart, and I find neither courage nor tranquility, O Vishnu!

25 दंष्ट्राकरालानि च ते मुखानि
दृष्ट्वैव कालानलसंनिभानि ।

दिशो न जाने न लभे च शर्म
प्रसीद देवेश जगन्निवास ।।

daṁṣṭrākarālāni ca te mukhāni
dṛṣṭvāiva kālānalasaṁnibhāni
diśo na jāne na labhe ca śarma
prasīda deveśa jagannivāsa

And having seen Your mouths, bearing many tusks, glowing like the fires of universal destruction, I lose my sense of direction, and I do not find comfort. Have mercy! Lord of Gods, abode of the universe!

26 अमी च त्वां धृतराष्ट्रस्य पुत्राः
सर्वे सहैवावनिपालसंघैः ।
भीष्मो द्रोणः सूतपुत्रस् तथासौ
सहास्मदीयैर् अपि योधमुख्यैः ।।

amī ca tvāṁ dhṛtarāṣṭrasya putrāḥ
sarve sahāivāvanipālasaṁghāih
bhīsmo dronah sūtaputras tathāsāu
sahāsmadīyāir api yodhamukhyāiḥ

And entering into You, all the sons of Dhritarashtra, along with the throngs of kings, Bhishma, Drona, and Karna, the son of the charioteer, and also with our chief warriors,

27 दंष्ट्राकरालानि भयानकानि ।
वक्त्राणि ते त्वरमाणा विशन्ति
केचिद् विलग्ना दशनान्तरेषु
संदृश्यन्ते चूर्णितैर् उत्तमाङ्गैः ।।

vaktrāṇi te tvaramāṇā viśanti
daṁṣṭrākarālāni bhayānakāni
kecid vilagnā daśanāntareṣu
saṁdṛśyante cūrṇitāir uttamāṅgāiḥ

They quickly enter Your fearful mouths, which gape with many tusks; some are seen with crushed heads, clinging between Your teeth.

28 यथा नदीनां बहवो ऽम्बुवेगाः
समुद्रम् एवाभिमुखा द्रवन्ति ।
तथा तवामी नरलोकवीरा
विशन्ति वक्त्राण्य् अभिविज्वलन्ति ॥
yathā nadīnāṁ bahavo 'mbuvegāḥ
samudram evābhimukhā dravanti
tathā tavāmī naralokavīrā
viśanti vaktrāṇy abhivijvalanti

As the many torrents of the rivers flow toward the ocean, so those heroes of the world of men enter Your flaming mouths.

29 यथा प्रदीप्तं ज्वलनं पतङ्गा
विशन्ति नाशाय संमृद्धवेगाः ।
तथैव नाशाय विशन्ति लोकास्
तवापि वक्त्राणि समृद्धवेगाः ॥
yathā pradīptaṁ jvalanaṁ pataṅgā
viśanti nāśāya saṁṛddhavegāḥ
tathāiva nāśāya viśanti lokās
tavāpi vaktrāṇi samṛddhavegāḥ

As moths enter a blazing flame to their destruction with great speed, so also, these creatures swiftly enter Your mouths to their destruction.

30 लेलिह्यसे ग्रसमानः समन्ताल्
लोकान् समग्रान् वदनैर् ज्वलद्भिः ।
तेजोभिर् आपूर्य जगत् समग्रं
भासस् तवोग्राः प्रतपन्ति विष्णो ॥

lelihyase grasamānaḥ samantāl
lokān samagrān vadanāir jvaladbhiḥ
tejobhir āpūrya jagat samagraṁ
bhāsas tavogrāḥ pratapanti viṣṇo

You lick up , swallowing on all sides all the worlds, with Your flaming mouths. Filling all the universe with splendor, Your terrible rays blaze forth, O Vishnu!

31 आख्याहि मे को भवान् उग्ररूपो
नमो ऽस्तु ते देववर प्रसीद ।
विज्ञातुम् इच्छामि भवन्तम् आद्यं
न हि प्रजानामि तव प्रवृत्तिम् ॥

ākhyāhi me ko bhavān ugrarūpo
namo 'stu te devavara prasīda
vijñātum icchāmi bhavantam ādyaṁ
na hi prajānāmi tava pravṛttim

Tell me who You are, of so terrible a form. Salutations to You, O Best of Gods; have mercy! I wish to understand You, primal One; indeed, I do not comprehend what You are doing.

32 श्रीभगवान् उवाच । *śrībhagavān uvāca*

कालो ऽस्मि लोकक्षयकृत् प्रवृद्धो
लोकान् समाहर्तुम् इह प्रवृत्तः ।
ऋते ऽपि त्वां न भविष्यन्ति सर्वे
ये ऽवस्थिताः प्रत्यनीकेषु योधाः ॥

kālo 'smi lokakṣayakṛt pravṛddho
lokān samāhartum iha pravṛttaḥ
ṛte 'pi tvāṁ na bhaviṣyanti sarve
ye 'vasthitāḥ pratyanīkeṣu yodhāḥ

The Blessed Lord spoke:

I am Time, the mighty cause of world destruction, who has come forth to annihilate the worlds. Even without any action of yours, all these warriors who are arrayed in the opposing ranks, shall cease to exist.

33 तस्मात् त्वम् उत्तिष्ठ यशो लभस्व
जित्वा शत्रून् भुङ्क्ष्व राज्यं समृद्धम् ।
मयैवैते निहताः पूर्वम् एव
निमित्तमात्रं भव सव्यसाचिन् ॥

tasmāt tvam uttiṣṭha yaśo labhasva
jitvā śatrūn bhuṅkṣva rājyaṁ samṛddham
mayāivāite nihatāḥ pūrvam eva
nimittamātraṁ bhava savyasācin

Therefore stand up and attain glory! Having conquered the enemy, enjoy prosperous kingship. These have already been struck down by Me; be the mere instrument, O Arjuna.

34 द्रोणं च भीष्मं च जयद्रथं च
कर्णं तथान्यान् अपि योधवीरान् ।
मया हतांस् त्वं जहि मा व्यथिष्ठा
युध्यस्व जेतासि रणे सपत्नान् ।।

droṇaṁ ca bhīṣmaṁ ca jayadrathaṁ ca
karṇaṁ tathānyān api yodhavīrān
mayā hatāṅs tvaṁ jahi mā vyathiṣṭhā
yudhyasva jetāsi raṇe sapatnān

Drona, Bhishma, Jayadratha, and Karna too, others also, warrior heroes, have been killed by Me. Do not hesitate! Kill! Fight! You shall conquer the enemy in battle.

35 संजय उवाच । *sañjaya uvāca*

एतच् छ्रुत्वा वचनं केशवस्य
कृताञ्जलिर् वेपमानः किरीटी ।
नमस्कृत्वा भूय एवाह कृष्णं
सगद्गदं भीतभीतः प्रणम्य ।।

etac chrutvā vacanaṁ keśavasya
kṛtāñjalir vepamānaḥ kirīṭī
namaskṛtvā bhūya evāha kṛṣṇaṁ
sagadgadaṁ bhītabhītaḥ praṇamya

Sanjaya spoke:

Having heard this utterance of Krishna, Arjuna, with joined palms, trembling, prostrating himself, terrified, and bowing down, thus spoke in a choked voice to Krishna:

36 अर्जुन उवाच । *arjuna uvāca*

स्थाने हृषीकेश तव प्रकीर्त्या
जगत् प्रहृष्यत्य् अनुरज्यते च ।
रक्षांसि भीतानि दिशो द्रवन्ति
सर्वे नमस्यन्ति च सिद्धसंघा : ।।

sthāne hṛṣīkeśa tava prakīrtyā
jagat prahṛṣyaty anurajyate ca
rakṣāṁsi bhītāni diśo dravanti
sarve namasyanti ca siddhasaṁghāḥ

Arjuna spoke:

Rightly, O Krishna, the universe rejoices and is gratified by Your praise. The demons, terrified, flee in all directions; and all the throngs of the perfected ones bow before You.

37 कस्माच् च ते न नमेरन् महात्मन्
गरीयसे ब्रह्मणो ऽप्य् आदिकर्त्रे ।
अनन्त देवेश जगन्निवास
त्वम् अक्षरं सद् असत् तत्परं यत् ।।

kasmāc ca te na nameran mahātman
garīyase brahmaṇo 'py ādikartre
ananta deveśa jagannivāsa
tvam akṣaraṁ sad asat tatparaṁ yat

And why should they not bow to You, O great One, who are the original Creator, greater even than Brahma! Infinite Lord of Gods, you are the dwelling place of the universe, the imperishable, the existent, the non-existent, and that which is beyond both.

38 त्वम् आदिदेवः पुरुषः पुराणस्
त्वम् अस्य विश्वस्य परं निधानम् ।
वेत्तासि वेद्यं च परं च धाम
त्वया ततं विश्वम् अनन्तरूप ॥

tvam ādidevaḥ puruṣaḥ purāṇas
tvam asya viśvasya paraṁ nidhānam
vettāsi vedyaṁ ca paraṁ ca dhāma
tvayā tataṁ viśvam anantarūpa

You are the primal God, the ancient Spirit; You are the supreme resting place of all the universe; You are the knower, the object of knowledge, and the supreme state. All the universe is pervaded by You, O One of infinite forms.

39 वायुर् यमो ऽग्निर् वरुणः शशाङ्कः
प्रजापतिस् त्वं प्रपितामहश्च ।
नमो नमस् ते ऽस्तु सहस्रकृत्वः
पुनश्च भूयो ऽपि नमो नमस् ते ॥

vāyur yamo 'gnir varuṇaḥ śaśāṅkaḥ
prajāpatis tvaṁ prapitāmahaś ca
namo namas te 'stu sahasrakṛtvaḥ
punaśca bhūyo 'pi namo namas te

You are Vayu, Yama, Agni, Varuna, the Moon, the Lord of creatures, and the great grandfather. Salutations to You a thousand times, and again saluations, salutations to You!

40 नमः पुरस्ताद् अथ पृष्ठतस् ते
नमो ऽस्तु ते सर्वत एव सर्व ।

अनन्तवीर्यामितविक्रमस् त्वं
सर्वं समाप्नोषि ततो ऽसि सर्वः ॥
namaḥ purastād atha pṛṣṭhatas te
namo 'stu te sarvata eva sarva
anantavīryāmitavikramas tvaṁ
sarvaṁ samāpnoṣi tato 'si sarvaḥ

Salutations to You from in front and behind, salutations to You on all sides also, O All. You are infinite valor and boundless might. You pervade all, therefore You are all.

41 सखेति मत्वा प्रसभं यद् उक्तं हे कृष्ण हे यादव हे सखेति ।
अजानता महिमानं तवेदं मया प्रमादात् प्रणयेन वापि ॥
sakheti matvā prasabhaṁ yad uktaṁ
he kṛṣṇa he yādava he sakheti
ajānatā mahimānaṁ tavedaṁ
mayā pramādāt praṇayena vāpi

Whatever I have said impetuously as if in ordinary friendship, "Oh Krishna, Oh Son of Yadu, Oh Comrade," in ignorance of Your majesty, through negligence or even through affection,

42 यच् चावहासार्थम् असत्कृतो ऽसि
विहारशय्यासनभोजनेषु ।
एको ऽथवाप्य् अच्युत तत्समक्षं
तत् क्षामये त्वाम् अहम् अप्रमेयम् ॥
yac cāvahāsārtham asatkṛto 'si
vihāraśayyāsanabhojaneṣu

eko 'thavāpy acyuta tatsamakṣaṁ
tat kṣāmaye tvām aham aprameyam

And if, with humorous purpose, You were disrespectfully treated, while at play, resting, while seated or while dining, when alone, O Krishna, or even before the eyes of others, for that I ask forgiveness of You, immeasurable One.

43 पितासि लोकस्य चराचरस्य
त्वम् अस्य पूज्यश्च गुरुर् गरीयान् ।
न त्वत्समो ऽस्त्य् अभ्यधिकः कुतो ऽन्यो
लोकत्रये ऽप्य् अप्रतिमप्रभाव ॥
pitāsi lokasya carācarasya
tvam asya pūjyaśca gurur garīyān
na tvatsamo 'sty abhyadhikaḥ kuto 'nyo
lokatraye 'py apratimaprabhāva

You are the father of the world, of all things moving and motionless. You are to be adored by this world. You are the most venerable Guru. There is nothing like You in the three worlds. How then could there be another greater, O Being of incomparable glory?

44 तस्मात् प्रणम्य प्रणिधाय कायं
प्रसादये त्वाम् अहम् ईशम् ईड्यम् ।
पितेव पुत्रस्य सखेव सख्युः
प्रियः प्रियायार्हसि देव सोढुम् ॥
tasmāt praṇamya praṇidhāya kāyaṁ
prasādaye tvām aham īśam īḍyam

piteva putrasya sakheva sakhyuḥ
priyaḥ priyāyārhasi deva soḍhum

Therefore, bowing down, prostrating my body, I ask forgiveness of You, O Lord; as is a father to a son, a friend to a friend, a lover to a beloved, please, O God, be merciful!

45 अदृष्टपूर्वं हृषितो ऽस्मि दृष्ट्वा भयेन च प्रव्यथितं मनो मे ।
तद् एव मे दर्शय देव रूपं प्रसीद देवेश जगन्निवास ।।
adṛṣṭapūrvaṁ hṛṣito 'smi dṛṣṭvā
bhayena ca pravyathitaṁ mano me
tad eva me darśaya deva rūpaṁ
prasīda deveśa jagannivāsa

Having seen that which has never been seen before, I am delighted, and yet my mind trembles with fear. Show me that form, O God, in which You originally appeared. Have mercy, Lord of Gods, dwelling of the universe.

46 किरीटिनं गदिनं चक्रहस्तम्
इच्छामि त्वां द्रष्टुम् अहं तथैव ।
तेनैव रूपेण चतुर्भुजेन
सहस्रबाहो भव विश्वमूर्ते ।।
kirīṭinaṁ gadinaṁ cakrahastam
icchāmi tvāṁ draṣṭum ahaṁ tathāiva
tenāiva rūpeṇa caturbhujena
sahasrabāho bhava viśvamūrte

I desire to see You wearing a crown, armed with a club, discus in hand, as be-

fore; become that four-armed form, O thousand armed One, O You who have all forms.

47 श्रीभगवान् उवाच । *śrībhagavān uvāca*

मया प्रसन्नेन तवार्जुनेदं
रूपं परं दर्शितम् आत्मयोगात् ।
तेजोमयं विश्वम् अनन्तम् आद्यं
यन् मे त्वदन्येन न दृष्टपूर्वम् ॥

mayā prasannena tavārjunedaṁ
rūpaṁ paraṁ darśitam ātmayogāt
tejomayaṁ viśvam anantam ādyaṁ
yan me tvadanyena na dṛṣṭapūrvam

The Blessed Lord spoke:

By My grace toward you, Arjuna, this supreme form has been manifested through My own power, this form of Mine, made up of splendor, universal, infinite, primal, which has never before been seen by other than you.

48 न वेदयज्ञाध्ययनैर् न दानैर्
न च क्रियाभिर् न तपोभिर् उग्रैः ।
एवंरूपः शक्य अहं नृलोके
द्रष्टुं त्वदन्येनकुरुप्रवीर ॥

na vedayajñādhyayanāir na dānāir
na ca kriyābhir na tapobhir ugrāiḥ
evaṁrūpaḥ śakya ahaṁ nṛloke
draṣṭuṁ tvadanyena kurupravīra

Not by Vedic sacrifice nor (Vedic) recitation, not by gifts, and not by ritual acts nor by severe austerities, can I be seen in such a form in the world of men by any other than you, Arjuna.

49 मा ते व्यथा मा च विमूढभावो
दृष्ट्वा रूपं घोरम् ईदृङ्ममेदम् ।
व्यपेतभीः प्रीतमनाः पुनस् त्वं
तद् एव मे रूपम् इदं प्रपश्य ॥
mā te vyathā mā ca vimūḍhabhāvo
dṛṣṭvā rūpaṁ ghoram īdṛṅ mamedam
vyapetabhīḥ prītamanāḥ punas tvaṁ
tad eva me rūpam idaṁ prapaśya

Have no fear or confusion on seeing this terrible form of Mine; be again free from fear and cheered in heart. Behold, My (previous) form!

50 संजय उवाच । *sañjaya uvāca*

इत्य् अर्जुनं वासुदेवस् तथोक्त्वा
स्वकं रूपं दर्शयाम् आस भूयः ।
आश्वासयाम् आस च भीतम् एनं
भूत्वा पुनः सौम्यवपुर् महात्मा ॥
ity arjunam vāsudevas tathoktvā
svakaṁ rūpaṁ darśayām āsa bhūyaḥ
āśvāsayām āsa ca bhītam enaṁ
bhūtvā punaḥ sāumyavapur mahātmā

Sanjaya spoke:

Having spoken thus to Arjuna, Krishna revealed His own (previous) form again. Having resumed His gentle, wonderful ap-

pearance, He calmed Arjuna, who was terrified.

51 अर्जुन उवाच *arjuna uvāca*

दृष्ट्वेदं मानुषं रूपं तव सौम्यं जनार्दन ।
इदानीम् अस्मि संवृत्तः सचेताः प्रकृतिं गतः ॥

dṛṣṭvedaṁ mānuṣaṁ rūpaṁ
tava sāumyaṁ janārdana
idānīm asmi saṁvṛttaḥ
sacetāḥ prakṛtiṁ gataḥ

Arjuna spoke:

Seeing Your gentle human form, O Krishna, now I am composed and my mind is restored to normal.

52 श्रीभगवान् उवाच । *śrībhagavān uvāca*

सुदुर्दर्शम् इदं रूपं दृष्टवान् असि यन् मम ।
देवा अप्य् अस्य रूपस्य नित्यं दर्शनकाङ्क्षिणः ॥

sudurdarśam idaṁ rūpaṁ
dṛṣṭavān asi yan mama
devā apy asya rūpasya
nityaṁ darśanakāṅkṣiṇaḥ

The Blessed Lord spoke:

This form of Mine which you have beheld is difficult to see; even the gods are constantly longing to behold it.

53 नाहं वेदैर् न तपसा न दानेन न चेज्यया ।
शक्य एवंविधो द्रष्टुं दृष्टवान् असि मां यथा ॥

nāhaṁ vedāir na tapasā
na dānena na cejyayā
śakya evaṁvidho draṣṭum
dṛṣṭavān asi mām yathā

Not through study of the Vedas, not through austerity, not through gifts, and not through sacrifice can I be seen in this form as you have beheld Me.

54 भक्त्या त्व् अनन्यया शक्य अहम् एवंविधो ऽर्जुन ।
ज्ञातुं द्रष्टुं च तत्त्वेन प्रवेष्टुं च परतप ॥
bhaktyā tv ananyayā śakya
aham evaṁvidho 'rjuna
jñātuṁ draṣṭuṁ ca tattvena
praveṣṭuṁ ca paraṁtapa

By undistracted devotion alone can I be known, and be truly seen in this form, and be entered into, Arjuna.

55 मत्कर्मकृन् मत्परमो मद्भक्तः सङ्गवर्जितः ।
निर्वैरः सर्वभूतेषु यः स माम् एति पाण्डव ॥
matkarmakṛn matparamo
madbhaktaḥ saṅgavarjitaḥ
nirvāiraḥ sarvabhūteṣu
yaḥ sa mām eti pāṇḍava

He who does all work for Me, considers Me as the Supreme, is devoted to Me, abandons all attachment, and is free from enmity toward any being, comes to Me, Arjuna.

Hari Om Tat Sat
Iti Srimad Bhagavadgītāsūpaniṣatsu Brahmavidyāyām
Yogaśāstre Sri Kriṣnārjunasamvāde
Visrarūpa Darśanayogo Nāma Ekādaśoddhyāyaḥ.

Thus ends the eleventh Chapter, entitled "The Vision of the Cosmic Form," of the venerated Bhagavad Gita Upanishad, the Knowledge of the Absolute, the scripture of Yoga, the dialogue between Sri Krishna and Arjuna.

TWELVE

The Yoga of Devotion

atha dvādaśoddhyāyaḥ

1 अर्जुन उवाच । *arjuna uvāca*

एवं सततयुक्ता ये भक्तास् त्वां पर्युपासते ।
ये चाप्य् अक्षरम् अव्यक्तं तेषां के योगवित्तमाः ॥
evaṁ satatayuktā ye
bhaktās tvāṁ paryupāsate
ye cāpy akṣaram avyaktam
teṣāṁ ke yogavittamāḥ
Arjuna spoke:

The constantly steadfast devotees who worship You with devotion, and those who worship the eternal unmanifest; which of these has the better knowledge of yoga?

2 श्रीभगवान् उवाच । *śrībhagavān uvāca*

मय्यावेश्य मनो ये मां नित्ययुक्ता उपासते ।
श्रद्धया परयोपेतास् ते मे युक्ततमा मताः ॥
mayyāveśya mano ye māṁ
nityayuktā upāsate
śraddhayā parayopetās
te me yuktatamā matāḥ

The Blessed Lord spoke:

Those who are eternally steadfast, who

worship Me, fixing their minds on Me, endowed with supreme faith; I consider them to be the most devoted to Me.

3 ये त्व् अक्षरम् अनिर्देश्यम् अव्यक्तं पर्युपासते ।
सर्वत्रगम् अचिन्त्यं च कूटस्थम् अचलं ध्रुवम् ॥
ye tv akṣaram anirdeśyam
avyaktaṁ paryupāsate
sarvatragam acintyaṁ ca
kūtaṣtham acalaṁ dhruvam

But those who honor the imperishable, the indefinable, the unmanifest, the all-pervading and unthinkable, the unchanging, the immovable, the eternal,

4 संनियम्येन्द्रियग्रामं सर्वत्र समबुद्धयः ।
ते प्राप्नुवन्ति माम् एव सर्वभूतहिते रताः ॥
saṁniyamyendriyagrāmaṁ
sarvatra samabuddhayaḥ
te prāpnuvanti mām eva
sarvabhūtahite ratāḥ

Controlling all the senses, even-minded on all sides, rejoicing in the welfare of all creatures, they also attain Me.

5 क्लेशो ऽधिकतरस् तेषाम् अव्यक्तासक्तचेतसाम् ।
अव्यक्ता हि गतिर् दुःखं देहवद्भिर् अवाप्यते ॥
kleśo 'dhikataras teṣām
avyaktāsaktacetasām
avyaktā hi gatir duḥkhaṁ
dehavadbhir avāpyate

The trouble of those whose minds are fixed on the unmanifest is greater, for the goal of the unmanifest is attained with difficulty by embodied beings.

6 ये तु सर्वाणि कर्माणि मयि संन्यस्य मत्पराः।
अनन्येनैव योगेन मां ध्यायन्त उपासते॥
ye tu sarvāṇi karmāṇi
mayi saṁnyasya matparāḥ
ananyenāiva yogena
māṁ dhyāyanta upāsate

But those who, renouncing all actions in Me, and regarding Me as the Supreme, worship Me, meditating on Me with undistracted yoga,

7 तेषाम् अहं समुद्धर्ता मृत्युसंसारसागरात्।
भवामि नचिरात् पार्थ मय्यावेशितचेतसाम्॥
teṣām ahaṁ samuddhartā
mṛtyusaṁsārasāgarāt
bhavāmi nacirāt pārtha
mayyāveśitacetasām

Of those whose thoughts have entered into Me, I am soon the deliverer from the ocean of death and transmigration, Arjuna.

8 मय्य् एव मन आधत्स्व मयि बुद्धिं निवेशय।
निवसिष्यसि मय्येव अत ऊर्ध्वं न संशयः॥
mayy eva mana ādhatsva
mayi buddhiṁ niveśaya

nivasiṣyasi mayyeva
ata ūrdhvaṁ na saṁśayaḥ

Keep your mind on Me alone, your intellect on Me. Thus you shall dwell in Me hereafter. There is no doubt of this.

9 अथ चित्तं समाधातुं न शक्नोषि मयि स्थिरम् ।
अभ्यासयोगेन ततो माम् इच्छाप्तुं धनंजय ॥
atha cittaṁ samādhātuṁ
na śaknoṣi mayi sthiram
abhyāsayogena tato
mām icchāptuṁ dhanaṁjaya

Or if you are not able to keep your mind steadily on Me, then seek to attain Me by the constant practice of yoga, Arjuna.

10 अभ्यासे ऽप्य् असमर्थो ऽसि मत्कर्मपरमो भव ।
मदर्थम् अपि कर्माणि कुर्वन् सिद्धिम् अवाप्स्यसि ॥
abhyāse 'py asamartho 'si
matkarmaparamo bhava
madartham api karmāṇi
kurvan siddhim avāpsyasi

If you are incapable even of practice, be intent on My work; even performing actions for My sake, you shall attain perfection.

11 अथैतद् अप्य् अशक्तो ऽसि कर्तुं मद्योगम् आश्रितः ।
सर्वकर्मफलत्यागं ततः कुरु यतात्मवान् ॥
athāitad apy aṡakto 'si
kartuṁ madyogam āsritaḥ

sarvakarmaphalatyāgaṁ
tataḥ kuru yatātmavān

But if you are unable even to do this, then, resorting to devotion to Me, and abandoning all the fruits of action, act with self-restraint.

12 श्रेयो हि ज्ञानम् अभ्यासाज् ज्ञानाद् ध्यानं विशिष्यते ।
ध्यानात् कर्मफलत्यागस् त्यागाच् छान्तिर् अनन्तरम् ॥
śreyo hi jñānam abhyāsāj
jñānād dhyānaṁ viśiṣyate
dhyānāt karmaphalatyāgas
tyāgāc chāntir anantaram

Knowledge is indeed better than practice; meditation is superior to knowledge; renunciation of the fruit of action is better than meditation; peace immediately follows renunciation.

13 अद्वेष्टा सर्वभूतानां मैत्रः करुण एव च ।
निर्ममो निरहंकारः समदुःखसुखः क्षमी ॥
adveṣṭā sarvabhūtānāṁ
māitraḥ karuṇa eva ca
nirmamo nirahaṁkārah
samaduḥkhasukhaḥ kṣamī

He who hates no being, friendly and compassionate, free from attachment to possessions, free from egotism, indifferent to pain and pleasure, patient,

14 संतुष्टः सततं योगी यतात्मा दृढनिश्चयः ।
मय्य् अर्पितमनोबुद्धिर् यो मद्भक्तः स मे प्रियः ॥
saṁtuṣṭaḥ satataṁ yogī
yatātmā dṛḍhaniścayaḥ
mayy arpitamanobuddhir
yo madbhaktaḥ sa me priyaḥ

The yogin who is always contented and balanced in mind, who is self-controlled, and whose conviction is firm, whose mind and intellect are fixed on Me, and who is devoted to Me, is dear to Me.

15 यस्मान् नोद्विजते लोको लोकान् नोद्विजते च यः ।
हर्षामर्षभयोद्वेगैर् मुक्तो यः स च मे प्रियः ॥
yasmān nodvijate loko
lokān nodvijate ca yaḥ
harṣāmarṣabhayodvegāir
mukto yaḥ sa ca me priyaḥ

He from whom the world does not shrink, and who does not shrink from the world, who is freed from joy, envy, fear, and distress, is dear to Me.

16 अनपेक्षः शुचिर् दक्ष उदासीनो गतव्यथः ।
सर्वारम्भपरित्यागी यो मद्भक्तः स मे प्रियः ॥
anapekṣaḥ śucir dakṣa
udāsīno gatavyathaḥ
sarvārambhaparityāgī
yo madbhaktaḥ sa me priyaḥ

He who is free from wants, pure, capable, disinterested, free from anxiety, who has abandoned all undertakings and is devoted to Me, is dear to Me.

17 यो न हृष्यति न द्वेष्टि न शोचति न काङ्क्षति ।
शुभाशुभपरित्यागी भक्तिमान् यः स मे प्रियः ॥
yo na hṛṣyati na dveṣṭi
na śocati na kāṅkṣati
śubhāśubhaparityāgī
bhaktimān yaḥ sa me priyaḥ

He who neither rejoices nor hates, nor grieves nor desires, has renounced good and evil, and is full of devotion, is dear to Me.

18 समः शत्रौ च मित्रे च तथा मानापमानयोः ।
शीतोष्णसुखदुःखेषु समः सङ्गविवर्जितः ॥
samaḥ śatrāu ca mitre ca
tathā mānāpamānayoḥ
śītoṣṇasukhaduḥkheṣu
samaḥ saṅgavivarjitaḥ

Alike toward enemy and friend, the same in honor and disgrace, alike in cold and heat, pleasure and pain, freed from attachment,

19 तुल्यनिन्दास्तुतिर् मौनी संतुष्टो येन केनचित् ।
अनिकेतः स्थिरमतिर् भक्तिमान् मे प्रियो नरः ॥
tulyanindāstutir māunī
saṁtuṣṭo yena kenacit
aniketaḥ sthiramatir
bhaktimān me priyo naraḥ

Indifferent to blame or praise, silent, content with anything whatever, homeless, steady-minded, full of devotion; this man is dear to Me.

20 ये तु धर्म्यामृतम् इदं यथोक्तं पर्युपासते ।
श्रद्दधाना मत्परमा भक्तास् ते ऽतीव मे प्रियाः ॥
ye tu dharmyāmṛtam idaṁ
yathoktaṁ paryupāsate
śraddadhānā matparamā
bhaktās te 'tīva me priyāḥ

Those who honor this immortal law described above, endowed with faith, devoted and intent on Me as the Supreme; they are exceedingly dear to Me.

Hari Om Tat Sat
Iti Srimad Bhagavadgītāsūpaniṣatsu Brahmavidyāyām
Yogaśāstre Sri Kriṣnārjunasamvāde
Bhaktiyogo Nāma Dvādaśoddhyāyaḥ.

Thus ends the twelfth Chapter, entitled "The Yoga of Devotion," of the venerated Bhagavad Gita Upanishad, the Knowledge of the Absolute, the scripture of Yoga, the dialogue between Sri Krishna and Arjuna.

THIRTEEN

The Yoga of the Distinction between the Field and the Knower of the Field

atha trayodaśoddhyāyaḥ

1 अर्जुन उवाच । *arjuna uvāca*
प्रकृतिं पुरुषं चैव क्षेत्रं क्षेत्रज्ञम् एव च ।
एतद् वेदितुम् इच्छामि ज्ञानं ज्ञेयं च केशव ॥
prakṛtiṁ puruṣaṁ cāiva
kṣetraṁ kṣetrajñam eva ca
etad veditum icchāmi
jñānaṁ jñeyaṁ ca keśava

Arjuna said:
Prakriti and Purusha, the field and the knower of the field, knowledge and the knower of knowledge, I wish to know about these, Krishna.

2 श्रीभगवान् उवाच । *śrībhagavān uvāca*
इदं शरीरं कौन्तेय क्षेत्रम् इत्य् अभिधीयते ।
एतद् यो वेत्ति तं प्राहुः क्षेत्रज्ञ इति तद्विदः ॥
idaṁ śarīraṁ kāunteya
kṣetram ity abhidhīyate
etad yo vetti taṁ prāhuḥ
kṣetrajña iti tadvidaḥ

The Blessed Lord spoke:
This body, Arjuna, is said to be the field;

he who knows this is called the knower of the field by those who are wise in such things.

3 तत् क्षेत्रं यच् च यादृक् च यद्विकारि यतश्च यत् ।
स च यो यत्प्रभावश्च तत् समासेन मे शृणु ॥
kṣetrajñaṁ cāpi māṁ viddhi
sarvakṣetreṣu bhārata
kṣetrakṣetrajñayor jñānaṁ
yat taj jñānaṁ mataṁ mama

Know also that I am the knower of the field in all fields, Arjuna; knowledge of the field and of the knower of the field, that is considered by Me to be true knowledge.

4 क्षेत्रज्ञं चापि मां विद्धि सर्वक्षेत्रेषु भारत ।
क्षेत्रक्षेत्रज्ञयोर् ज्ञानं यत् तज् ज्ञानं मतं मम ॥
tat kṣetraṁ yac ca yādṛk ca
yadvikāri yataśca yat
sa ca yo yatprabhāvaśca
tat samāsena me śṛṇu

This field, what it is, and of what kind, what its modifications are and whence they come, and who he (the knower of the field) is, and what are his powers, that, in brief, hear from Me:

5 ऋषिभिर् बहुधा गीतं छन्दोभिर् विविधैः पृथक् ।
ब्रह्मसूत्रपदैश्चैव हेतुमद्भिर् विनिश्चितैः ॥
ṛṣibhir bahudhā gītaṁ
chandobhir vividhāiḥ pṛthak
brahmasūtrapadāiścāiva
hetumadbhir viniścitāiḥ

Sages have sung of it in many ways, distinctly, in various sacred (Vedic) hymns, and with quotations concerning Brahman, full of reasoning.

6 महाभूतान्य् अहंकारो बुद्धिर् अव्यक्तम् एव च ।
इन्द्रियाणि दशैकं च पञ्च चेन्द्रियगोचराः ॥
mahābhūtāny ahaṁkāro
buddhir avyaktam eva ca
indriyāṇi daśāikaṁ ca
pañca cendriyagocarāḥ

The great elements, egoism, intellect and the unmanifest, the senses, ten and one, and the five objects of the senses,

7 इच्छा द्वेषः सुखं दुःखं संघातश्चेतना धृतिः ।
एतत् क्षेत्रं समासेन सविकारम् उदाहृतम् ॥
icchā dveṣaḥ sukhaṁ duḥkhaṁ
saṁghātaścetanā dhṛtiḥ
etat kṣetraṁ samāsena
savikāram udāhṛtam

Desire, hatred, pleasure, pain, the body, intelligence, steadfastness—this briefly is described as the field with its modifications.

8 अमानित्वम् अदम्भित्वम् अहिंसा क्षान्तिर् आर्जवम् ।
आचार्योपासनं शौचं स्थैर्यम् आत्मविनिग्रहः ॥
amānitvam adambhitvam
ahiṁsā kṣāntir ārjavam
ācāryopāsanaṁ śāucaṁ
sthāiryam ātmavinigrahaḥ

Absence of pride, freedom from hypocrisy, non-violence, patience, rectitude, service of the teacher, purity, constancy, self-restraint,

9 इन्द्रियार्थेषु वैराग्यम् अनहंकार एव च ।
जन्ममृत्युजराव्याधि- दुःखदोषानुदर्शनम् ॥
indriyārtheṣu vāirāgyam
anahaṁkāra eva ca
janmamṛtyujarāvyādhi-
duḥkhadoṣānudarśanam

Indifference to the objects of sense, and absence of egotism; keeping in view the evils of birth, death, old age, disease, and pain;

10 असक्तिर् अनभिष्वङ्ग पुत्रदारगृहादिषु ।
नित्यं च समचित्तत्वम् इष्टानिष्टोपपत्तिषु ॥
asaktir anabhiṣvaṅga
putradāragṛhādiṣu
nityaṁ ca samacittatvam
iṣṭāniṣṭopapattiṣu

Non-attachment, absence of clinging to son, wife, home, and so on, and constant even-mindedness toward desired and undesired events;

11 मयि चानन्ययोगेन भक्तिर् अव्यभिचारिणी ।
विविक्तदेशसेवित्वम् अरतिर् जनसंसदि ॥
mayi cānanyayogena
bhaktir avyabhicāriṇī

viviktadeśasevitvam
aratir janasaṁsadi

And unswerving devotion to Me with single-minded yoga, frequenting secluded places, distaste for the society of men,

12 अध्यात्मज्ञाननित्यत्वं तत्त्वज्ञानार्थदर्शनम् ।
एतज् ज्ञानम् इति प्रोक्तम् अज्ञानं यद् अतो ऽन्यथा ॥

adhyātmajñānanityatvaṁ
tattvajñānārthadarśanam
etaj jñānam iti proktam
ajñānaṁ yad ato 'nyathā

Constancy in knowledge of the supreme Spirit, observing the goal of knowledge of the truth; this is declared to be true knowledge. Ignorance is what is contrary to this.

13 ज्ञेयं यत् तत् प्रवक्ष्यामि यज् ज्ञात्वा ऽमृतम् अश्नुते ।
अनादिमत् परं ब्रह्म न सत् तन् नासद् उच्यते ॥

jñeyaṁ yat tat pravakṣyāmi
yaj jñātvā 'mṛtam aśnute
anādimat paraṁ brahma
na sat tan nāsad ucyate

I shall declare that which has to be known, knowing which, one attains immortality; it is the beginningless supreme Brahman, which is said to be neither existent nor non-existent.

14 सर्वतःपाणिपादं तत् सर्वतो ऽक्षिशिरोमुखम् ।
सर्वतःश्रुतिमल् लोके सर्वम् आवृत्य तिष्ठति ।।

sarvataḥpāṇipādaṁ tat
sarvato 'kṣiśiromukham
sarvataḥśrutimal loke
sarvam āvṛtya tiṣṭhati

Having hands and feet everywhere, eyes, heads and faces everywhere, having ears everywhere, That stands, enveloping everything in the world,

15 सर्वेन्द्रियगुणाभासं सर्वेन्द्रियविवर्जितम् ।
असक्तं सर्वभृच् चैव निर्गुणं गुणभोक्तृ च ।।

sarvendriyaguṇābhāsaṁ
sarvendriyavivarjitam
asaktaṁ sarvabhṛc cāiva
nirguṇaṁ guṇabhoktṛ ca

Shining by the function of the senses, yet freed from all the senses, unattached yet maintaining all, free from the qualities yet experiencing the qualities;

16 बहिर् अन्तश्च भूतानाम् अचरं चरम् एव च ।
सूक्ष्मत्वात् तद् अविज्ञेयं दूरस्थं चान्तिके च तत् ।।

bahir antaś ca bhūtānam
acaraṁ caram eva ca
sūkṣmatvāt tad avijñeyaṁ
dūrasthaṁ cāntike ca tat

Outside and inside beings, those that are moving and not moving, because of its subtlety This is not comprehended. This is far away and also near.

17 अविभक्तं च भूतेषु विभक्तम् इव च स्थितम् ।
भूतभर्तृ च तज् ज्ञेयं ग्रसिष्णु प्रभविष्णु च ॥

avibhaktaṁ ca bhūteṣu
vibhaktam iva ca sthitam
bhūtabhartṛ ca taj jñeyaṁ
grasiṣṇu prabhaviṣṇu ca

Undivided yet remaining as if divided in all beings, This is to be known as the sustainer of beings, their devourer and creator.

18 ज्योतिषां अपि तज् ज्योतिस् तमसः परम् उच्यते ।
ज्ञानं ज्ञेयं ज्ञानगम्यं हृदि सर्वस्य विष्ठितम् ॥

jyotiṣāṁ api taj jyotis
tamasaḥ param ucyate
jñānaṁ jñeyaṁ jñānagamyaṁ
hṛdi sarvasya viṣṭhitam

Also This is said to be the light of lights that is beyond darkness; it is knowledge, the object of knowledge and that which is to be attained through knowledge. It is seated in the hearts of all.

19 इति क्षेत्रं तथा ज्ञानं ज्ञेयं चोक्तं समासतः ।
मद्भक्त एतद् विज्ञाय मद्भावायोपपद्यते ॥

iti kṣetraṁ tathā jñānaṁ
jñeyaṁ coktaṁ samāsataḥ
madbhakta etad vijñāya
madbhāvāyopapadyate

Thus the field, knowledge, and the object of knowledge have been briefly described. My devotee, understanding this, enters into My state of being.

20 प्रकृतिं पुरुषं चैव विद्ध्य् अनादी उभाव् अपि ।
विकारांस् च गुणांस् चैव विद्धि प्रकृतिसंभवान् ॥
prakṛtiṁ puruṣaṁ cāiva
viddhy anādi ubhāv api
vikārāṇś ca guṇāṅś cāiva
viddhi prakṛtisaṁbhavān

Know that material nature and Spirit are both beginningless, and know also that the modifications of the field, and the qualities, too, arise from material nature.

21 कार्यकारणकर्तृत्वे हेतुः प्रकृतिर् उच्यते ।
पुरुषः सुखदुःखानां भोक्तृत्वे हेतुर् उच्यते ॥
kāryakāraṇakartṛtve
hetuḥ prakṛtir ucyate
puruṣaḥ sukhaduḥkhānāṁ
bhoktṛtve hetur ucyate

Material nature is said to be the cause in the producing of cause and effect. The Spirit is said to be the cause in the experiencing of pleasure and pain.

22 पुरुषः प्रकृतिस्थो हि भुङ्क्ते प्रकृतिजान् गुणान् ।
कारणं गुणसङ्गो ऽस्य सदसद्योनिजन्मसु ॥
puruṣaḥ prakṛtistho hi
bhuṅkte prakṛtijān guṇān

kāraṇaṁ guṇasaṅgo 'sya
sadasadyonijanmasu

For the Spirit, abiding in material nature, experiences the qualities born of material nature. Attachment to the qualities is the cause of its birth in good and evil wombs.

23 उपद्रष्टानुमन्ता च भर्ता भोक्ता महेश्वरः ।
परमात्मेति चाप्य् उक्तो देहे ऽस्मिन् पुरुषः परः ॥
upadraṣṭānumantā ca
bhartā bhoktā maheśvaraḥ
paramātmeti cāpy ukto
dehe 'smin puruṣaḥ paraḥ

The highest Spirit in this body is called the witness, the consenter, the supporter, the experiencer, the great Lord, and also the supreme Spirit.

24 य एवं वेत्ति पुरुषं प्रकृतिं च गुणैः सह ।
सर्वथा वर्तमानो ऽपि न स भूयो ऽभिजायते ॥
ya evaṁ vetti puruṣaṁ
prakṛtiṁ ca guṇāiḥ saha
sarvathā vartamāno 'pi
na sa bhūyo 'bhijāyate

He who in this way knows the Spirit and material nature, along with the qualities, in whatever stage of transmigration he may exist, is not born again.

25 ध्यानेनात्मनि पश्यन्ति केचिद् आत्मानम् आत्मना ।
अन्ये सांख्येन योगेन कर्मयोगेन चापरे ॥

dhyānenātmani paśyanti
kecid ātmānam ātmanā
anye sāṁkhyena yogena
karmayogena cāpare

Some perceive the Self in the Self by the Self through meditation; others by the discipline of Sankhya and still others by the yoga of action.

26 अन्ये त्व् एवम् अजानन्तः श्रुत्वान्येभ्य उपासते ।
ते ऽपि चातितरन्त्य् एव मृत्युं श्रुतिपरायणाः ॥
anye tv evam ajānantaḥ
śrutvānyebhya upāsate
te 'pi cātitaranty eva
mrtyuṁ śrutiparāyaṇāḥ

Yet others, not knowing this, worship, having heard it from others, and they also cross beyond death, devoted to what they have heard.

27 यावत् संजायते किंचित् सत्त्वं स्थावरजङ्गमम् ।
क्षेत्रक्षेत्रज्ञसंयोगात् तद् विद्धि भरतर्षभ ॥
yāvat saṁjāyate kiṁcit
sattvaṁ sthāvarajaṅgamam
kṣetrakṣetrajñasaṁyogāt
tad viddhi bharatarṣabha

Know, Arjuna, that any being whatever that is born, moving or unmoving, arises from the union of the field and the knower of the field.

28 समं सर्वेषु भूतेषु तिष्ठन्तं परमेश्वरम् ।
विनश्यत्स्व् अविनश्यन्तं यः पश्यति स पश्यति ।।
samaṁ sarveṣu bhūteṣu
tiṣṭhantaṁ parameśvaram
vinaśyatsv avinaśyantaṁ
yaḥ paśyati sa paśyati

He who sees the Supreme Lord, existing alike in all beings, not perishing when they perish, truly sees.

29 समं पश्यन् हि सर्वत्र समवस्थितम् ईश्वरम् ।
न हिनस्त्य् आत्मना ऽत्मानं ततो याति परां गतिम् ।।
samaṁ paśyan hi sarvatra
samavasthitam īśvaram
na hinasty ātmanā 'tmānaṁ
tato yāti parāṁ gatim

Seeing indeed the same Lord established everywhere, he does not injure the Self by the self. Thereupon he goes to the supreme goal.

30 प्रकृत्यैव च कर्माणि क्रियमाणानि सर्वशः ।
यः पश्यति तथात्मानम् अकर्तारं स पश्यति ।।
prakṛtyāiva ca karmāṇi
kriyamāṇāni sarvaśaḥ
yaḥ paśyati tathātmānam
akartāraṁ sa paśyati

He who sees that all actions are performed exclusively by material nature, and thus the Self is not the doer, truly sees.

31 यदा भूतपृथग्भावम् एकस्थम् अनुपश्यति।
तत एव च विस्तारं ब्रह्म संपद्यते तदा॥
yadā bhūtapṛthagbhāvam
ekastham anupaśyati
tata eva ca vistāraṁ
brahma saṁpadyate tadā

When he perceives the various states of being as resting in the One, and from That alone spreading out, then he attains Brahman.

32 अनादित्वान् निर्गुणत्वात् परमात्मायम् अव्ययः।
शरीरस्थो ऽपि कौन्तेय न करोति न लिप्यते॥
anāditvān nirguṇatvāt
paramātmāyam avyayaḥ
śarīrastho 'pi kāunteya
na karoti na lipyate

This imperishable supreme Self is beginningless and without qualities; even though situated in the body, Arjuna, it does not act, and is not tainted.

33 यथा सर्वगतं सौक्ष्म्याद् आकाशं नोपलिप्यते।
सर्वत्रावस्थितो देहे तथात्मा नोपलिप्यते॥
yathā sarvagataṁ saukṣmyād
ākāśaṁ nopalipyate
sarvatrāvasthito dehe
tathātmā nopalipyate

As the all-pervading ether, because of its subtlety, is not tainted, so the Self, seated in the body, is not tainted in any case.

34 यथा प्रकाशयत्य् एकः कृत्स्नं लोकम् इमं रविः ।
क्षेत्रं क्षेत्री तथा कृत्स्नं प्रकाशयति भारत ॥

yathā prakāśayaty ekaḥ
kṛtsnaṁ lokam imaṁ raviḥ
kṣetraṁ kṣetrī tathā kṛtsnaṁ
prakāśayati bhārata

As the sun alone illumines this entire world, so the Lord of the field illumines the entire field, Arjuna.

35 क्षेत्रक्षेत्रज्ञयोर् एवम् अन्तरं ज्ञानचक्षुषा ।
भूतप्रकृतिमोक्षं च ये विदुर् यान्ति ते परम् ॥

kṣetrakṣetrajñayor evam
antaraṁ jñānacakṣuṣā
bhūtaprakṛtimokṣaṁ ca
ye vidur yānti te param

They who know, through the eye of knowledge, the distinction between the field and the knower of the field, as well as the liberation of beings from material nature, go to the Supreme.

Hari Om Tat Sat
Iti Srimad Bhagavadgītāsūpaniṣatsu Brahmavidyāyām Yogaśāstre Sri Krisnārjunasamvāde Kṣetrakṣetrajñavibhāgayogo Nāma Trayodaśoddhyāyaḥ.

Thus ends the thirteenth Chapter, entitled "The Yoga of the Distinction between the Field and the Knower of the Field," of the venerated Bhagavad Gita Upanishad, the Knowledge of the Absolute, the scripture of Yoga, the dialogue between Sri Krishna and Arjuna.

FOURTEEN

The Yoga of the Differentiation of the Three Qualities

atha caturdaśoddhyāyaḥ

1 श्रीभगवान् उवाच । *śrībhagavān uvāca*
परं भूयः प्रवक्ष्यामि ज्ञानानां ज्ञानम् उत्तमम् ।
यज् ज्ञात्वा मुनयः सर्वे परां सिद्धिम् इतो गताः ॥
paraṁ bhūyaḥ pravakṣyāmi
jñānānāṁ jñānam uttamam
yaj jñātvā munayaḥ sarve
parāṁ siddhim ito gatāḥ

The Blessed Lord spoke:
I shall declare, further, the highest knowledge, the best of all knowledge, having known which all the sages have gone from here to supreme perfection.

2 इदं ज्ञानम् उपाश्रित्य मम साधर्म्यम् आगताः ।
सर्गे ऽपि नोपजायन्ते प्रलये न व्यथन्ति च ॥
idaṁ jñānam upāśritya
mama sādharmyam āgatāḥ
sarge 'pi nopajāyante
pralaye na vyathanti ca

Resorting to this knowledge, and arriving at a state of identity with Me, even at the creation of the world they are not born, nor do they tremble at its dissolution.

3 मम योनिर् महद् ब्रह्म तस्मिन् गर्भं दधाम्य् अहम् ।
संभवः सर्वभूतानां ततो भवति भारत ॥
mama yonir mahad brahma
tasmin garbhaṁ dadhāmy aham
saṁbhavaḥ sarvabhūtānāṁ
tato'bhavati bhārata

Great Brahma is My womb. In it I place the seed. The origin of all beings exists from that, Arjuna.

4 सर्वयोनिषु कौन्तेय मूर्तयः संभवन्ति याः ।
तासां ब्रह्म महद् योनिर् अहं बीजप्रदः पिता ॥
sarvayoniṣu kāunteya
mūrtayaḥ saṁbhavanti yāḥ
tāsāṁ brahma mahad yonir
ahaṁ bījapradaḥ pitā

Whatever forms are produced in any womb, Arjuna, the great Brahma is their womb, and I am the seed-sowing father.

5 सत्त्वं रजस् तम इति गुणाः प्रकृतिसंभवाः ।
निबध्नन्ति महाबाहो देहे देहिनम् अव्ययम् ॥
sattvaṁ rajas tama iti
guṇāḥ prakṛtisambhavāḥ
nibadhnanti mahābāho
dehe dehinam avyayam

Sattva, rajas, tamas, thus, the qualities born of material nature, bind fast in the body, O Arjuna, the imperishable embodied One (the atman).

6 तत्र सत्त्वं निर्मलत्वात् प्रकाशकम् अनामयम् ।
सुखसङ्गेन बध्नाति ज्ञानसङ्गेन चानघ ॥
tatra sattvaṁ nirmalatvāt
prakāśakam anāmayam
sukhasaṅgena badhnati
jñānasaṅgena cānagha

Of these, sattva, free from impurity, illuminating and free from disease, binds by attachment to happiness and by attachment to knowledge, Arjuna.

7 रजो रागात्मकं विद्धि तृष्णासङ्गसमुद्भवम् ।
तन् निबध्नाति कौन्तेय कर्मसङ्गेन देहिनम् ॥
rajo rāgātmakaṁ viddhi
tṛṣṇāsaṅgasamudbhavam
tan nibadhnāti kāunteya
karmasaṅgena dehinam

Know that rajas is characterized by passion arising from thirst and attachment. This binds fast the embodied one, Arjuna, by attachment to action.

8 तमस् त्व् अज्ञानजं विद्धि मोहनं सर्वदेहिनाम् ।
प्रमादालस्यनिद्राभिस् तन् निबध्नाति भारत ॥
tamas tv ajñānajaṁ viddhi
mohanaṁ sarvadehinām
pramādālasyanidrābhis
tan nibadhnāti bhārata

Know indeed that tamas is born of ignorance, which confuses all embodied beings.

This binds fast, Ajuna, with negligence, indolence, and sleepiness.

9 सत्त्वं सुखे सञ्जयति रजः कर्मणि भारत ।
ज्ञानम् आवृत्य तु तमः प्रमादे सञ्जयत्य् उत ॥
sattvaṁ sukhe sañjayati
rajaḥ karmaṇi bhārata
jñānam āvṛtya tu tamaḥ
pramāde sañjayaty uta

Sattva causes attachment to happiness, rajas to action, Arjuna; tamas, obscuring knowledge, causes attachment to negligence.

10 रजस् तमश्चाभिभूय सत्त्वं भवति भारत ।
रजः सत्त्वं तमश्चैव तमः सत्त्वं रजस् तथा ॥
rajas tamaścābhibhūya
sattvaṁ bhavati bhārata
rajaḥ sattvaṁ tamaścāiva
tamaḥ sattvaṁ rajas tathā

When prevailing over rajas and tamas, sattva arises, Arjuna; rajas prevailing over sattva and tamas also comes to be; likewise tamas prevailing over sattva and rajas.

11 अप्रकाशो ऽप्रवृत्तिश्च प्रमादो मोह एव च ।
तमस्य् एतानि जायन्ते विवृद्धे कुरुनन्दन ॥
sarvadvāreṣu dehe 'smin
prakāśa upajāyate
jñānaṁ yadā tadā vidyād
vivṛddhaṁ sattvam ity uta

When the light of knowledge shines through all the gates of this body, then it should be known that sattva is dominant.

12 सर्वद्वारेषु देहेऽस्मिन् प्रकाश उपजायते ।
ज्ञानं यदा तदा विद्याद् विवृद्धं सत्त्वम् इत्य् उत ॥
lobhaḥ pravṛttir ārambhaḥ
karmaṇām aśamaḥ spṛhā
rajasy etāni jāyante
vivṛddhe bharatarṣabha

Greed, activity and the undertaking of actions, restlessness, desire; these are born when rajas is dominant, Arjuna.

13 लोभः प्रवृत्तिर् आरम्भः कर्मणाम् अशमः स्पृहा ।
रजस्य् एतानि जायन्ते विवृद्धे भरतर्षभ ॥
aprakāśo 'pravṛttiśca
pramādo moha eva ca
tamasy etāni jāyante
vivṛddhe kurunandana

Darkness and inertness, heedlessness and confusion; these are born when tamas is dominant, Arjuna.

14 यदा सत्त्वे प्रवृद्धे तु प्रलयं याति देहभृत् ।
तदोत्तमविदां लोकान् अमलान् प्रतिपद्यते ॥
yadā sattve pravṛddhe tu
pralayaṁ yāti dehabhṛt
tadottamavidāṁ lokān
amalān pratipadyate

When an embodied being goes to dissolution (death) under the dominance of sattva, then he attains the stainless worlds of those who know the highest.

15 रजसि प्रलयं गत्वा कर्मसङ्गिषु जायते ।
तथा प्रलीनस् तमसि मूढयोनिषु जायते ॥

rajasi pralayaṁ gatvā
karmasaṅgiṣu jāyate
tathā pralīnas tamasi
mūḍhayoniṣu jāyate

He who goes to dissolution (death) when rajas is dominant, is reborn among those attached to action; likewise, dissolved (dying) when tamas is dominant, he is reborn from the wombs of the deluded.

16 कर्मणः सुकृतस्याहुः सात्त्विकं निर्मलं फलम् ।
रजसस् तु फलं दुःखम् अज्ञानं तमसः फलम् ॥

karmaṇaḥ sukṛtasyāhuḥ
sāttvikaṁ nirmalaṁ phalam
rajasas tu phalaṁ duḥkham
ajñānaṁ tamasaḥ phalam

They say the fruit of good action is sattvic and without impurity, but the fruit of rajasic action is pain, and the fruit of tamasic action is ignorance.

17 सत्त्वात् संजायते ज्ञानं रजसो लोभ एव च ।
प्रमादमोहौ तमसो भवतो ऽज्ञानम् एव च ॥

sattvāt saṁjāyate jñānaṁ
rajaso lobha eva ca

pramādamohau tamaso
bhavato 'jñānam eva ca

From sattva knowledge is born, and from rajas desire; negligence and delusion arise from tamas, and ignorance too.

18 ऊर्ध्वं गच्छन्ति सत्त्वस्था मध्ये तिष्ठन्ति राजसाः ।
जघन्यगुणवृत्तिस्था अधो गच्छन्ति तामसाः ॥
ūrdhvaṁ gacchanti sattvasthā
madhye tiṣṭhanti rājasāḥ
jaghanyaguṇavṛttisthā
adho gacchanti tāmasāḥ

Those established in sattva go upward; the rajasic stay in the middle; the tamasic, established in the lowest quality, go downward.

19 नान्यं गुणेभ्यः कर्तारं यदा द्रष्टानुपश्यति ।
गुणेभ्यश्च परं वेत्ति मद्भावं सो ऽधिगच्छति ॥
nānyaṁ guṇebhyaḥ kartāraṁ
yadā draṣṭānupaśyati
guṇebhyaśca paraṁ vetti
madbhāvaṁ so 'dhigacchati

When the seer perceives no doer other than the qualities, and knows that which is higher than the qualities, he attains My being.

20 गुणान् एतान् अतीत्य त्रीन् देही देहसमुद्भवान् ।
जन्ममृत्युजरादुःखैर् विमुक्तो ऽमृतम् अश्नुते ॥
guṇān etān atītya trīn
dehī dehasamudbhavān

janmamṛtyujarāduḥkhāir
vimukto 'mrtam aśnute

When an embodied being transcends these three qualities, which are the source of the body, released from birth, death, old age, and pain, he attains immortality.

21 अर्जुन उवाच । *arjuna uvāca*

कैर् लिङ्गैस् त्रीन् गुणान् एतान् अतीतो भवति प्रभो ।
किमाचारः कथं चैतांस् त्रीन् गुणान् अतिवर्तते ।।
kāir liṅgāis trīn guṇān etān
atīto bhavati prabho
kimācāraḥ kathaṁ cāitāṅs
trīn guṇān ativartate

Arjuna spoke:

By what marks is he recognized who has transcended these three qualities, O Lord? What is his conduct? And how does he go beyond these three qualities?

22 श्रीभगवान् उवाच । *śrībhagavān uvāca*

प्रकाशं च प्रवृत्तिं च मोहम् एव च पाण्डव ।
न द्वेष्टि संप्रवृत्तानि न निवृत्तानि काङ्क्षति ।।
prakāśaṁ ca pravṛttiṁ ca
moham eva ca pāṇḍava
na dveṣṭi saṁpravṛttāni
na nivṛttāni kāṅkṣati

The Blessed Lord spoke:

He neither hates nor desires the presence

or the absence of light or activity or delusion, Arjuna.

23 उदासीनवद् आसीनो गुणैर् यो न विचाल्यते ।
गुणा वर्तन्त इत्य् एव यो ऽवतिष्ठति नेङ्गते ॥

udāsīnavad āsīno
guṇāir yo na vicālyate
guṇā vartanta ity eva
yo 'vatiṣṭhati neṅgate

He who is seated as if indifferent, who is not disturbed by the qualities, thinking "the qualities are operating," and who stands firm and does not waver,

24 समदुःखसुखः स्वस्थः समलोष्टाश्मकाञ्चनः ।
तुल्यप्रियाप्रियो धीरस् तुल्यनिन्दात्मसंस्तुतिः ॥

samaduḥkhasukhaḥ svasthaḥ
samaloṣṭāśmakāñcanaḥ
tulyapriyāpriyo dhīras
tulyanindātmasaṁstutiḥ

To whom pain and pleasure are equal, who dwells in the Self, to whom a clod, a stone, and gold are the same, to whom the loved and the unloved are alike, who is steadfast, to whom blame and praise of himself are alike,

25 मानापमानयोस् तुल्यस् तुल्यो मित्रारिपक्षयोः ।
सर्वारम्भपरित्यागी गुणातीतः स उच्यते ॥

mānāpamānayos tulyas
tulyo mitrāripakṣayoḥ

sarvārambhaparityāgī
guṇātītaḥ sa ucyate

To whom honor and dishonor are equal, dispassionate toward the side of friend or foe, renouncing all undertakings—he is said to transcend the qualities.

26 मां च यो ऽव्यभिचारेण भक्तियोगेन सेवते ।
स गुणान् समतीत्यैतान् ब्रह्मभूयाय कल्पते ॥

māṁ ca yo 'vyabhicāreṇa
bhaktiyogena sevate
sa guṇān samatītyāitān
brahmabhūyāya kalpate

And he who serves Me with the yoga of unswerving devotion, transcending these qualities, is ready for absorption in Brahman.

27 ब्रह्मणो हि प्रतिष्ठाहम् अमृतस्याव्ययस्य च ।
शाश्वतस्य च धर्मस्य सुखस्यैकान्तिकस्य च ॥

brahmaṇo hi pratiṣṭhāham
amṛtasyāvyayasya ca
śāśvatasya ca dharmasya
sukhasyāikāntikasya ca

For I am the abode of Brahman, of the immortal and the imperishable, of everlasting virtue, and of absolute bliss.

Hari Om Tat Sat
Iti Srimad Bhagavadgītāsūpaniṣatsu Brahmavidyāyām
Yogaśāstre Sri Kriṣnārjunasamvāde
Gunatrayavibhāgayogo Nāma Caturdaśoddhyāyaḥ.

Thus ends the fourteenth Chapter, entitled "The Yoga of the Differentiation of the Three Qualities," of the venerated Bhagavad Gita Upanishad, the Knowledge of the Absolute, the scripture of Yoga, the dialogue between Sri Krishna and Arjuna.

FIFTEEN

The Yoga of the Supreme Being

atha pancadaśoddhyāyaḥ

1 श्रीभगवान् उवाच । *śrībhagavān uvāca*

ऊर्ध्वमूलम् अधःशाखम् अश्वत्थं प्राहुर् अव्ययम् ।
छन्दांसि यस्य पर्णानि यस् तं वेद स वेदवित् ॥

ūrdhvamūlaṃ adhaḥśākham
aśvatthaṁ prāhur avyayam
chandāṁsi yasya parṇāni
yas taṁ veda sa vedavit

The Blessed Lord spoke:

They speak of the eternal ashvattha tree, having its roots above and branches below, whose leaves are the (Vedic) hymns. He who knows this is a knower of the Vedas.

2 गुणप्रवृद्धा विषयप्रवालाः ।
अधश्चोर्ध्वं प्रसृतास् तस्य शाखा
अधश्च मूलान्य् अनुसंततानि
कर्मानुबन्धीनि मनुष्यलोके ॥

adhaścordhvaṁ prasṛtās tasya śākhā
guṇapravṛddhā viṣayapravālāḥ
adhaśca mūlāny anusaṁtatāni
karmānubandhīni manuṣyaloke

Below and above its branches spread, nourished by the qualities, with objects of the senses as sprouts; and below its roots stretch forth engendering action in the world of men.

3 न रूपम् अस्येह तथोपलभ्यते
नान्तो न चादिर् न च संप्रतिष्ठा ।
अश्वत्थम् एनं सुविरूढमूलम्
असङ्गशस्त्रेण दृढेन छित्त्वा ॥
na rūpam asyeha tathopalabhyate
nānto na cādir na ca saṁpratiṣṭhā
aśvattham enaṁ suvirūḍhamūlam
asaṅgaśastreṇa dṛḍhena chittvā

Its form is not perceptible here in the world, not its end, nor its beginning, nor its existence. Cutting this ashvattha tree, with its well grown root, by the strong axe of non-attachment,

4 ततः पदं तत् परिमार्गितव्यं
यस्मिन् गता न निवर्तन्ति भूयः ।
तम् एव चाद्यं पुरुषं प्रपद्ये
यतः प्रवृत्तिः प्रसृता पुराणी ॥
tataḥ padaṁ tat parimārgitavyaṁ
yasmin gatā na nivartanti bhūyaḥ
tam eva cādyaṁ puruṣaṁ prapadye
yataḥ pravṛttiḥ prasṛtā purāṇī

Then that goal is to be sought from which, having gone, no one returns. In that primal Spirit I take refuge, whence the primeval energy streamed forth.

5 निर्मानमोहा जितसङ्गदोषा
अध्यात्मनित्या विनिवृत्तकामाः ।
द्वन्द्वैर् विमुक्ताः सुखदुःखसंज्ञैर्
गच्छन्त्य् अमूढाः पदम् अव्ययं तत् ॥
nirmānamohā jitasaṅgadoṣā
adhyātmanityā vinivṛttakāmāḥ
dvandvāir vimuktāḥ sukhaduḥkhasaṁjñāir
gacchanty amūḍhāḥ padam avyayaṁ tat

Without arrogance or delusion, with the evils of attachment conquered, dwelling constantly in the supreme Self, with desires turned away, released from the dualities known as pleasure and pain, the undeluded go to that imperishable goal.

6 न तद् भासयते सूर्यो न शशाङ्को न पावकः ।
यद् गत्वा न निवर्तन्ते तद् धाम परमं मम ॥
na tad bhāsayate sūryo
na śaśāṅko na pāvakaḥ
yad gatvā na nivartante
tad dhāma paramaṁ mama

The sun does not illumine, nor the moon, nor fire, that place to which, having gone, no one returns; that is My supreme abode.

7 ममैवांशो जीवलोके जीवभूतः सनातनः ।
मनःषष्ठानीन्द्रियाणि प्रकृतिस्थानि कर्षति ॥
mamāivāṁśo jīvaloke
jīvabhūtaḥ sanātanaḥ
manaḥ ṣaṣṭhānīndriyāṇī
prakṛtisthāni karṣati

Merely a fragment of Myself, becoming an eternal (individual) soul in the world of the living, draws to itself the senses, of which the sixth is the mind, that exist in material nature.

8 शरीरं यद् अवाप्नोति यच् चाप्य् उत्क्रामतीश्वरः ।
गृहीत्वैतानि संयाति वायुर् गन्धान् इवाशयात् ॥

śarīraṁ yad avāpnoti
yac cāpy utkrāmatīśvaraḥ
gṛhītvāitāni saṁyāti
vāyur gandhān ivāśayāt

When the Lord acquires a body, and also when He departs from it, He goes, taking them along, like the wind blowing perfumes from their source.

9 श्रोत्रं चक्षुः स्पर्शनं च रसनं घ्राणम् एव च ।
अधिष्ठाय मनश्चायं विषयान् उपसेवते ॥

śrotraṁ cakṣuḥ sparśanaṁ ca
rasanaṁ ghrāṇam eva ca
adhiṣṭhāya manaścāyaṁ
viṣayān upasevate

Presiding over hearing, sight and touch, taste and smell, as well as the mind, He (i.e. the fragment of the Lord incarnated as the individual soul) enjoys the objects of the senses.

10 उत्क्रामन्तं स्थितं वापि भुञ्जानं वा गुणान्वितम् ।
विमूढा नानुपश्यन्ति पश्यन्ति ज्ञानचक्षुषः ॥
utkrāmantaṁ sthitaṁ vāpi
bhuñjānaṁ vā guṇānvitam
vimūḍhā nānupaśyanti
paśyanti jñānacakṣuṣaḥ

When He departs, remains, or enjoys (sense objects) while accompanied by the qualities, the deluded do not perceive Him. Those with the eye of knowledge see Him.

11 यतन्तो योगिनश्चैनं पश्यन्त्य् आत्मन्य् अवस्थितम् ।
यतन्तो ऽप्य् अकृतात्मानो नैनं पश्यन्त्य् अचेतसः ॥
yatanto yoginaścāinaṁ
paśyanty ātmany avasthitam
yatanto 'py akṛtātmāno
nāinaṁ paśyanty acetasaḥ

The yogins, striving, see Him (the embodied fraction of the Lord) situated in the Self, but the unthinking, those of unperfected selves, strive but do not see Him.

12 यद् आदित्यगतं तेजो जगद् भासयते ऽखिलम् ।
यच् चन्द्रमसि यच् चाग्नौ तत् तेजो विद्धि मामकम् ॥
yad ādityagataṁ tejo
jagad bhāsayate 'khilam
yac candramasi yac cāgnau
tat tejo viddhi māmakam

That brilliance which resides in the sun, which illumines the entire universe, which is in the moon and which is in fire, know that brilliance to be Mine.

13 गाम् आविश्य च भूतानि धारयाम्य् अहम् ओजसा ।
पुष्णामि चौषधीः सर्वाः सोमो भूत्वा रसात्मकः ॥
gām āviśya ca bhūtāni
dhārayāmy aham ojasā
puṣṇāmi cāuṣadhīḥ sarvāḥ
somo bhūtvā rasātmakaḥ

Entering the earth, I support all beings with energy, and, having become the watery moon, I cause all the plants to thrive.

14 अहं वैश्वानरो भूत्वा प्राणिनां देहम् आश्रितः ।
प्राणापानसमायुक्तः पचाम्य् अन्नं चतुर्विधम् ॥
ahaṁ vāiśvānaro bhūtvā
prāṇināṁ deham āśritaḥ
prāṇāpānasamāyuktaḥ
pacāmy annaṁ caturvidham

Having become the digestive fire of all men, I abide in the body of all living beings; and joining with the prana and apana, I (digest) the four kinds of food.

15 सर्वस्य चाहं हृदि संनिविष्टो
मत्तः स्मृतिर् ज्ञानम् अपोहनं च ।
वेदैश्च सर्वैर् अहम् एव वेद्यो
वेदान्तकृद् वेदविद् एव चाहम् ॥
sarvasya cāhaṁ hṛdi saṁniviṣṭo
mattaḥ smṛtir jñānam apohanaṁ ca

vedāiśca sarvāir aham eva vedyo
vedāntakṛd vedavid eva cāham

I have entered into the hearts of all beings; from Me come memory and knowledge, as well as their loss. I alone am that which is to be known in all the Vedas; I am the author of the Vedanta and the knower of the Vedas.

16 द्वाव् इमौ पुरुषौ लोके क्षरश्चाक्षर एव च ।
क्षरः सर्वाणि भूतानि कूटस्थोऽक्षर उच्यते ॥
dvāv imāu puruṣāu loke
kṣaraścākṣara eva ca
kṣaraḥ sarvāṇi bhūtāni
kūṭastho 'kṣara ucyate

There are these two spirits in the world—the perishable and the imperishable. All beings are the perishable; the unchanging is called the imperishable.

17 उत्तमः पुरुषस् त्व् अन्यः परमात्मेत्य् उदाहृतः ।
यो लोकत्रयम् आविश्य बिभर्त्य् अव्यय ईश्वरः ॥

uttamaḥ puruṣas tv anyaḥ
paramātmety udāhṛtaḥ
yo lokatrayam āviśya
bibharty avyaya īśvaraḥ

But the highest Spirit is another, called the supreme Self, who, entering the three worlds as the eternal Lord, supports them.

18 यस्मात् क्षरम् अतीतो ऽहम् अक्षराद् अपि चोत्तमः।
अतो ऽस्मि लोके वेदे च प्रथितः पुरुषोत्तमः॥
yasmāt kṣaram atīto 'ham
akṣarād api cottamaḥ
ato 'smi loke vede ca
prathitaḥ puruṣottamaḥ

Since I transcend the perishable and am higher than the imperishable, therefore I am, in the world, and in the Vedas, celebrated as the supreme Spirit.

19 यो माम् एवम् असंमूढो जानाति पुरुषोत्तमम्।
स सर्वविद् भजति मां सर्वभावेन भारत॥
yo mām evam asaṁmūḍho
jānāti puruṣottamam
sa sarvavid bhajati māṁ
sarvabhāvena bhārata

He who, thus undeluded, knows Me as the supreme Spirit, he, all-knowing, worships Me with his whole being, Arjuna.

20 इति गुह्यतमं शास्त्रम् इदम् उक्तं मया ऽनघ।
एतद् बद्ध्वा बुद्धिमान् स्यात् कृतकृत्यश्च भारत॥
iti guhyatamaṁ śāstram
idam uktaṁ mayā 'nagha
etad buddhvā buddhimān syāt
krtakṛtyaśca bhārata

Thus this most secret doctrine has been taught by Me, O Arjuna; having awakened to this, a man becomes wise and fulfills all his duties, Arjuna.

Hari Om Tat Sat
Iti Srimad Bhagavadgītāsūpaniṣatsu Brahmavidyāyām
Yogaśāstre Sri Krişnārjunasamvāde
Puruṣottamayogo Nāma Pancadaśoddhyāyaḥ.

Thus ends the fifteenth Chapter, entitled "The Yoga of the Supreme Being," of the venerated Bhagavad Gita Upanishad, the Knowledge of the Absolute, the scripture of Yoga, the dialogue between Sri Krishna and Arjuna.

SIXTEEN

The Yoga of the Distinction between the Divine and the Demoniacal

atha ṣoḍaśoddhyāyaḥ

1 श्रीभगवान् उवाच । *śrībhagavān uvāca*

अभयं सत्त्वसंशुद्धिर् ज्ञानयोगव्यवस्थितिः ।
दानं दमश्च यज्ञश्च स्वाध्यायस् तप आर्जवम् ॥

abhayaṁ sattvasaṁśuddhir
jñānayogavyavasthitiḥ
dānaṁ damaśca yajñaśca
svādhyāyas tapa ārjavam

The Blessed Lord spoke:

Fearlessness, purity of being, perseverance in yoga and knowledge, giving, self-restraint and sacrifice, study of sacred texts, austerity, and uprightness,

2 अहिंसा सत्यम् अक्रोधस् त्यागः शान्तिर् अपैशुनम् ।
दया भूतेषु् अलोलुप्त्वं मार्दवं ह्रीर् अचापलम् ॥

ahiṁsā satyam akrodhas
tyāgaḥ śāntir apāiśunam
dayā bhūteṣv aloluptvaṁ
mārdavaṁ hrīr acāpalam

Non-violence, truth, absence of anger, renunciation, serenity, absence of calumny, compassion for all beings, freedom from desire, gentleness, modesty, absence of fickleness,

3 तेजः क्षमा धृतिः शौचम् अद्रोहो नातिमानिता ।
भवन्ति संपदं दैवीम् अभिजातस्य भारत ॥

tejaḥ kṣamā dhṛtiḥ śāucam
adroho nātimānitā
bhavanti saṁpadaṁ dāivīm
abhijātasya bhārata

Vigor, forgiveness, fortitude, purity, freedom from malice, freedom from pride; these are the endowment of those born to a divine destiny, Arjuna.

4 दम्भो दर्पो ऽभिमानश्च क्रोधः पारुष्यम् एव च ।
अज्ञानं चाभिजातस्य पार्थ संपदम् आसुरीम् ॥
dambho darpo 'bhimānaśca
krodhaḥ pāruṣyam eva ca
ajñānaṁ cābhijātasya
pārtha saṁpadam āsurīm

Hypocrisy, arrogance, pride, anger, insolence, and ignorance, are the endowment of those born to a demoniacal destiny, Arjuna.

5 दैवी संपद् विमोक्षाय निबन्धायासुरी मता ।
मा शुचः संपदं दैवीम् अभिजातो ऽसि पाण्डव ॥
dāivī saṁpad vimokṣāya
nibandhāyāsurī matā
mā śucaḥ saṁpadaṁ dāivīm
abhijāto 'si pāṇḍava

The divine destiny leads to liberation; the demoniacal to bondage, it is thought. Do not grieve! You are born to a divine destiny, Arjuna.

6 द्वौ भूतसर्गौ लोके ऽस्मिन् दैव आसुर एव च ।
दैवो विस्तरशः प्रोक्त आसुरं पार्थ मे शृणु ।।
dvāu bhūtasargāu loke 'smin
dāiva āsura eva ca
dāivo vistaraśaḥ prokta
āsuraṁ pārtha me śṛṇu

There are two classes of created beings in this world—the divine and the demoniacal. The divine has been explained at length; now hear from Me, Arjuna, about the demoniacal.

7 प्रवृत्तिं च निवृत्तिं च जना न विदुर् आसुराः ।
न शौचं नापि चाचारो न सत्यं तेषु विद्यते ।।
pravṛttiṁ ca nivṛttiṁ ca
janā na vidur āsurāḥ
na śaucaṁ nāpi cācāro
na satyaṁ teṣu vidyate

Demoniacal men do not understand when to act and when to refrain from action. Neither purity, nor good conduct, nor truth is found in them.

8 असत्यम् अप्रतिष्ठं ते जगद् आहुर् अनीश्वरम् ।
अपरस्परसंभूतं किम् अन्यत् कामहैतुकम् ।।

asatyam apratiṣṭhaṁ te
jagad āhur anīśvaram
aparasparasaṁbhūtaṁ
kim anyat kāmahāitukam

"The universe," they say, "is without truth, without basis, without a God; brought about by a mutual union. How else? It is caused by lust alone."

9 एतां दृष्टिम् अवष्टभ्य नष्टात्मानो ऽल्पबुद्धयः ।
प्रभवन्त्य् उग्रकर्माणः क्षयाय जगतो ऽहिताः ॥
etāṁ dṛṣṭim avaṣṭabhya
naṣṭātmāno 'lpabuddhayaḥ
prabhavanty ugrakarmāṇaḥ
kṣayāya jagato 'hitāḥ

Holding this view, these men of lost souls, of small intelligence, and of cruel actions, come forth as enemies of the world for its destruction.

10 कामम् आश्रित्य दुष्पूरं दम्भमानमदान्विताः ।
मोहाद् गृहीत्वा ऽसद्ग्राहान् प्रवर्तन्ते ऽशुचिव्रताः ॥
kāmam āśritya duṣpūraṁ
dambhamānamadānvitāḥ
mohād gṛhītvā 'sadgrāhān
pravartante 'śucivratāḥ

Attached to insatiable desire, full of hypocrisy, arrogance, and pride, having accepted false notions through delusion, they work with unclean resolves,

11 चिन्ताम् अपरिमेयां च प्रलयान्ताम् उपाश्रिताः ।
कामोपभोगपरमा एतावद् इति निश्चिताः ॥
cintām aparimeyāṁ ca
pralayāntām upāśritāḥ
kāmopabhogaparamā
etāvad iti niścitāḥ

Clinging to immeasurable anxiety, ending only in death, with gratification of desire as their highest aim, convinced that this is all;

12 आशापाशशतैर् बद्धाः कामक्रोधपरायणाः ।
ईहन्ते कामभोगार्थम् अन्यायेनार्थसंचयान ॥
āśāpāśaśatāir baddhāḥ
kāmakrodhaparāyaṇāḥ
īhante kāmabhogārtham
anyāyenārthasaṁcayān

Bound by a hundred snares of hope, devoted to desire and anger, they seek to obtain, by unjust means, hoards of wealth for the gratification of their desires.

13 इदम् अद्य मया लब्धम् इदं प्राप्स्ये मनोरथम् ।
इदम् अस्तीदम् अपि मे भविष्यति पुनर् धनम् ॥
idam adya mayā labdham
idaṁ prāpsye manoratham
idam astīdam api me
bhaviṣyati punar dhanam

This has been obtained by me today; this desire I shall attain; this is mine, and this wealth also shall be mine.

14 असौ मया हतः शत्रुर् हनिष्ये चापरान् अपि ।
ईश्वरो ऽहम् अहं भोगी सिद्धो ऽहं बलवान् सुखी ॥
asāu mayā hataḥ śatrur
haniṣye cāparān api
īśvaro 'ham ahaṁ bhogī
siddho 'haṁ balavān sukhī

"That enemy has been slain by me, and I shall slay others too; I am a lord, I am the enjoyer, I am successful, powerful, and happy,

15 आढ्यो ऽभिजनवान् अस्मि को ऽन्यो ऽस्ति सदृशो मया ।
यक्ष्ये दास्यामि मोदिष्य इत्य् अज्ञानविमोहिताः ॥
āḍhyo 'bhijanavān asmi
ko 'nyo 'sti sadṛśo mayā
yakṣye dāsyāmi modiṣya
ity ajñānavimohitāḥ

"I am wealthy and high born. Who else is equal to me? I shall sacrifice, I shall give, I shall rejoice." Thus, they are deluded by ignorance.

16 अनेकचित्तविभ्रान्ता मोहजालसमावृताः ।
प्रसक्ताः कामभोगेषु पतन्ति नरके ऽशुचौ ॥
anekacittavibhrāntā
mohajālasamāvṛtāḥ
prasaktāḥ kāmabhogeṣu
patanti narake 'śucāu

Led astray by many imaginings, enveloped in a net of delusion, attached to the gratification of desires, they fall into a foul hell.

17 आत्मसंभाविताः स्तब्धा धनमानमदान्विताः ।
यजन्ते नामयज्ञैस् ते दम्भेनाविधिपूर्वकम् ॥
ātmasambhāvitāḥ stabdhā
dhanamānamadānvitāḥ
yajante nāmayajñāis te
dambhenāvidhipūrvakam

Self-conceited, stubborn, filled with the pride and arrogance of wealth, they perform sacrifices only in name, with hypocrisy, and not according to Vedic injunction.

18 अहंकारं बलं दर्पं कामं क्रोधं च संश्रिताः ।
माम् आत्मपरदेहेषु प्रद्विषन्तो ऽभ्यसूयकाः ॥
ahaṁkāraṁ balaṁ darpaṁ
kāmaṁ krodhaṁ ca saṁśritāḥ
mām ātmaparadeheṣu
pradviṣanto 'bhyasūyakāḥ

Clinging to egotism, force, insolence, desire, and anger, those malicious people hate Me in their own and others' bodies.

19 तान् अहं द्विषतः क्रूरान् संसारेषु नराधमान् ।
क्षिपाम्य् अजस्रम् अशुभान् आसुरीषु एव योनिषु ॥
tān ahaṁ dviṣataḥ krūrān
saṁsāreṣu narādhamān
kṣipāmy ajasram aśubhān
āsurīṣv eva yoniṣu

Those cruel haters, the worst of men, I constantly hurl into the wombs of demons in the cycles of rebirth.

20 आसुरीं योनिम् आपन्ना मूढा जन्मनि जन्मनि ।
माम् अप्राप्यैव कौन्तेय ततो यान्त्य् अधमां गतिम् ॥
āsurīṁ yonim āpannā
mūḍhā janmani janmani
mām arāpryāiva kāunteya
tato yānty adhamāṁ gatim

Having entered the wombs of demons, those who are deluded, not attaining Me in birth after birth, Arjuna, from there go to a condition still lower than that.

21 त्रिविधं नरकस्येदं द्वारं नाशनम् आत्मनः ।
कामः क्रोधस् तथा लोभस् तस्माद् एतत् त्रयं त्यजेत् ॥
trividhaṁ narakasyedaṁ
dvāraṁ nāśanam ātmanaḥ
kāmaḥ krodhas tathā lobhas
tasmād etat trayaṁ tyajet

This is the threefold gate of hell, destructive of the self: desire, anger, and greed. Therefore one should abandon these three.

22 एतैर् विमुक्तः कौन्तेय तमोद्वारैस् त्रिभिर् नरः ।
आचरत्य् आत्मनः श्रेयस् ततो याति परां गतिम् ॥
etāir vimuktaḥ kāunteya
tamodvārāis tribhir naraḥ
ācaraty ātmanaḥ śreyas
tato yāti parāṁ gatim

Released from these three gates to darkness, Arjuna, a man does what is best for himself. Then he goes to the highest goal.

23 यः शास्त्रविधिम् उत्सृज्य वर्तते कामकारतः ।
न स सिद्धिम् अवाप्नोति न सुखं न परां गतिम् ॥
yaḥ śāstravidhim utsṛjya
vartate kāmakārataḥ
na sa siddhim avāpnoti
na sukhaṁ na parāṁ gatim

He who acts under the impulse of desire, casting aside the injunctions of the scriptures, does not attain perfection, nor happiness, nor the highest goal.

24 तस्माच् छास्त्रं प्रमाणं ते कार्याकार्यव्यवस्थितौ ।
ज्ञात्वा शास्त्रविधानोक्तं कर्म कर्तुम् इहार्हसि ॥
tasmāc chāstraṁ pramāṇaṁ te
kāryākāryavyavasthitāu
jñātvā śāstravidhānoktaṁ
karma kartum ihārhasi

Therefore, determining your standard by the scriptures, as to what is and what is not to be done, knowing the scriptural injunction prescribed, you should perform action here in this world.

Hari Om Tat Sat
Iti Srimad Bhagavadgītāsūpaniṣatsu Brahmavidyāyām

Yogaśāstre Sri Krișnārjunasamvāde
Daivāsurasampadvibhāgayogo Nāma Șodaśoddhyāyaḥ.

Thus ends the sixteenth Chapter, entitled "The Yoga of the Distinction between the Divine and the Demoniacal," of the venerated Bhagavad Gita Upanishad, the Knowledge of the Absolute, the scripture of Yoga, the dialogue between Sri Krishna and Arjuna.

SEVENTEEN

The Yoga of the Threefold Division of Faith

atha saptadaśoddhyāyaḥ

1 अर्जुन उवाच। *arjuna uvāca*

ये शास्त्रविधिम् उत्सृज्य यजन्ते श्रद्धयान्विताः।
तेषां निष्ठा तु का कृष्ण सत्त्वम् आहो रजस् तमः॥

ye śāstravidhim utsṛjya
yajante śraddhayānvitāḥ
teṣāṁ niṣṭhā tu kā kṛṣṇa
sattvam āho rajas tamaḥ

Arjuna spoke:

Those who sacrifice casting the injunctions of the scriptures aside, but filled with faith, what is their condition, Krishna? Is it sattva, rajas, or tamas?

2 श्रीभगवान् उवाच। *śrībhagavān uvāca*

त्रिविधा भवति श्रद्धा देहिनां सा स्वभावजा।
सात्त्विकी राजसी चैव तामसी चेति तां शृणु॥

trividhā bhavati śraddhā
dehināṁ sā svabhāvajā
sāttvikī rājasī cāiva
tāmasī ceti tāṁ śṛṇu

The Blessed Lord spoke:

The faith of embodied beings is of three

kinds, born of their innate nature; it is sattvic, rajasic, and tamasic. Now hear of this.

3 सत्त्वानुरूपा सर्वस्य श्रद्धा भवति भारत।
श्रद्धामयो ऽयं पुरुषो यो यच्छ्रद्धः स एव सः॥
sattvānurūpā sarvasya
śraddhā bhavati bhārata
śraddhāmayo 'yam puruṣo
yo yacchraddhaḥ sa eva saḥ

Faith is in accordance with the truth (nature) of each, Arjuna. Man is made of faith. Whatever faith he has, thus he is.

4 यजन्ते सात्त्विका देवान् यक्षरक्षांसि राजसाः।
प्रेतान् भूतगणांश्चान्ये यजन्ते तामसा जनाः॥
yajante sāttvikā devān
yakṣarakṣāṁsi rājasāḥ
pretān bhūtagaṇāṅścānye
yajante tāmasā janāḥ

The sattvic worship the gods, the rajasic worship the Yakshas and demons; the others, the tamasic men, worship the ghosts and the hordes of nature spirits.

5 अशास्त्रविहितं घोरं तप्यन्ते ये तपो जनाः।
दम्भाहंकारसंयुक्ताः कामरागबलान्विताः॥
aśāstravihitaṁ ghoraṁ
tapyante ye tapo janāḥ
dambhāhaṁkārasaṁyuktāḥ
kāmarāgabalānvitāḥ

Men who undergo terrible austerities not enjoined by the scriptures, accompanied by hypocrisy and egotism, along with desire and passion,

6 कर्षयन्तः शरीरस्थं भूतग्रामम् अचेतसः ।
मां चैवान्तः शरीरस्थं तान्विद्ध्य् आसुरनिश्चयान् ।।

karṣayantaḥ śarīrasthaṁ
bhūtagrāmam acetasaḥ
māṁ cāivāntaḥ śarīrasthaṁ
tān viddhy āsuraniścayān

The unthinking, torturing within the body the aggregate of elements, and also torturing Me thus within the body, know them to be of demoniacal resolves.

7 आहारस् त्व् अपि सर्वस्य त्रिविधो भवति प्रियः ।
यज्ञस् तपस् तथा दानं तेषां भेदम् इमं शृणु ।।

āhāras tv api sarvasya
trividho bhavati priyaḥ
yajñas tapas tạthā dānaṁ
teṣāṁ bhedam imaṁ śṛṇu

But also the food preferred by all is of three kinds, as are their sacrifices, austerities, and gifts. Hear now the distinction between them.

8 आयुः सत्त्वबलारोग्य-सुखप्रीतिविवर्धनाः ।
रस्याः स्निग्धाः स्थिरा हृद्या आहाराः सात्त्विकप्रियाः ।।

āyuḥsattvabalārogya-
sukhaprītivivardhanāḥ

rasyāḥ snigdhāḥ sthirā hṛdyā
āhārāḥ sāttvikapriyāḥ

Promoting life, virtue, strength, health, happiness, and satisfaction, which are savory, smooth, firm, and pleasant to the stomach; such foods are dear to the sattvic.

9 कट्वम्ललवणात्युष्ण तीक्ष्णरूक्षविदाहिनः ।
आहारा राजसस्येष्टा दुःखशोकामयप्रदाः ॥
kaṭvamlalavaṇātyuṣṇa-
tīkṣṇarūkṣavidāhinaḥ
āhārā rājasasyeṣṭā
duḥkhaśokāmayapradāḥ

Causing pain, misery, and sickness, bitter, sour, salty, excessively hot, pungent, dry, and burning; such foods are desired by the rajasic.

10 यातयामं गतरसं पूति पर्युषितं च यत् ।
उच्छिष्टम् अपि चामेध्यं भोजनं तामसप्रियम् ॥
yātayāmaṁ gatarasaṁ
pūti paryuṣitaṁ ca yat
ucchiṣṭam api cāmedhyaṁ
bhojanaṁ tāmasapriyam

Stale, tasteless, putrid, rotten, and refuse as well as the impure, is the food which is dear to the tamasic.

11 अफलाकाङ्क्षिभिर् यज्ञो विधिदृष्टो य इज्यते ।
यष्टव्यम् एवेति मनः समाधाय स सात्त्विकः ॥

aphalākāṅkṣibhir yajño
vidhidṛṣṭo ya ijyate
yaṣṭavyam eveti manaḥ
samādhāya sa sāttvikaḥ

Sacrifice which is offered, observing the scriptures, by those who do not desire the fruit, concentrating the mind only on the thought "this is to be sacrificed;" that sacrifice is sattvic.

12 अभिसंधाय तु फलं दम्भार्थम् अपि चैव यत् ।
इज्यते भरतश्रेष्ठ तं यज्ञं विद्धि राजसम् ॥
abhisaṁdhāya tu phalaṁ
dambhārtham api cāiva yat
ijyate bharataśreṣṭha
taṁ yajñaṁ viddhi rājasam

But sacrifice which is offered with a view to the fruit, Arjuna, and also for the purpose of ostentation; know that to be rajasic.

13 विधिहीनम् असृष्टान्नं मन्त्रहीनम् अदक्षिणम् ।
श्रद्धाविरहितं यज्ञं तामसं परिचक्षते ॥
vidhihīnam asṛṣṭānnaṁ
mantrahīnam adakṣiṇam
śraddhāvirahitaṁ yajñam
tāmasaṁ paricakṣate

Sacrifice devoid of faith, contrary to scriptural ordinances, with no food offered, without mantras and without gifts (to the presiding priest), they regard as tamasic.

14 देवद्विजगुरुप्राज्ञ पूजनं शौचम् आर्जवम् ।
ब्रह्मचर्यम् अहिंसा च शारीरं तप उच्यते ॥

devadvijagurupräjña-
pūjanaṁ śāucam ārjavam
brahmacaryam ahiṁsā ca
śārīraṁ tapa ucyate

Worship of the gods, the twice-born, teachers, and wise men; purity, rectitude, celibacy, and non-violence; these are called austerities of the body.

15 अनुद्वेगकरं वाक्यं सत्यं प्रियहितं च यत् ।
स्वाध्यायाभ्यसनं चैव वाङ्मयं तप उच्यते ॥

anudvegakaraṁ vākyaṁ
satyaṁ priyahitaṁ ca yat
svādhyāyābhyasanaṁ cāiva
vāṅmayaṁ tapa ucyate

Words that do not cause distress, truthful, agreeable, and beneficial; and practice in the recitation of sacred texts; these are called austerities of speech.

16 मनःप्रसादः सौम्यत्वं मौनम् आत्मविनिग्रहः ।
भावसंशुद्धिर् इत्य् एतत् तपो मानसम् उच्यते ॥

manaḥprasādaḥ sāumyatvaṁ
māunam ātmavinigrahaḥ
bhāvasaṁśuddhir ity etat
tapo mānasam ucyate

Peace of mind, gentleness, silence, self-restraint, purity of being; these are called austerities of the mind.

17 श्रद्धया परया तप्तं तपस् तत् त्रिविधं नरैः ।
अफलाकाङ्क्षिभिर् युक्तैः सात्त्विकं परिचक्षते ॥
śraddhayā parayā taptaṁ
tapas tat trividhaṁ narāiḥ
aphalākāṅkṣibhir yuktāiḥ
sāttvikaṁ paricakṣate

This threefold austerity practiced with the highest faith by men who are not desirous of fruits and are steadfast, they regard as sattvic.

18 सत्कारमानपूजार्थं तपो दम्भेन चैव यत् ।
क्रियते तद् इह प्रोक्तं राजसं चलम् अध्रुवम् ॥
satkāramānapūjārthaṁ
tapo dambhena cāiva yat
kriyate tad iha proktaṁ
rājasaṁ calam adhruvam

Austerity which is practiced with hypocrisy for the sake of honor, respect, and reverence; that, here in the world, is declared to be rajasic, unsteady, and impermanent.

19 मूढग्राहेणात्मनो यत् पीडया क्रियते तपः ।
परस्योत्सादनार्थं वा तत् तामसम् उदाहृतम् ॥
mūḍhagrāheṇātmano yat
pīḍayā kriyate tapaḥ
parasyotsādanārthaṁ vā
tat tāmasam udāhṛtam

Austerity which is performed with deluded notions and with self-torture, or with the aim of destroying another, is declared to be tamasic.

20 दातव्यम् इति यद् दानं दीयते ऽनुपकारिणे ।
देशे काले च पात्रे च तद् दानं सात्त्विकं स्मृतम् ॥

dātavyam iti yad dānaṁ
dīyate 'nupakāriṇe
deśe kāle ca pātre ca
tad dānaṁ sāttvikaṁ smṛtam

The gift which is given only with the thought "it is to be given," to a worthy person who has done no prior favor, at the proper place and time; that gift is held to be sattvic.

21 यत् तु प्रत्युपकारार्थं फलम् उद्दिश्य वा पुनः ।
दीयते च परिक्लिष्टं तद् दानं राजसं स्मृतम् ॥

yat tu pratyupakārārthaṁ
phalam uddiśya vā punaḥ
dīyate ca parikliṣṭaṁ
tad dānaṁ rājasaṁ smṛtam

But that gift which is given grudgingly, with the aim of recompense or gain, with regard to fruit, is considered rajasic.

22 अदेशकाले यद् दानम् अपात्रेभ्यश्च दीयते ।
असत्कृतम् अवज्ञातं तत् तामसम् उदाहृतम् ॥

adeśakāle yad dānam
apātrebhyaśca dīyate

asatkṛtam avajñātaṁ
tat tāmasam udāhṛtam

That gift which is given at the wrong place and time to the unworthy, without paying respect, or with contempt, is declared to be tamasic.

23 ओं तत् सद् इति निर्देशो ब्रह्मणस् त्रिविधः स्मृतः ।
ब्राह्मणास् तेन वेदाश्च यज्ञाश्च विहिताः पुरा ॥
oṁ tat sad iti nirdeśo
brahmaṇas trividhaḥ smṛtaḥ
brāhmaṇās tena vedāśca
yajñāśca vihitāḥ purā

"Om tat sat"—this has been taught as the threefold designation of Brahman. By this the brahmins, the Vedas, and the sacrifices were created in ancient times.

24 तस्मादो इत्य् उदाहृत्य यज्ञदानतपःक्रियाः ।
प्रवर्तन्ते विधानोक्ताः सततं ब्रह्मवादिनाम् ॥
tasmād om ity udāhṛtya
yajñadānatapaḥkriyāḥ
pravartante vidhānoktāḥ
satataṁ brahmavādinām

Therefore, acts of sacrifice, giving, and austerity are always begun uttering the syllable "Om" by the students of Brahman, as prescribed in the Vedic injunctions.

25 तद् इत्य् अनभिसंधाय फलं यज्ञतपःक्रियाः ।
दानक्रियाश्च विविधाः क्रियन्ते मोक्षकाङ्क्षिभिः ॥

tad ity anabhisaṁdhāya
phalaṁ yajñatapaḥkriyāḥ
dānakriyāśca vividhāḥ
kriyante mokṣakāṅkṣibhiḥ

Uttering "tat" and without aiming at fruits, acts of sacrifice and austerity and acts of giving of various sorts are performed by those who desire liberation.

26 सद्भावे साधुभावे च सद् इत्य् एतत् प्रयुज्यते ।
प्रशस्ते कर्मणि तथा सच्छब्दः पार्थ युज्यते ॥
sadbhāve sādhubhāve ca
sad ity etat prayujyate
praśaste karmaṇi tathā
sacchabdaḥ pārtha yujyate

"Sat" is used in its meaning of "reality" and in its meaning of "goodness." Also the word "sat" is used for an auspicious act, Arjuna.

27 यज्ञे तपसि दाने च स्थितिः सद् इति चोच्यते ।
कर्म चैव तदर्थीयं सद् इत्य् एवाभिधीयते ॥
yajñe tapasi dāne ca
sthitiḥ sad iti cocyate
karma cāiva tadarthīyaṁ
sad ity evābhidhīyate

Steadfastness in sacrifice, austerity, and giving is also called "sat," and action relating to these is likewise designated as "sat."

28 अश्रद्धया हुतं दत्तं तपस् तप्तं कृतं च यत् ।
असद् इत्य् उच्यते पार्थ न च तत् प्रेत्य नो इह ॥

aśraddhayā hutaṁ dattaṁ
tapas taptaṁ kṛtaṁ ca yat
asad ity ucyate pārtha
na ca tat pretya no iha

An oblation offered or an austerity practiced without faith is called "asat," Arjuna, and is nothing in the hereafter or here in the world.

Hari Om Tat Sat
Iti Srimad Bhagavadgītāsūpaniṣatsu Brahmavidyāyām
Yogaśāstre Sri Kriṣnārjunasamvāde
Śraddhātrayavibhāgayogo Nāma Saptadaśoddhyāyaḥ.

Thus ends the seventeenth Chapter, entitled "The Yoga of the Threefold Division of Faith," of the venerated Bhagavad Gita Upanishad, the Knowledge of the Absolute, the scripture of Yoga, the dialogue between Sri Krishna and Arjuna.

EIGHTEEN

The Yoga of Liberation by Renunciation

atha aṣṭādaśoddhyāyaḥ

1 अर्जुन उवाच । *arjuna uvāca*

संन्यासस्य महाबाहो तत्त्वम् इच्छामि वेदितुम् ।
त्यागस्य च हृषीकेश पृथक् केशिनिषूदन ॥

saṁnyāsasya mahābāho
tattvam icchāmi veditum
tyāgasya ca hṛṣīkeśa
pṛthak keśiniṣūdana

Arjuna spoke:
I wish to know the truth of sannyasa, Krishna, and of renunciation, and the difference between them.

2 श्रीभगवान् उवाच । *śrībhagavān uvāca*

काम्यानां कर्मणां न्यासं
संन्यासं कवयो विदुः ।
सर्वकर्मफलत्यागं
प्राहुस् त्यागं विचक्षणाः ॥

kāmyānāṁ karmaṇāṁ nyāsaṁ
saṁnyāsaṁ kavayo viduḥ
sarvakarmaphalatyāgaṁ
prāhus tyāgaṁ vicakṣaṇāḥ

The Blessed Lord spoke:

The relinquishment of actions prompted by desire the sages understand as sannyasa; the relinquishment of the fruit of all action the wise declare to be renunciation.

3 त्याज्यं दोषवद् इत्य् एके कर्म प्राहुर् मनीषिणः ।
यज्ञदानतपःकर्म न त्याज्यम् इति चापरे ॥
tyājyaṁ doṣavad ity eke
karma prāhur manīṣiṇaḥ
yajñadānatapaḥkarma
na tyājyam iti cāpare

Some men of wisdom declare that action is to be abandoned and is full of evil, and others say that acts of sacrifice, giving, and austerity are not to be abandoned.

4 निश्चयं शृणु मे तत्र त्यागे भरतसत्तम ।
त्यागो हि पुरुषव्याघ्र त्रिविधः संप्रकीर्तितः ॥
niścayaṁ śṛṇu me tatra
tyāge bharatasattama
tyāgo hi puruṣavyāghra
trividhaḥ saṁprakīrtitaḥ

Hear My conclusion in this matter concerning renunciation, Arjuna. Renunciation is declared to be of three kinds:

5 यज्ञदानतपःकर्म न त्याज्यं कार्यम् एव तत् ।
यज्ञो दानं तपश्चैव पावनानि मनीषिणाम् ॥
yajñadānatapaḥkarma
na tyājyaṁ kāryam eva tat

yajño dānaṁ tapaścaiva
pāvanāni manīṣiṇām

Acts of sacrifice, giving, and austerity are not to be abandoned, but rather to be performed; sacrifice, giving, and austerity are purifiers of those who are wise.

6 एतान्य् अपि तु कर्माणि सङ्गं त्यक्त्वा फलानि च ।
कर्तव्यानीति मे पार्थ निश्चितं मतम् उत्तमम् ॥
etāny api tu karmāṇi
saṅgaṁ tyaktvā phalāni ca
kartavyānīti me pārtha
niścitaṁ matam uttamam

These actions, however, are to be performed abandoning attachment to the fruits. This is My definite and highest belief, Arjuna.

7 नियतस्य तु संन्यासः कर्मणो नोपपद्यते ।
मोहात् तस्य परित्यागस् तामसः परिकीर्तितः ॥
niyatasya tu saṁnyāsaḥ
karmaṇo nopapadyate
mohāt tasya parityāgas
tāmasaḥ parikīrtitaḥ

But renunciation of obligatory action is not proper; the abandonment of it through delusion is proclaimed to be tamasic.

8 दुःखम् इत्येव यत् कर्म कायक्लेशभयात् त्यजेत् ।
स कृत्वा राजसं त्यागं नैव त्यागफलं लभेत् ॥

duḥkham ityeva yat karma
kāyakleśabhayāt tyajet
sa kṛtvā rājasaṁ tyāgaṁ
nāiva tyāgaphalaṁ labhet

He who abandons action merely because it is difficult, or because of fear of bodily suffering, performs rajasic renunciation. He does not obtain the fruit of that renunciation.

9 कार्यम् इत्येव यत् कर्म नियतं क्रियते ऽर्जुन ।
सङ्गं त्यक्त्वा फलं चैव स त्यागः सात्त्विको मतः ॥

kāryam ityeva yat karma
niyataṁ kriyate 'rjuna
saṅgaṁ tyaktvā phalaṁ cāiva
sa tyāgaḥ sāttviko mataḥ

When action is done because it is a duty, Arjuna, and abandoning attachment to the fruit, such renunciation is thought to be sattvic.

10 न द्वेष्ट्य् अकुशलं कर्म कुशले नानुषज्जते ।
त्यागी सत्त्वसमाविष्टो मेधावी छिन्नसंशयः ॥

na dveṣṭy akuśalaṁ karma
kuśale nānuṣajjate
tyāgī sattvasamāviṣṭo
medhāvī chinnasaṁśayaḥ

The man of renunciation, the wise man whose doubt is cut away, filled with goodness, does not hate disagreeable action, nor is he attached to agreeable action.

11 न हि देहभृता शक्यं त्यक्तुं कर्माण्य् अशेषतः।
यस् तु कर्मफलत्यागी स त्यागीत्य् अभिधीयते ॥

na hi dehabhṛtā śakyaṁ
tyaktuṁ karmāṇy aśeṣataḥ
yas tu karmaphalatyāgī
sa tyāgīty abhidhīyate

Indeed embodied beings are not able to abandon actions entirely; he, then, who abandons the fruit of action, is called a man of renunciation.

12 अनिष्टम् इष्टं मिश्रं च त्रिविधं कर्मणः फलम्।
भवत्य् अत्यागिनां प्रेत्य न तु संन्यासिनां क्वचित् ॥

aniṣṭam iṣṭaṁ miśraṁ ca
trividhaṁ karmaṇaḥ phalam
bhavaty atyāgināṁ pretya
na tu saṁnyāsinām kvacit

The fruit of action for those who have not renounced when they depart (die) is threefold: evil, good, and mixed; but for the renouncers there is none whatever.

13 पञ्चैतानि महाबाहो कारणानि निबोध मे।
सांख्ये कृतान्ते प्रोक्तानि सिद्धये सर्वकर्मणाम् ॥

pañcāitāni mahābāho
kāranāṇi nibodha me
sāṁkhye kṛtānte proktāni
siddhaye sarvakarmaṇām

Learn from Me, O Arjuna, these five factors, declared in the Sankhya doctrine for the accomplishment of all actions:

14 अधिष्ठानं तथा कर्ता करणं च पृथग्विधम् ।
विविधाश्च पृथक्चेष्टा दैवं चैवात्र पञ्चमम् ॥
adhiṣṭhānaṁ tathā kartā
karaṇaṁ ca pṛthagvidham
vividhāśca pṛthakceṣṭā
daivaṁ cāivātra pañcamam

The seat of action (the body), the doer, the various organs, and the various separate activities, with the presiding deities as the fifth;

15 शरीरवाङ्मनोभिर् यत् कर्म प्रारभते नरः ।
न्याय्यं वा विपरीतं वा पञ्चैते तस्य हेतवः ॥
śarīravāṅmanobhir yat
karma prārabhate naraḥ
nyāyyaṁ vā viparītaṁ vā
pañcāite tasya hetavaḥ

Whatever action a man undertakes with his body, speech or mind, either right or wrong, these are its five factors.

16 तत्रैवं सति कर्तारम् आत्मानं केवलं तु यः ।
पश्यत्य् अकृतबुद्धित्वान् न स पश्यति दुर्मतिः ॥
tatrāivaṁ sati kartāram
ātmānaṁ kevalaṁ tu yaḥ
paśyaty akṛtabuddhitvān
na sa paśyati durmatiḥ

This being so, he who sees his Self as the doer does not really see, because of the fact that he has not perfected his understanding.

17 यस्य नाहंकृतो भावो बुद्धिर् यस्य न लिप्यते ।
हत्वापि स इमाँल् लोकान् न हन्ति न निबध्यते ।।

yasya nāhaṁkṛto bhāvo
buddhir yasya na lipyate
hatvāpi sa imāṁl lokān
na hanti na nibadhyate

He whose state of mind is not egoistic, whose intellect is not tainted, even though he slays these people, he does not slay, and is not bound (by his actions).

18 ज्ञानं ज्ञेयं परिज्ञाता त्रिविधा कर्मचोदना ।
करणं कर्म कर्तेति त्रिविधः कर्मसंग्रहः ।।

jñānaṁ jñeyaṁ parijñātā
trividhā karmacodanā
karaṇaṁ karma karteti
trividhaḥ karmasaṁgrahaḥ

Knowledge, the process of knowing, and the knower are the threefold impulse to action; the instrument, the action, and the doer are the threefold basis of action.

19 ज्ञानं कर्म च कर्ता च त्रिधैव गुणभेदतः ।
प्रोच्यते गुणसंख्याने यथावच् छृणु तान्य् अपि ।।

jñānaṁ karma ca kartā ca
tridhāiva guṇabhedataḥ

procyate guṇasaṁkhyāne
yathāvac chṛṇu tāny api

It is declared in Sankhya that knowledge, action, and the doer are of three kinds, distinguished according to the qualities. Hear about these also:

20 सर्वभूतेषु येनैकं भावम् अव्ययम् ईक्षते।
अविभक्तं विभक्तेषु तज् ज्ञानं विद्धि सात्त्विकम्॥
sarvabhūteṣu yenāikaṁ
bhāvam avyayam īkṣate
avibhaktaṁ vibhakteṣu
taj jñānaṁ viddhi sāttvikam

That knowledge by which one sees one imperishable Being in all beings, undivided in separate beings; know that knowledge to be sattvic.

21 पृथक्त्वेन तु यज् ज्ञानं नानाभावान् पृथग्विधान्।
वेत्ति सर्वेषु भूतेषु तज् ज्ञानं विद्धि राजसम्॥
pṛthaktvena tu yaj jñānaṁ
nānābhāvān pṛthagvidhān
vetti sarveṣu bhūteṣu
taj jñānaṁ viddhi rājasam

But that knowledge which sees in all beings separate entities of various kinds, by differentiation, know that knowledge to be rajasic.

22 यत् तु कृत्स्नवद् एकस्मिन् कार्ये सक्तम् अहैतुकम्।
अतत्त्वार्थवद् अल्पं च तत् तामसम् उदाहृतम्॥

yat tu kṛtsnavad ekasmin
kārye saktam ahāitukam
atattvārthavad alpaṁ ca
tat tāmasam udāhṛtam

That (knowledge), however, which is attached to one single effect as if it were all, and without reason, without a real purpose and small in significance, is declared to be tamasic.

23 नियतं सङ्गरहितम् अरागद्वेषतः कृतम् ।
अफलप्रेप्सुना कर्म यत् तत् सात्त्विकम् उच्यते ।।
niyataṁ saṅgarahitam
arāgadveṣataḥ kṛtam
aphalaprepsunā karma
yat tat sāttvikam ucyate

That action which is ordained and free from attachment, performed without desire or hate, with no wish to obtain fruit, is said to be sattvic.

24 यत् तु कामेप्सुना कर्म साहंकारेण वा पुनः ।
क्रियते बहुलायासं तद् राजसम् उदाहृतम् ।।
yat tu kāmepsunā karma
sāhaṁkāreṇa vā punaḥ
kriyate bahulāyāsaṁ
tad rājasam udāhṛtam

But that action which is performed with a wish to obtain desires, with selfishness, or, again, with much effort, is declared to be rajasic.

25 अनुबन्धं क्षयं हिंसाम् अनपेक्ष्य च पौरुषम् ।
मोहाद् आरभ्यते कर्म यत् तत् तामसम् उच्यते ॥

anubandhaṁ kṣayaṁ hiṁsām
anapekṣya ca pāuruṣam
mohād ārabhyate karma
yat tat tāmasam ucyate

That action which is undertaken because of delusion, disregarding consequences, loss, or injury to others, as well as one's own ability, is said to be tamasic.

26 मुक्तसङ्गो ऽनहंवादी धृत्युत्साहसमन्वितः ।
सिद्ध्यसिद्ध्योर् निर्विकारः कर्ता सात्त्विक उच्यते ॥

muktasaṅgo 'nahaṁvādī
dhṛtyutsāhasamanvitaḥ
siddhyasiddhyor nirvikāraḥ
kartā sāttvika ucyate

Released from attachment, free from ego, endowed with steadfastness and resolution, unperturbed in success or failure; such a doer is said to be sattvic.

27 रागी कर्मफलप्रेप्सुर् लुब्धो हिंसात्मको ऽशुचिः ।
हर्षशोकान्वितः कर्ता राजसः परिकीर्तितः ॥

rāgī karmaphalaprepsur
lubdho hiṁsātmako 'śuciḥ
harṣaśokānvitaḥ kartā
rājasaḥ parikīrtitaḥ

Passionate, desiring the fruits of action, greedy, violent-natured, impure, subject to joy or sorrow; such a doer is proclaimed to be rajasic.

28 अयुक्तः प्राकृतः स्तब्धः शठो नैकृतिको ऽलसः ।
विषादी दीर्घसूत्री च कर्ता तामस उच्यते ॥
ayuktaḥ prākṛtaḥ stabdhaḥ
śaṭho nāikṛtiko 'lasaḥ
viṣādī dīrghasūtrī ca
kartā tāmasa ucyate

Undisciplined, vulgar, obstinate, wicked, deceitful, lazy, despondent, and procrastinating; such a doer is said to be tamasic.

29 बुद्धेर् भेदं धृतेश्चैव गुणतस् त्रिविधं शृणु ।
प्रोच्यमानम् अशेषेण पृथक्त्वेन धनंजय ॥
buddher bhedaṁ dhṛteścāiva
guṇatas trividhaṁ śṛṇu
procyamānam aśeṣeṇa
pṛthaktvena dhanaṁjaya

Now hear the threefold distinctions of intellect and also of firmness, according to the qualities, taught completely and separately, Arjuna:

30 प्रवृत्तिं च निवृत्तिं च कार्याकार्ये भयाभये ।
बन्धं मोक्षं च या वेत्ति बुद्धिः सा पार्थ सात्त्विकी ॥
pravṛttiṁ ca nivṛttiṁ ca
kāryākārye bhayābhaye
bandhaṁ mokṣaṁ ca yā vetti
buddhiḥ sā pārtha sāttvikī

That intellect which knows when to act and when not to act, what is to be done and what is not to be done, and what is to be feared and what is not to be feared, along with the knowledge of bondage and liberation, Arjuna, is sattvic.

31 यया धर्मम् अधर्मं च कार्यं चाकार्यम् एव च।
अयथावत् प्रजानाति बुद्धिः सा पार्थ राजसी॥

yayā dharmam adharmaṁ ca
kāryaṁ cākāryam eva ca
ayathāvat prajānāti
buddhiḥ sā pārtha rājasī

That intellect which distinguishes incorrectly between the right and the wrong, and between that which is to be done and that which is not to be done, is rajasic, Arjuna.

32 अधर्मं धर्मम् इति या मन्यते तमसावृता।
सर्वार्थान् विपरीतांश्च बुद्धिः सा पार्थ तामसी॥

adharmaṁ dharmam iti yā
manyate tamasāvṛtā
sarvārthān viparītaṁśca
buddhiḥ sā pārtha tāmasī

That intellect which, enveloped in darkness, imagines wrong to be right, and all things to be perverted, is tamasic, Arjuna.

33 धृत्या यया धारयते मनःप्राणेन्द्रियक्रियाः
योगेनाव्यभिचारिण्या धृतिः सा पार्थ सात्त्विकी॥

dhṛtyā yayā dhārayate
manaḥprāṇendriyakriyāḥ
yogenāvyabhicāriṇyā
dhṛtiḥ sā pārtha sāttvikī

The unswerving firmness by which, through yoga, one holds fast the functions of the mind, vital breath, and senses, that firmness, Arjuna, is sattvic.

34 यया तु धर्मकामार्थान् धृत्या धारयतेऽर्जुन ।
प्रसङ्गेन फलाकाङ्क्षी धृतिः सा पार्थ राजसी ॥
yayā tu dharmakamārthān
dhṛtyā dhārayate 'rjuna
prasaṅgena phalākāṅkṣī
dhṛtiḥ sā pārtha rājasī

But the firmness by which one holds to duty, pleasures, and wealth, with attachment and desire for the fruits of action, that firmness, Arjuna, is rajasic.

35 यया स्वप्नं भयं शोकं विषादं मदम् एव च ।
न विमुञ्चति दुर्मेधा धृतिः सा पार्थ तामसी ॥
yayā svapnaṁ bhayaṁ śokaṁ
viṣādaṁ madam eva ca
na vimuñcati durmedhā
dhṛtiḥ sā pārtha tāmasī

That firmness by which a stupid man does not abandon sleep, fear, grief, depression, and conceit, is tamasic, Arjuna.

36 सुखं त्व् इदानीं त्रिविधं शृणु मे भरतर्षभ।
अभ्यासाद् रमते यत्र दुःखान्तं च निगच्छति॥
sukhaṁ tv idānīṁ trividhaṁ
śṛṇu me bharatarṣabha
abhyāsād ramate yatra
duḥkhāntaṁ ca nigacchati

And now, hear from Me, Arjuna, the threefold happiness that one enjoys through practice, and in which one comes to the end of suffering.

37 यत् तद् अग्रे विषम् इव परिणामे ऽमृतोपमम्।
तत् सुखं सात्त्विकं प्रोक्तम् आत्मबुद्धिप्रसादजम्॥
yat tad agre viṣam iva
pariṇāme 'mṛtopamam
tat sukhaṁ sāttvikaṁ proktam
ātmabuddhiprasādajam

That which in the beginning is like poison but in the end like nectar; that happiness, born from the tranquility of one's own mind, is declared to be sattvic.

38 विषयेन्द्रियसंयोगाद् यत् तद् अग्रे ऽमृतोपमम्।
परिणामे विषम् इव तत् सुखं राजसं स्मृतम्॥
viṣayendriyasaṁyogād
yat tad agre 'mrtopamam
pariṇāme viṣam iva
tat sukhaṁ rājasaṁ smṛtam

That which in the beginning, through contact between the senses and their objects, is like nectar, and in the end like poison; that happiness is declared to be rajasic.

39 यद् अग्रे चानुबन्धे च सुखं मोहनम् आत्मनः ।
निद्रालस्यप्रमादोत्थं तत् तामसम् उदाहृतम् ॥

yad agre cānubandhe ca
sukhaṁ mohanam ātmanaḥ
nidrālasyapramādotthaṁ
tat tāmasam udāhṛtam

That happiness which both in the beginning and afterwards deludes the self, arising from sleep, indolence, and negligence, is declared to be tamasic.

40 न तद् अस्ति पृथिव्यां वा दिवि देवेषु वा पुनः ।
सत्त्वं प्रकृतिजैर् मुक्तं यद् एभिः स्यात् त्रिभिर् गुणैः ॥

na tad asti pṛthivyāṁ vā
divi deveṣu vā punaḥ
sattvaṁ prakṛtijāir muktaṁ
yad ebhiḥ syāt tribhir guṇāiḥ

There is no being, either on earth or yet in heaven among the gods, which can exist free from these three qualities born of material nature.

41 ब्राह्मणक्षत्रियविशां शूद्राणां च परंतप ।
कर्माणि प्रविभक्तानि स्वभावप्रभवैर् गुनैः ॥

brāhmaṇakṣatriyaviśāṁ
śūdrāṇāṁ ca paraṁtapa
karmāṇi pravibhaktāni
svabhāvaprabhavāir guṇāiḥ

The duties of the brahmins, the kshatriyas, the vaishyas, and of the shudras, Arjuna, are distributed according to the qualities which arise from their own nature.

42 शमो दमस् तपः शौचं क्षान्तिर् आर्जवम् एव च ।
ज्ञानं विज्ञानम् आस्तिक्यं ब्रह्मकर्म स्वभावजम् ॥
śamo damas tapaḥ śāucaṁ
kṣāntir ārjavam eva ca
jñānaṁ vijñānam āstikyaṁ
brahmakarma svabhāvajam

Tranquility, restraint, austerity, purity, forgiveness, and uprightness, knowledge, wisdom, and faith in God are the duties of the brahmins, born of their innate nature.

43 शौर्यं तेजो धृतिर् दाक्ष्यं युद्धे चाप्य् अपलायनम् ।
दानम् ईश्वरभावश्च क्षत्रं कर्म स्वभावजम् ॥
śāuryaṁ tejo dhṛtir dākṣyaṁ
yuddhe cāpy apalāyanam
dānam īśvarabhāvaśca
kṣātraṁ karma svabhāvajam

Heroism, majesty, firmness, skill, not fleeing in battle, generosity, and lordly spirit are the duties of the kshatriyas, born of their innate nature.

44 कृषिगौरक्ष्यवाणिज्यं वैश्यकर्म स्वभावजम् ।
परिचर्यात्मकम् कर्म शूद्रस्यापि स्वभावजम्
kṛṣigāurakṣyavāṇijyaṁ
vāiśyakarma svabhāvajam

paricaryātmakam karma
śūdrasyāpi svabhāvajam

Plowing, cow-herding, and trade are the duties of the vaishyas, born of their innate nature. Service is the duty of the shudras, born of their innate nature.

45 स्वे स्वे कर्मण्य् अभिरतः संसिद्धिं लभते नरः ।
स्वकर्मनिरतः सिद्धिं यथा विन्दति तच् छृणु ॥
sve sve karmaṇy abhirataḥ
saṁsiddhiṁ labhate naraḥ
svakarmanirataḥ siddhiṁ
yathā vindati tac chṛṇu

Devoted to his own duty, a man attains perfection. Hear then how one who is devoted to his own duty finds perfection:

46 यतः प्रवृत्तिर् भूतानां येन सर्वम् इदं ततम् ।
स्वकर्मणा तम् अभ्यर्च्य सिद्धिं विन्दति मानवः ॥
yataḥ pravṛttir bhūtānaṁ
yena sarvam idaṁ tatam
svakarmaṇā tam abhyarcya
siddhiṁ vindati mānavaḥ

By worshiping with his own proper duty Him from whom all beings have their origin, Him by whom all this universe is pervaded, man finds perfection.

47 श्रेयान् स्वधर्मो विगुणः परधर्मात् स्वनुष्ठितात् ।
स्वभावनियतं कर्म कुर्वन् नाप्नोति किल्बिषम् ॥

śreyān svadharmo viguṇaḥ
paradharmāt svanuṣṭhitāt
svabhāvaniyataṁ karma
kurvan nāpnoti kilbiṣam

Better one's own duty, though imperfect, than the duty of another well performed; performing the duty prescribed by one's own nature, one does not incur evil.

48 सहजं कर्म कौन्तेय सदोषम् अपि न त्यजेत् ।
सर्वारम्भा हि दोषेण धूमेनाग्निर् इवावृताः ॥
sahajaṁ karma kāunteya
sadoṣam api na tyajet
sarvārambhā hi doṣeṇa
dhūmenāgnir ivāvṛtāḥ

One should not abandon the duty to which one is born even though it be deficient, Arjuna. Indeed, all undertakings are enveloped by evil as fire is by smoke.

49 असक्तबुद्धिः सर्वत्र जितात्मा विगतस्पृहः ।
नैष्कर्म्यसिद्धिं परमां संन्यासेनाधिगच्छति ॥
asaktabuddhiḥ sarvatra
jitātmā vigataspṛhaḥ
nāiṣkarmyasiddhiṁ paramāṁ
saṁnyāsenādhigacchati

With his intellect unattached at all times, with conquered self, free from desire, by renunciation, one attains the supreme state of freedom from action.

50 सिद्धिं प्राप्तो यथा ब्रह्म तथाप्नोति निबोध मे ।
समासेनैव कौन्तेय निष्ठा ज्ञानस्य या परा ।।
siddhiṁ prāpto yathā brahma
tathāpnoti nibodha me
samāsenāiva kāunteya
niṣṭhā jñānasya yā parā

Learn from Me briefly, Arjuna, how one who has attained perfection also attains Brahman, which is the highest state of knowledge.

51 बुद्ध्या विशुद्धया युक्तो धृत्यात्मानं नियम्य च ।
शब्दादीन् विषयांस् त्यक्त्वा रागद्वेषौ व्युदस्य च ।।
buddhyā viśuddhayā yukto
dhṛtyātmānaṁ niyamya ca
śabdādīn viṣayāṅs tyaktvā
rāgadveṣāu vyudasya ca

Endowed with a pure intellect, controlling the self with firmness, abandoning sound and the other objects of sense, casting off attraction and hatred,

52 विविक्तसेवी लघ्वाशी यतवाक्कायमानसः ।
ध्यानयोगपरो नित्यं वैराग्यं समुपाश्रितः ।।
viviktasevī laghvāśī
yatavākkāyamānasaḥ
dhyānayogaparo nityaṁ
vāirāgyaṁ samupāśritaḥ

Dwelling in solitude, eating lightly, controlling speech, body, and mind, constantly devoted to yoga meditation, taking refuge in dispassion,

53 अहंकारं बलं दर्पं कामं क्रोधं परिग्रहम् ।
विमुच्य निर्ममः शान्तो ब्रह्मभूयाय कल्पते ॥
ahamkāraṁ balaṁ darpaṁ
kāmaṁ krodhaṁ parigrahaṁ
vimucya nirmamaḥ śānto
brahmabhūyāya kalpate

Relinquishing egotism, force, arrogance, desire, anger, and possession of property; unselfish, tranquil, he is fit for oneness with Brahman.

54 ब्रह्मभूतः प्रसन्नात्मा न शोचति न काङ्क्षति ।
समः सर्वेषु भूतेषु मद्भक्तिं लभते पराम् ॥
brahmabhūtaḥ prasannātmā
na śocati na kāṅkṣati
samaḥ sarveṣu bhūteṣu
madbhaktiṁ labhate parām

Absorbed in Brahman, he whose self is serene does not mourn, nor does he desire; impartial among all beings, he attains supreme devotion to Me.

55 भक्त्या माम् अभिजानाति यावान् यश्चास्मि तत्त्वतः ।
ततो मां तत्त्वतो ज्ञात्वा विशते तदनन्तरम् ॥
bhaktyā mām abhijānāti
yāvān yaścāsmi tattvataḥ
tato māṁ tattvato jñātvā
viśate tadanantaram

By devotion to Me he comes to know who I am in truth; then having known Me in truth, he enters Me immediately.

56 सर्वकर्माण्य् अपि सदा कुर्वाणो मद्व्यपाश्रयः ।
मत्प्रसादाद् अवाप्नोति शाश्वतं पदम् अव्ययम् ।।
sarvakarmāṇy api sadā
kurvāṇo madvyapāśrayaḥ
matprasādād avāpnoti
śāśvataṁ padam avyayam

Performing all actions, he whose reliance is always on Me, attains, by My grace, the eternal, imperishable abode.

57 चेतसा सर्वकर्माणि मयि संन्यस्य मत्परः ।
बुद्धियोगम् उपाश्रित्य मच्चित्तः सततं भव ।।
cetasā sarvakarmāṇi
mayi saṁnyasya matparaḥ
buddhiyogam upāśritya
maccittaḥ satataṁ bhava

Mentally renouncing all actions in Me, devoted to Me as the Supreme, taking refuge in the yoga of discrimination, constantly think of Me.

58 मच्चित्तः सर्वदुर्गाणि मत्प्रसादात् तरिष्यसि ।
अथ चेत् त्वम् अहंकारान् न श्रोष्यसि विनङ्क्ष्यसि ।।
maccittaḥ sarvadurgāṇi
matprasādāt tariṣyasi
atha cet tvam ahaṁkārān
na śroṣyasi vinaṅksyasi

Fixing your mind on Me, you shall pass over all difficulties, through My grace; but if, through egoism, you will not listen, then you shall perish.

59 यद् अहंकारम् आश्रित्य न योत्स्य इति मन्यसे ।
मिथ्यैष व्यवसायस् ते प्रकृतिस् त्वां नियोक्ष्यति ॥
yad ahaṁkāram āśritya
na yotsya iti manyase
mithyāiṣa vyavasāyas te
prakṛtis tvāṁ niyokṣyati

If, filled with egoism, you think, "I shall not fight," your resolve will be in vain; your own material nature will compel you.

60 स्वभावजेन कौन्तेय निबद्धः स्वेन कर्मणा ।
कर्तुं नेच्छसि यन् मोहात् करिष्यस्य् अवशो ऽपि तत् ॥
svabhāvajena kāunteya
nibaddhaḥ svena karmaṇā
kartuṁ necchasi yan mohāt
kariṣyasy avaśo 'pi tat

What you wish not to do, through delusion, you shall do that against your will, Arjuna, bound by your own karma, born of your own material nature.

61 ईश्वरः सर्वभूतानां हृद्देशे ऽर्जुन तिष्ठति ।
भ्रामयन् सर्वभूतानि यन्त्रारूढानि मायया ॥
īśvaraḥ sarvabhūtānāṁ
hṛddeśe 'rjuna tiṣṭhati

bhrāmayan sarvabhūtāni
yantrārūḍhāni māyayā

The Lord abides in the hearts of all beings, Arjuna, causing all beings to revolve, by the power of illusion, as if fixed on a machine.

62 तम् एव शरणं गच्छ सर्वभावेन भारत ।
तत्प्रसादात् परां शान्तिं स्थानं प्राप्स्यसि शाश्वतम् ।।
tam eva śaraṇaṁ gaccha
sarvabhāvena bhārata
tatprasādāt parāṁ śāntiṁ
sthānaṁ prāpsyasi śāśvatam

Fly unto Him alone for refuge with your whole being, Arjuna. From His grace, you shall attain supreme peace and the eternal abode.

63 इति ते ज्ञानम् आख्यातं गुह्याद् गुह्यतरं मया ।
विमृश्यैतद् अशेषेण यथेच्छसि तथा कुरु ।।
iti te jñānam ākhyātaṁ
guhyād guhyataraṁ mayā
vimṛśyāitad aśeṣeṇa
yathecchasi tathā kuru

Thus the knowledge that is more secret than all that is secret has been expounded to you by Me. Having reflected on this fully, do as you please.

64 सर्वगुह्यतमं भूयः शृणु मे परमं वचः ।
इष्टो ऽसि मे दृढम् इति ततो वक्ष्यामि ते हितम् ।।

sarvaguhyatamaṁ bhūyaḥ
śṛṇu me paramaṁ vacaḥ
iṣṭo 'si me dṛḍham iti
tato vakṣyāmi te hitam

Hear again My supreme word, most secret of all. You are surely loved by Me; therefore, I shall speak for your good.

65 मन्मना भव मद्भक्तो मद्याजी मां नमस्कुरु ।
माम् एवैष्यसि सत्यं ते प्रतिजाने प्रियो ऽसि मे ।।
manmanā bhava madbhakto
madyājī māṁ namaskuru
mām evāiṣyasi satyaṁ te
pratijāne priyo 'si me

Fix your mind on Me, worshiping Me, sacrificing to Me, bowing down to Me; in this way you shall come truly to Me, I promise, for you are dear to Me.

66 सर्वधर्मान् परित्यज्य माम् एकं शरणं व्रज ।
अहं त्वा सर्वपापेभ्यो मोक्षयिष्यामि मा शुचः ।।
sarvadharmān parityajya
mām ekaṁ śaraṇaṁ vraja
ahaṁ tvā sarvapāpebhyo
mokṣayiṣyāmi mā śucaḥ

Abandoning all duties, take refuge in Me alone. I shall liberate you from all evils; do not grieve.

67 इदं ते नातपस्काय नाभक्ताय कदाचन ।
न चाशुश्रूषवे वाच्यं न च मां यो ऽभ्यसूयति ।।

idaṁ te nātapaskāya
nābhaktāya kadācana
na cāśuśrūṣave vācyaṁ
na ca māṁ yo 'bhyasūyati

This shall not be spoken of by you to one who is without austerity, nor to one who is without devotion, nor to one who does not render service, nor to one who does not desire to listen, nor to one who speaks evil of Me.

68 य इदं परमं गुह्यं मद्भक्तेष्व् अभिधास्यति ।
भक्तिं मयि परां कृत्वा माम् एवैष्यत्य् असंशयः ।।
ya idaṁ paramaṁ guhyaṁ
madbhakteṣv abhidhāsyati
bhaktiṁ mayi parāṁ kṛtvā
mām evāiṣyaty asaṁśayaḥ

He who shall teach this supreme secret to My worshipers, having performed the highest devotion to Me, shall come to Me, without doubt.

69 न च तस्मान् मनुष्येषु कश्चिन् मे प्रियकृत्तमः ।
भविता न च मे तस्माद् अन्यः प्रियतरो भुवि ।।
na ca tasmān manuṣyeṣu
kaścin me priyakṛttamaḥ
bhavitā na ca me tasmād
anyaḥ priyataro bhuvi

And no one among men shall do more pleasing service to Me than he, and no other on earth shall be dearer to Me.

70 अध्येष्यते च य इमं धर्म्यं संवादम् आवयोः ।
ज्ञानयज्ञेन तेनाहम् इष्टः स्याम् इति मे मतिः ॥

adhyeṣyate ca ya imaṁ
dharmyaṁ saṁvādam āvayoḥ
jñānayajñena tenāham
iṣṭaḥ syām iti me matiḥ

And he who shall study this sacred dialogue of ours, by him I shall have been worshiped with the wisdom sacrifice; such is My conviction.

71 श्रद्धावान् अनसूयश्च शृणुयाद् अपि यो नरः ।
सो ऽपि मुक्तः शुभाँल् लोकान् प्राप्नुयात् पुण्यकर्मणाम् ॥

śraddhāvān anasūyaśca
śṛṇuyād api yo naraḥ
so 'pi muktaḥ śubhāṅl lokān
prāpnuyāt puṇyakarmaṇām

Even the man who hears it with faith and free from malice, he also, liberated, shall attain the happy worlds of those whose actions are pure.

72 कच्चिद् एतच् छ्रुतं पार्थ त्वयैकाग्रेण चेतसा ।
कच्चिद् अज्ञानसंमोहः प्रणष्टस् ते धनंजय ॥

kaccid etac chrutaṁ pārtha
tvayāikāgreṇa cetasā
kaccid ajñānasaṁmohaḥ
praṇaṣṭas te dhanaṁjaya

Has this been heard by you, Arjuna, with a concentrated mind? Have your ignorance and delusion been destroyed?

73 अर्जुन उवाच । *arjuna uvāca*

नष्टो मोहः स्मृतिर् लब्धा त्वत्प्रसादान् मयाच्युत ।
स्थितो ऽस्मि गतसंदेहः करिष्ये वचनं तव ॥
naṣṭo mohaḥ smṛtir labdhā
tvatprasādān mayācyuta
sthito 'smi gatasaṁdehaḥ
kariṣye vacanaṁ tava

Arjuna spoke:

My delusion is destroyed and I have gained wisdom through Your grace, Krishna. My doubts are gone. I shall do as You command.

74 संजय उवाच । *sañjaya uvāca*

इत्य् अहं वासुदेवस्य पार्थस्य च महात्मनः ।
संवादम् इमम् अश्रौषम् अद्भुतं रोमहर्षणम् ॥
ity ahaṁ vāsudevasya
pārthasya ca mahātmanaḥ
saṁvādam imam aśrāuṣam
adbhutaṁ romaharṣaṇam

Sanjaya spoke:

Thus I have heard from Krishna and the great-souled Arjuna, this wondrous dialogue which causes the hair to stand on end.

75 व्यासप्रसादाच् छ्रुतवान् एतद् गुह्यम् अहं परम् ।
योगं योगेश्वरात् कृष्णात् साक्षात् कथयतः स्वयम् ॥

vyāsaprasādāc chrutavān
etad guhyam ahaṁ param
yogaṁ yogeśvarāt kṛṣṇāt
sākṣāt kathayataḥ svayam

By the grace of Vyasa I have heard this supreme and most secret yoga which Krishna, the Lord of Yoga, has divulged directly, speaking Himself.

76 राजन् संस्मृत्य संस्मृत्य संवादम् इमम् अद्भुतम् ।
केशवार्जुनयोः पुण्यं हृष्यामि च मुहुर् मुहुः ॥
rājan saṁsmṛtya saṁsmṛtya
saṁvādam imam adbhutam
keśavārjunayoḥ puṇyaṁ
hṛṣyāmi ca muhur muhuḥ

O King, remembering again and again this marvelous and holy dialogue of Krishna and Arjuna, I rejoice again and again.

77 तच् च संस्मृत्य संस्मृत्य रूपम् अत्यद्भुतं हरेः ।
विस्मयो मे महान् राजन् हृष्यामि च पुनः पुनः ॥
tac ca samsmṛtya saṁsmṛtya
rūpam atyadbhutaṁ hareḥ
vismayo me mahān rājan
hṛṣyāmi ca punaḥ punaḥ

And remembering again and again that marvelous form of Krishna, my amazement is great, O King, and I rejoice again and again.

78 यत्र योगेश्वरः कृष्णो यत्र पार्थो धनुर्धरः ।
तत्र श्रीर् विजयो भूतिर् ध्रुवा नीतिर् मतिर् मम ॥

yatra yogeśvaraḥ kṛṣṇo
yatra pārtho dhanurdharaḥ
tatra śrir vijayo bhūtir
dhruvā nītir matir mama

Wherever there is Krishna, Lord of Yoga, wherever there is Arjuna, the archer, there will surely be splendor, victory, wealth, and righteousness; this is my conviction.

Hari Om Tat Sat
Iti Srimad Bhagavadgītāsūpaniṣatsu Brahmavidyāyām
Yogaśāstre Sri Kriṣṇārjunasamvāde
Mokṣasannyāsayogo Nāma Aṣṭādaśoddhyāyaḥ.

Thus ends the eighteenth Chapter, entitled "The Yoga of Liberation by Renunciation," of the venerated Bhagavad Gita Upanishad, the Knowledge of the Absolute, the scripture of Yoga, the dialogue between Sri Krishna and Arjuna.